THE PERFECT RECIPE FOR

Losing Weight & Eating Great

THE PERFECT RECIPE FOR Losing Weight & Eating Great

PAM ANDERSON

PHOTOGRAPHS BY MAURA McEVOY

Houghton Mifflin Company

Boston • New York

www.houghtonmifflinbooks.com

Library of Congress Cataloging-in-Publication Data
Anderson, Pam, date.
The perfect recipe for losing weight and eating great / Pam Anderson; photographs by Maura McEvoy.
p. cm.
Includes index.
ISBN-13: 978-0-618-83596-6
ISBN-10: 0-618-83596-2
1. Reducing diets—Recipes. 2. Weight loss. I. Title.
RM222.2.A518 2008
613.2'5—dc22 2007039801

Book design by Kris Tobiassen
Food styling by Frank Mentesana
Prop styling by Vicki Petro-Conroy
Hair and makeup styling by Sarah Johnson
Wardrobe styling by Sarah Parlow

Printed in the United States of America

QWT 10 9 8 7 6 5 4 3 2 1

To Terrie, my old same

ACKNOWLEDGMENTS

Thanks to:

Terrie Brown, for standing with me from the first lost pound to the last tested recipe; my therapist, Mary Siegel, for helping me heal emotionally; my doctor, Alan Lebowitz, and acupuncturist, Babs Meade, for helping me heal physically; my husband, David Anderson, for being a loving witness to my life for over thirty years now and for allowing me to share a little of our story; my daughters, Maggy Keet and Sharon Anderson, for loving, respecting, and supporting me, even when I started buying more clothes for myself; my parents, Flynn and Della Skipper, for being such wonderful parents (despite my turning Yankee); my brother-in-law, Michael Anderson, for leading the way; my editor, Rux Martin, for being such an insightful, gifted, and reasonable editor; Sarah Jane Freymann, agent and friend, for always looking out for me with such grace and style; and all who had a hand in making this book beautiful, clean, and inviting—Maura McEvoy, Frank Mentesana, Vicki Petro-Conroy, Sarah Johnson, Sarah Parlow, Kris Tobiassen, Eugenie Delaney, Michaela Sullivan, Susan Dickinson, Jacinta Monniere, and registered dietician Tammi Hancock, for her calorie analysis of the recipes.

Thanks as well to Adam Ried, who generously shared his knowledge about kitchen equipment; my friends and colleagues at *USA Weekend*—especially my editor Connie Kurz—for allowing me to be the paper's culinary voice; my friends and colleagues at *Fine Cooking* magazine, for giving me a regular presence in their pages; and my new friends and colleagues at *Better Homes and Gardens,* for letting me be their monthly "Celebrate" columnist.

contents

FOREWORD xi

INTRODUCTION 1

Yo-Yo Mama 1

Change in Motion 5

Face the Numbers 6

Bringing Home the Bacon, Packing on the Pork 8

Get Physical 11

No More Diets! 14

Eat What You Love, Love What You Eat 17

A Medical "Happily Ever After" 18

Run—or Walk—Toward Yourself 21

Sit Still to Lose Weight 22

About the Calorie Analysis 23

STOCK UP 25

THE RECIPES 35

Eat (or Drink) Your Breakfast 37

Big Lunch in a Bowl 83

Time for Tea 139

Before-Dinner Nibbles 165

Dinners—Fast and Faster 181

Dessert Too 277

INDEX 297

FOREWORD

Not long ago my husband and I were in Knoxville, Tennessee, helping celebrate his father's eighty-seventh birthday. As a gift, one of my brothers-in-law, who's a whiz with computers, had digitized all the old Anderson family slides.

During the birthday dinner, the Anderson siblings, eager to see the family pictures that had been hidden in those ancient carousel trays for twenty-five years, prevailed upon Charley to present his gift now. He walked to a table nearby and started the show.

At first I watched from a distance. These weren't my family pictures, and all the inside jokes were lost on me. But suddenly I noticed something. I got up, left the table, and went for a closer look. The pictures were vintage 1950s and '60s in the town and outlying farms of Yankton, South Dakota. Women smiled as they served up baked beans and corn on the cob from a farmhouse picnic table. Couples posed in front of bulky, finned automobiles. Six women laughed as they drank coffee and gossiped around a kitchen table. The shots were grainy, the fashion and hairstyles wonderfully dated, but what struck me was how *slim* these average, hardworking Midwesterners were. I was sure they must have lived ordinary lives out there on the prairie, but as the images kept pulsing on the monitor, my only thought was, "These people looked good!"

I returned to the table and immediately recognized the next generation of family pictures in the making. The Andersons—along with in-laws and adult grandchildren—were drinking coffee and chatting about upcoming weddings, the merits of the next set of presidential candidates, and the latest ADD meds. My God, I thought, what a contrast. We may have become worldlier, but most of us around that table were at least ten to fifty pounds heavier than those South Dakotans. We were Exhibit A for the recent CDC (Centers for Disease Control and Prevention) report declaring two-thirds of Americans overweight or obese.

What's happened to us in my short lifetime? I was one of those two-thirds—overweight, teetering on the brink of obesity. Not only do I know what happened, I know what we need to do about it.

INTRODUCTION

Yo-Yo Mama

I'm guessing you're a veteran dieter. If you're like me, you've got a bunch of weight loss books gathering dust in various corners of the house. Remember the Scarsdale Diet? (I tried that back when I needed to shed just ten pounds to look good.) Then there was the Rotation Diet, my bible for serious post-baby weight loss, and the Liquid Diet—I went on that and kept it up for over a month. When I reached my premarriage weight, I bought a bag of Doritos and haven't seen that number since. And how about all the diets you photocopied? Did you try the one "doctors use" to get fatties ready for heart surgery? Hot dogs, carrots, and ice cream for supper on Tuesday night, bananas and skim milk on Thursday. I tortured myself twice on that and never lost a pound. What the hell was I thinking? Remember the Cabbage Soup Diet? Did you flush it after week two?

> After several decades of yo-yo dieting, I finally tossed out my scales nearly ten years ago and vowed never to diet again.

By the time Atkins and South Beach came along, I had already sworn off diets. I figured any plan that restricts an entire food category is really just another form of calorie control in disguise. I mean, how much bacon and eggs can you down before you just want a piece of toast with jelly, or how big a steak can you face before craving an ear of corn or a baked potato? And who could permanently live without pasta, French fries, or a glazed doughnut now and again? Besides, any diet that guilts you for two of life's most basic pleasures—bread and wine—is just wrongheaded.

After several decades of yo-yo dieting, I finally tossed out my scales nearly ten years ago, packed my diet books into a box destined for the attic, and vowed never to diet again. I said if I could figure out a way to change my life, I'd do it, but I'd never again follow an unrealistic program only to fall off the wagon a few days, a few weeks, a few months later.

In fact, I already knew what to do. My best friend had just been to the doctor and complained of not being able to lose weight. The physician's response was infuriatingly simple. "You just need to exercise a little more and eat a little less." He was right, of course. We all know what to do. If knowledge were enough, we'd all be thin. So how *do* you turn knowledge into permanent motivation? We've all got legitimate excuses. For years, mine was my job.

Not only do I love to eat, I have to eat. As a cookbook author and food writer, I make my living testing and tasting recipes. It's not unusual for me to have to sample three dozen versions of chocolate cake or sixteen different pot roasts on a given day. As a wife and mother, I'm also committed to family meals, so between those astounding numbers of tastes, I usually serve up—and eat—breakfast, lunch, and dinner.

Since I don't test recipes alone, there's always another person alongside me in the kitchen. I was always puzzled that out of all the people who have worked with me over the years, none was overweight. In fact, some were downright skinny. It didn't seem fair.

And then there was my husband. I frequently enlisted him to taste, and he still ate three meals a day. How come he could still wear pants from high school, while I couldn't even fit into last summer's shorts? We seemed to eat identically, so why was I the only one five pounds heavier after each book project?

If you've spent the better part of your life trying to lose weight, you've probably had similar feelings. You think, "Why can't I be more like my sister, coworker, or friend?" They make looking slim seem so effortless. You've tried diets often enough to know they don't work, but a piece of you still holds out hope for the next miracle drug, food, or plan that will make weight loss painless and permanent.

You already know lifestyle change is the only way to go, that "you just need to exercise a little more and eat a little less," and you've tried that too. You know the story. Your eating's out of control, and you're miserable. No gimmicks this time. You're just going to eat healthy and exercise every day.

Day one: you set the alarm an hour early and head out for a brisk walk or long-overdue trip to the gym. Exercise, an invigorating shower, a quick bowl of oatmeal—you feel great. You take time to make a big salad for lunch, and when the midafternoon hunger pangs hit, you confidently reach for an apple instead of cookies or a candy bar. Wow, you're good. For dinner you bypass the usual haunts—Chinese or takeout pizza—and stop at the grocery store for salmon fillets, salad greens, and a bunch of broccoli. While you're there, you think ahead and grab a container of blueberries, a carton of yogurt, and a loaf of whole wheat bread for breakfast. "This makes so much sense," you say. "Why didn't I change my life sooner?"

My desire to change my life began more than two years before I shed a single pound.

Dinner's reasonably satisfying, but by 9:00 you start to feel antsy and a little cranky. Normally a bowl of ice cream would take care of both feelings, but it's not part of the plan, so you head for bed instead. Your hunger gnaws at you in the night, and when the alarm goes off on day two (or five or seven or ten), you hit snooze. Since you wake up late, you skip the gym and opt for coffee and a muffin instead. As you toss the carton of mold-skinned yogurt into the trash a month later, you're reminded of your long-lost good intentions.

You gave this lifestyle-change thing your best shot, so what happened? Why did it feel wonderful, yet so impossible to sustain? How *do* you change—for good?

Change in Motion

My desire to change my life began more than two years before I shed a single pound. You may be at that point right now. In the winter of 2002, I attended a retreat at The Greenbrier, a resort in White Sulphur Springs, West Virginia. I gave two cooking demonstrations that chilly January weekend, but presenters were encouraged to attend other retreat seminars. Among the offerings was an exercise class. A blend of yoga, aerobics, and dance, the experience promised to energize the body and spirit. With nothing else to do, I decided to give it a try. Maybe this would do it for me.

A plump middle-aged food writer prancing around a mirrored room, I felt a little silly. But the experience not only forced me to see my present self but also made me long for what I could be. At the final session, the retreat coordinator asked us to tell a fellow attendee what we had learned from the weekend and what we wanted to change. I knew my experience had been significant, but I wasn't ready to share something so personal. Since I had never learned to dance (I was raised a strict Baptist), I longed to feel confident and comfortable moving my body, and even though I had already sworn off diets at this point, I suspected weight loss was part of the solution. I packed and headed toward my car. Then, on impulse, I returned to the auditorium and found my instructor. Someday, I told her, I wanted to be proud of the way I looked.

A year passed. I started writing another cookbook, put on a few more pounds, and got my younger daughter through high school graduation and college acceptance, my vow gently simmering on the back burner. Then, after eleven years of working in Pennsylvania, my husband took a new job in Connecticut. I found myself dealing with a big move and transitioning two grumpy teens to a new town, with barely enough time to unpack before my younger daughter headed off for her freshman year of college and my older daughter went abroad for a year. After I dropped her at the airport, I breathed a sigh of relief. I'd made it. Things had been difficult, for sure, but now it was time to get back to work. I'd heard all the empty-nest stories—women who couldn't even walk into their daughter's room for weeks without crying, women who had lost their purpose. I felt insulated from those problems: I'd had a fulfilling career during my child-rearing years, and I enjoyed a good partnership with my husband.

I sat down to finish the cookbook, only to discover I lacked direction and motivation. During the move, I had developed a severe pain in my right shoulder, and because I hadn't taken time to fix it, it had deteriorated to the point where I couldn't hook my bra or put away dishes above the first shelf.

Feeling old and emotionally spent, I just wanted to go away and hide somewhere. My husband, ordinarily my go-to person, was preoccupied with his new job. After a time of despair, I realized I had three choices. I could do nothing and continue to marinate in my misery, I could walk away, or I could get up and do something.

Fortunately, I decided it was time for healing and scheduled a visit with my new doctor. And then I did something much harder for me: for the first time in my life, I made an appointment to see a psychotherapist.

Face the Numbers

Though I didn't know it at the time, the very act of setting up an appointment with my doctor was crucial for setting in motion the changes I'd eventually make. When I finally stepped on the scale, I asked the nurse who weighed me to keep the number to herself. As a sign of her disapproval, she wrote "192" in bold marker within eye's view. At the time, I was annoyed, but in retrospect, her making me face the numbers was a really good thing. There was no wiggling out of my weight or explaining it away. The scale was accurate. My shoes were off, and my clothes weighed less than a pound. I didn't have my period. I was out of excuses. Not that I was

> Not that I was ready to do anything about it yet, but I was just a bag of chips away from 200 pounds.

IF THE SUIT DOESN'T FIT . . . WEAR IT

It took me a long time to realize that losing weight is as much—or more—about what's in your head as what's on your hips or gut. Healing the body and mind isn't a guaranteed-thirty-days-or-your-money-back proposition. It takes time, and you can't rush it. After all, you've spent a lifetime becoming yourself. No weight loss drink, plan, or machine is going to instantly transform you into someone slender. You can force your body to submit for a time, but to lose weight and keep it off, you must start from within.

If you're not quite ready to see the doctor or set up an appointment with a therapist, start with little steps. Try getting up, showering, and making yourself look as good as you can five days of the week. Dig out those eye-catching earrings or that sporty shirt you haven't felt up to wearing for a while. Pull out the suit in the back of the closet that surely doesn't fit. Slip it on anyway, see where you are, imagine yourself fitting into it. Try nibbling on a couple of cookies rather than devouring your usual five or six. Vow, if you can, to walk just three times a week. Approach these assignments not as work, but as the first steps toward taking care of yourself, toward changing your life from the inside.

Before long, you'll sense a subtle shift within and feel a little lighter in spirit. And when the time is right, when the moment presents itself, you'll be ready, and you'll know it.

ready to do anything about it yet, but I was just a bag of chips away from 200 pounds.

Thankfully, my doctor didn't beat up on me about my weight, and he heartily approved of my seeing a psychotherapist. An MRI revealed that the cause of my shoulder pain was tendinitis. I could go the conventional route and see a specialist, but before trying that, he suggested I try acupuncture.

Not only did acupuncture cure my ailing shoulder, but the weekly sessions, which included massage, had a healing effect on my whole body. After the needle pricking (it didn't hurt, by the way), the acupuncturist put on a CD and turned on a heat lamp. Restorative music soothing my mind, warmth and light enveloping my body, I lay in a meditative state for nearly an hour. Some weeks, I felt slight improvements immediately after the session. Other weeks, healing was slower than a turtle's pace. Whatever my shoulder's state, however, I always left feeling calm, cared for, centered, and refreshed. Over time, the energy started to flow again, and my newly energized body, in turn, helped bring one of its ailing members back to life.

Bringing Home the Bacon, Packing on the Pork

Recognizing the need to see a therapist was long in coming. For years I viewed therapy as a pricey whining session. Many people I knew who "indulged" in it never seemed to change. Besides, I had a built-in counselor, my clergy spouse. We had gotten pretty good at listening to and advising each other. I thought it was enough, but it wasn't. I needed objective help outside the family. I called a respected therapist in town and described the kind of person I hoped to see and got a referral.

Weekly sessions helped me realize that I had shouldered too much and asked too little of others. For years I had tried to be what I thought everyone else wanted or needed me to be. I started to see how my chronic weight problem might be related to these things. To address such deep-seated issues, I had to confront the two most important and basic relationships in my life: my parents and my spouse.

It wasn't easy revisiting the almost fifty-year-old relationship with my mother and father. When I left home, I moved from small-town Florida to take my first job in Chicago, and I was living in a world my parents could hardly understand. I developed my own ideas on women's issues, marriage roles, politics, and religion. And when I had children, I had very different notions from my parents about how to raise them. My mother and father made it clear they did not approve of my choices. As an only child and the mother of their only two grandchildren, I didn't want to risk alienation. So, as best I could, when I went home or they visited me, I hid the person I was becoming.

PICK UP THAT PHONE!

A sore knee, chronic headaches, high blood pressure, back pain—what's standing in the way of your efforts to lose weight? Before you can make any major lifestyle change, especially one as fundamental as a change in your weight, you'll need to deal with your overall health. Postpone that Pap smear, mammogram, root canal, or annual physical; skip your vitamins or medications; ignore the creaky knee or ailing eye; and you're telling yourself that you're not worth taking care of.

If you're like me, it may be the dreaded scale that keeps you from making the appointment with your doctor. As long as you can postpone it, your weight is your secret, and as long as there's not a real number, you don't have a problem. Are you too "busy" to keep those appointments? Afraid to set up those visits?

As best you can, you have to start the process of healing the body before changing your life. Since mind and body are so interwoven, it's impossible to fix one if the other's out of whack.

Rather than stand up for what I believed (and confirm what they already knew), I fell silent during conflict. By keeping my mouth shut, I believed I was taking the high road. Surely they'd eventually catch on. But as I turned more sullen, they grew more vocal.

Who knew why it took so long to simply be myself? I arranged for a quick trip home. In those brief few days, on walks with my mother, sitting beside the grill with my father, I told them who I was and what I cared about. I assured them I loved them and wanted nothing to come between us. They were gracious, gentle, and loving. My inability to be honest with them had stunted our relationship. Now, finally, it could grow.

My therapist also helped me revisit the more-than-twenty-five-year relationship with my husband. I was an overachiever. As a child, I had been encouraged to excel, yet at the same time, I was taught that men were better—more important—than women.

The achiever side of me brought home the bacon and put my husband through his master's and Ph.D. programs and then seminary. Working full-time, I ran a catering business on the side. Like most other American parents, I juggled frantically, taking charge of the cleaning, cooking, child rearing, bill paying, vacation planning, entertaining, and family life. I had parish responsibilities as well. Last on my list of priorities—something I never quite got around to dealing with—was me. I'd rant about this once or twice a year. My husband usually agreed that life wasn't fair, but things never seemed to change. Therapy helped me realize that I worked too hard and demanded too little of my spouse. It had never occurred to me to say simply, "This is what I need. This is what you can expect from me. This is what you can't." If I couldn't set reasonable boundaries for what I would do and what I expected him to do, how could I set healthy food boundaries?

My weight gain compounded the problem. The heavier I got, the more insecure I felt and the more I overcompensated by taking on even more responsibilities to justify my existence. I wanted equality in my marriage but believed I had to work twice as hard to get it.

As they tell you on an airplane: first put on your own oxygen mask, then you can help others.

Breaking relational habits isn't easy, but weekly therapy helped me see the issues clearly and gave me the courage to deal head-on. To initiate lasting change, I had to stop caring about what people thought of me and stop worrying about what they might do if I departed from the approved script. I had to speak my mind. I would continue to extend the same opportunity to every other person in my life, but I would no longer be the one who always deferred. That didn't help me or anyone else. As they tell you on an airplane: first put on your own oxygen mask, then you can help others.

At first this new way of relating to my husband felt strange—almost cold. After years out of whack, I had to recalibrate my emotions: *this is what healthy and good feels like.* My pulling back and demanding more made my husband take me more seriously, and our relationship actually started to change. Caring less about what he "needed" enabled me to attend to my legitimate needs. And the funny thing was, the more I cared for myself, the more he did too.

Get Physical

Gradually I started to heal: my shoulder was now nearly back to normal, my energy had begun to flow. Though I hadn't lost a pound yet, I was starting to feel confident and take pride in myself. At about that time, our family took a long-planned trip to Rome and Florence. In establishing our daily budget, we had decided that food and fun were more important than transportation. Instead of using taxis and buses to get around, we walked everywhere—kilometer after kilometer—every day. Perhaps the extra walking and summer heat curbed my appetite, or unconsciously I wanted to save the calories I had worked so hard to burn, or I was just feeling good about myself. In any case, by the end of those ten days, I noticed my pants were ever so loose. A few weeks later, my best friend and I took a little trip to her family farm. As when I was on the family vacation, I was eating well—not dieting—and getting lots of exercise. I felt great.

I came home but stayed in vacation mode, finding a way to eat less and exercise more in the real world. After vacation and that little retreat, I walked briskly for a couple of miles in the morning, and I threw in an extra walk at the end of the day. Continuing to gain strength, I realized I could get done a lot sooner (and burn more calories) if I picked up the pace, so I began to alternate walking with bursts of running. Walk, run, walk, run, walk. Gradually the intervals of running became longer as my stamina increased, until finally I was running two short runs a day. I quickly discovered that the extra activity was both appetite-curbing and calorie-burning.

I quickly discovered that extra activity was both appetite-curbing and calorie-burning.

WHAT'S EATING *YOU*?

Do your children treat you disrespectfully? Do you hate your job? Has it been years since you've talked with your sister? Is your spouse out of love with you? Until you get your head straight, your body's not going to cooperate—at least not for long.

Is talking regularly with a friend good enough? Friendships are mutual—two friends helping each other. Therapy has one focus: you. The experience of an hour devoted solely to you may feel like an incredible luxury. But if it's good, therapy will also keep the focus on you even when you'd rather it not. Eventually you're brought face-to-face with how you need to change. No friendship can do this.

It's true that therapy isn't cheap. I was lucky that my insurance covered part of the cost. Some of my friends, I reasoned, were willing to spend money on diet systems and elaborate exercise equipment to lose weight. I knew that would be a waste of money until I got to the heart of why I ate more than I should.

Since I had friends who'd gone through three or four therapists before finding the right person, I didn't bother with the Yellow Pages. If you have a physician you trust, he or she can be a resource. Make calls; ask around.

Once you get there, how do you know your therapist is right for you? It should feel good all around. If it's not working for you—three sessions max—pull the plug. Therapy is too expensive and your time too valuable to waste on someone who's not helping you progress.

When certain people or situations come to mind, do you shake your head and say, "No way, I'm not going there"? If so, it may be time to get help and prepare for the wonderful growth opportunities ahead of you.

For eight months during the weight loss phase, as often as I could manage, I went on short walk/runs before each meal. On a quiet day, I'd do it three times. I'd usually head out feeling a little lethargic and hungry, I'd return energized, happy, alive—a great time to sit down at the table.

During that time, I practically lived in running clothes, but I trashed my shoddy sweats and invested in smart spandex. At the end of every day, I took time to clean up and slip into a nice pair of jeans in time for a glass of wine and the evening news. It didn't go unnoticed.

That December, it was time to host our annual holiday party for the parish. Our first year in town, in typical fashion, I had cooked for more than 200 people, devoting over a week to the shopping and cooking. It was time for a change. I made the event a potluck, with a team of volunteers to run the party. At 5:00—just two hours before the first guests would arrive—I was out on my evening run. How far I'd come in just one year! The old me would have taken full responsibility for the party (though no one ever asked me to), and I would have never had time for the run.

No More Diets!

One thing I knew: I couldn't lose weight for good by going on a diet. Most diets prescribe a rigid, artificial way of eating that can't be sustained. Diets are like trying to sell everyone the same style and size shoe. What if you're allergic to seafood, nuts, or yogurt? What if you despise tuna, eggs, or grapefruit? And what do you do when the mission is accomplished? If this way of eating is forced and not really you, you'll revert back to your old patterns every time. Better to find a way to eat for life.

> Diets are like trying to sell everyone the same style and size shoe.

I sat down and figured out what foods and meals I needed and came up with a personalized eating plan. I wanted the big three—breakfast, lunch, and dinner—but since I had started taking care of myself, afternoon tea with a little sweet was important too. I usually enjoyed a glass of wine before dinner. Most diets frown upon drinking. Did I want to live a dry life? If not, why give it up to lose weight, guiltily adding it back post-diet?

Most important, I didn't want to be tied down or restricted—nothing was off-limits if I really wanted it. If I wanted toast with peanut butter and jelly for breakfast, I could pop in some good bread. If I wanted pizza or pasta for dinner, I could reach for a whole wheat pizza

COMMIT TO A 20-MINUTE WALK IN THE PARK. YES, *YOU.*

You might be thinking you're not physically able or don't have the time to exercise twenty to thirty minutes two or three times a day during the weight loss phase. Certainly the old me would never have imagined I could do it. I would have immediately pictured myself on a treadmill at the eighty-ninth minute—bored, sweaty, sore, and miserable. Utterly depressed, I wouldn't have even bothered to try.

You don't have to. After you start to take pride in yourself, you'll figure out what's right for you. From the beginning, commit only to the exercise you can theoretically keep up. To have to scale back is demoralizing. You can always increase your activity—and if you're doing it right, you probably will as you gain strength.

You know your schedule and what's realistically possible. If the desire is there, however, think about how you could fit exercise into your schedule two or three times a day for a short period in your life. If you got up a little earlier, could you manage twenty to thirty minutes on a treadmill or a walk around the neighborhood?

Although most people get a full hour for lunch, most rarely take it. Remembering that this isn't forever, could you walk or run for a half hour before you eat? Or go to the gym, then eat at your desk? If you're losing weight, I'll bet you'd get a lot of support. You might even get some company.

If you've got a full-time job, evenings can be difficult, but before or after dinner, can you get to the gym for a quick one? Got kids? Maybe your spouse would agree to be on duty for a couple of nights a week. If not, why not?

You'll know you've done the inner work if exercising isn't a task you have to force yourself to do. At least most of the time, you should look forward to walking, running, rowing, biking, doing the elliptical, or whatever it is you've decided to do. The first five or ten minutes can be daunting—until the endorphins kick in.

If you're not sure what kind of exercise you like, think about what kind of person you are. Do you like exercising with a group, or one or two other people, or are you a loner? Are you competitive, or do you just want to have fun? If your joints are achy, what about swimming for an effective, low-impact workout?

HUSH UP AND LISTEN—TO YOURSELF

How much food do I really need? How much can I exercise? If you're in a good place, you'll think small and realistically to start, and if you're listening, your body will let you know.

After all, this is not a race to complete and get over with as soon as possible. This new way of life is about giving yourself what you legitimately need and want. How about that midafternoon candy bar you love so much? In the past, you indulged in the large variety. Check the numbers and do the math. Maybe you settle for a miniature size. If you're willing to exercise a little more, maybe you can even afford two.

You crave a sandwich for lunch. Can you make it open-faced or stuff it in a lower-calorie pita? Love a big double chocolate cookie with that afternoon latte? How about a biscotti instead? Look forward to that nightly martini? Can you slowly savor a well-made jigger? Better to give yourself a little dose of what you love than to deprive yourself, then overindulge.

crust or whole wheat pasta, but there was no rule saying I couldn't have the white varieties if I wanted. I didn't feel the need for a regular dessert, but after a special dinner, I could have a sliver instead of a slice.

Of course, I couldn't eat unlimited quantities of whatever I wanted. But rather than letting someone else tell me what I could and could not eat, I finally put myself in charge and found I was actually fairly responsible. I vaguely kept score on calories, figuring 1,800 to 2,000 on weekdays—400 to 500 for breakfast, 400 to 500 for lunch, 150 for teatime, 250 for my predinner nibble, and 600 for dinner. Maybe a few hundred more on the weekends.

My only restriction was *when* I could eat. I now feed myself well and regularly. Early-morning tea and half a banana is the perfect energy boost before exercise so that I can eat breakfast a bit later. I usually don't give food another thought until midday. I always treat myself to an afternoon cup of tea and a couple of small cookies, a sure cure for lethargy and hunger. And before I prepare dinner, I enjoy a glass of wine and a handful of nuts or a deviled egg. I don't allow more than three waking hours to elapse between meals, so I'm never starved. If I am, I have to wait a bit. No more *I'm feeling a little hungry and need a midmorning snack* or *I've got a taste for a late-evening bar of chocolate.* No more grazing during prep as I make dinner (when many cooks consume the calorie equivalent of an entire meal) or eating at any hour of the day or night.

It's torture to be hungry, with celery sticks or grapefruit sections as the only option. Hunger becomes the focus. Rather than nibbling on no- or low-calorie snacks to get me to the next unsatisfying meal, I decided to give myself what I legitimately needed so that I was truly content. By putting boundaries around mealtimes and feeding myself well, I eventually fell into a satisfying rhythm. Every day my body knew what to expect and happily anticipated each ritual meal.

Eat What You Love, Love What You Eat

Although all the years of testing and tasting had clearly taken its toll on my body, it was my knowledge of food that ultimately helped me trim down. I was changing how I ate, yes—but that didn't mean I was willing to eat inferior food. If this was for life, I wanted to continue to enjoy all the foods I loved: filling soups, satisfying salads, jazzy pizzas, hearty pastas, tea and treats, nibbles and wine.

> I always treat myself to an afternoon cup of tea and a couple of small cookies.

Since I wanted to wake up excited about my first meal of the day, breakfast needed to set the right tone. Open-faced omelets are super-easy to make and look impressively big. I don't like preparing oatmeal from scratch in the morning (or the little instant packets), so I figured out how to mix my oatmeal the night before and fridge it or pop it into a slow oven so that it's ready when I get up. And for mornings when I have to hit the ground running, I created a blend-and-go smoothie.

Lunch has to be simple. I developed a meal-in-a-bowl formula for a main-course salad. During the warmer months, I keep on hand a "bar" of prepared ingredients: greens that are sold washed, cooked meats and seafood, hard-boiled eggs, canned beans, crumbled cheeses, toasted nuts, and dried fruit. I never get stuck eating the same boring meal day after day.

When the weather turns chilly, I start to crave soup. I don't have a taste for the stuff in a can, and I don't have time for the long-simmered ones, so I created a formula for a big-flavored 30-minute soup. For tea, I have found ways of making every bite count. I drizzle mini whole wheat pumpkin muffins with an orange glaze, so they don't need much sugar. Storing mini muffins in the freezer keeps them both fresh and out of sight—another form of calorie control. My Cardamom Pistachio and Chocolate Hazelnut refrigerator cookies are made from the same dough, and I can slice just a couple of rounds from the frozen log and bake them fresh.

Dinner is the one meal we share together as a family, so it has to be especially satisfying. Because everyone is always famished, I purposely developed dishes that are quick—most of them can be on the table in 15 to 30 minutes. I found a way to make creamy pasta without heavy cream, to bake pizzas with lots of fresh, inviting combinations, to serve faster-cooking cuts of meat with boldly flavored pan sauces. I also discovered new techniques that eighty-six the calories: succulent fish and vegetables all baked in the same pan (you don't even have to preheat the oven!) and mix-and-match foil packs of poultry, pork, or seafood with vegetables—all-in-one meals.

I've included calorie counts for all the recipes, so you can keep track if you want.

A Medical "Happily Ever After"

I lost 42 pounds over the course of eight months. That may sound like a lot, but in fact, it amounted to a generous pound a week—or just a little over five pounds a month. As with most weight loss, it came off more quickly at the beginning, tapering off as my body approached its comfort zone.

Before I started losing, I had asked my ob-gyn what she thought I should weigh. She turned the question back to me, asking how much I weighed the last time I felt good about my body. My answer was 140 pounds, where I was six weeks after delivering my first child (and a number I hadn't seen since). I set my sights on that, but as I approached 150 (I'm 5'4½"), I felt great, looked great, and had picked up good muscle weight from my running. My body just seemed to settle naturally there. Certainly I'm not skinny—I still love to eat and drink well—but it's a number I've been able to maintain for three years now.

I lost the weight by establishing new, normal eating patterns and exercising more during the weight loss phase. Having reached my target weight, I scaled back on the exercise to one 45-minute session a day.

I didn't rush the process. In fact, it was two years from the time I decided I wanted to be proud of my body to the moment I actually began to do something about it. And it all started with an extra walk.

The old me would have felt selfish taking that much time for myself each day. But guess who appreciated this new me the most? The people I would have thought I was "neglecting"—my husband and my daughters.

It all started with an extra walk.

On past diets, I had always kept my old clothes, just in case (I always eventually needed them). Over those eight months of weight loss, however, I cleaned out my closet several times and got rid of things as they started to bag.

When it came to food, my husband had always been the more disciplined. I would finish my meal, then thoughtlessly pick at everyone else's plates as I cleared the table. In my new life, I made a practice of stopping when I was satisfied.

Naturally my weight loss has had a dramatic impact on my health stats. Compared with my 2004 physical, when I had tipped the scales at nearly 200 pounds, my 2006 physical looked like a medical "happily ever after." My total cholesterol had dropped dramatically, and I was now in the lowest risk category for heart disease. My bone-density numbers improved as well. My doctor, astounded, jokingly said I should be a poster child for weight loss.

Spicy Sausage and White Bean Soup with Winter Squash and Broccoli Rabe (PAGE 114)

Honeydew-Blackberry and Granola Parfait (PAGE 50)

Multigrain Pancakes (PAGE 66)

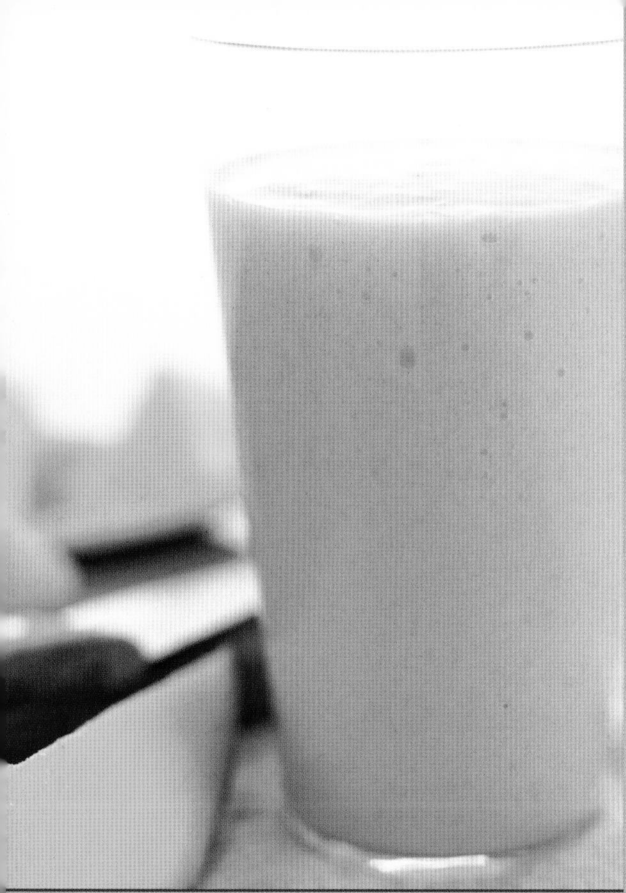

Mango Smoothie (PAGE 47)

Mini Whole Wheat Pumpkin Muffins with Orange Drizzle (PAGE 145)

Cardamom Pistachio Cookies (PAGE 151), Miniature Apricot-Cherry Bars (PAGE 156), Cherry Almond Biscotti (PAGE 163)

Gingerbread Straws (PAGE 158)

Seared Scallop, Black Bean, Orange, and Avocado Salad (PAGE 100)

Creamy Chili-Corn Soup with Chicken and Black Beans (PAGE 136)

Canadian Bacon and Cheese Pizza with Tomatoes and Basil (PAGE 60)

Asian Chicken Salad (PAGE 101)

Smoked Salmon Tartare (PAGE 177)

Sausage, Cilantro, and Creamy Salsa Verde Omelet (PAGE 75)

I Can't Believe They're Not Fried Tortilla Chips (PAGE 173) and Classic Texas Caviar (PAGE 178)

Asian Chicken Noodle Soup (PAGE 137)

Wine Biscuits with Cracked Black Pepper (PAGE 176)

Sausage and Caramelized Onion Flatbread with Kale and Parmesan (PAGE 194)

Mix-and-Match Foil Packets (PAGE 243)

Sear-and-Sauce Chicken Cutlets (PAGE 222) with Mushroom-Thyme Cream Sauce (PAGE 231)

Baked Fish with Green Beans and Capers (PAGE 238)

Fresh Tomato Flatbread with Arugula and Prosciutto (PAGE 193)

Sear-and-Sauce Pork Tenderloin (PAGE 225) with Marsala and Prunes (PAGE 233)

Creamy Pasta with Salmon, Asparagus, and Dill (PAGE 208)

Grilled Swordfish or Tuna Steaks (PAGE 254)

Pasta with Just-Right Red Sauce (PAGE 213)

Spicy Grilled Shrimp (PAGE 250)

Coconut Cream Tartlets (PAGE 293)

Light Orange Panna Cotta with Fresh Raspberries (PAGE 287)

Lemon Cheesecake (PAGE 295)

NO WEIGH!

Part of your reward is regularly checking the numbers on the scale, but from my experience, it's usually a disappointment. If you're like me, you think you've sacrificed so much, worked so hard, and yet you've never lost as much as you think you should have. Most of the time, it's just downright discouraging. I've also discovered that if I hop on the scale every day, my weight becomes an obsession. I've got better things to think about.

If you don't own scales, you may not want to invest just yet. (Ultimately you might want to, but not now.) If you have scales, give them to someone temporarily, or ask a family member to hide them, then find a consistent off-site spot to weigh yourself every month or two. Pop into your doctor's office or detour to the gym's changing rooms to occasionally check your progress. Make sure they're the same scales each time. They can vary, and depending on the discrepancy, they can falsely make or blow your day.

Rather than weigh frequently, let your clothes be your gauge. If they're baggin', you're losin'. Every ten pounds means a new size. There's no better feeling than slipping into that next-smaller-size jeans. Besides, if you're starting to feel good about how you look, what does it matter how much you weigh?

Run—or Walk—Toward Yourself

Once I had achieved my weight loss goal, I scaled back from my daily two or three short premeal walk/runs to just one cardio session a day. These days I run an average of 45 minutes on Mondays, Wednesdays, and Fridays. To keep the routine interesting and to exercise a different set of body parts, I head to the gym on Tuesdays and Thursdays to bike and row for 45 minutes.

Everyone who exercises needs one day off, and Saturday's mine. To keep myself motivated post–weight loss, I've started running races, so most Sundays I get up early and run a little longer to build my endurance.

Once you achieve your weight loss goal, you may rediscover that old strong, energetic, agile you. If running isn't your thing, what might be? I recently read a woman's account of returning to downhill ski racing after a twenty-year hiatus. Last summer a friend took up rowing, a sport he was passionate about in college. Is it finally time to pick up that racket again? Maybe you need a personal trainer to help tighten that trimmer body.

Whatever you do, find a routine that you can faithfully commit to week after week, one that keeps you motivated to eat a little less and exercise a little more every day for the rest of your life.

Sit Still to Lose Weight

Since losing weight was the result of a lifestyle change and not a strict diet, there was no "going off" once I reached my goal. For the first time in my yo-yo history, there wasn't that celebratory moment when I went out and feasted on all those things I'd given up for months.

Remembering previous weight loss experiences, I'd worry at first if I deviated from my normal pattern for a day or two. That voice would say, "See there, I told you this wasn't for real," or "You're on your way up again." And there was good reason to half listen. I had never lost weight and kept it off.

Although the voice isn't as strong as it was in the beginning, there's still a small part of me that frets a little now and again. It's taken a long time for me to trust that since I've changed at my core, reverting back would be almost impossible. These days if I've eaten more than normal at one meal, I naturally tend to cut back at the next. I pay less attention to whether I've eaten a bigger cookie at teatime or indulged in a jumbo muffin for breakfast and more attention to my behavior. Am I carrying more of the weight in my relationships, doing too much, overcompensating, letting people off the hook, avoiding necessary confrontation, working too hard?

> Somewhere along the line, I developed a built-in mechanism that tells me when to stop eating.

Besides taking care of myself, I find that living a ritualized life keeps me on track. I get up early, at which point my husband and I light an oil lamp, read a short spiritual essay, then meditate for twenty minutes. Among other things, these few minutes of sitting quietly center and calm, making clear what's really important before the day starts to overwhelm. As with my scheduled eating, this meditation reinforces that I am in control of my time; my time does not control me.

Somewhere along the line, I developed a built-in mechanism that tells me when to stop eating—and it's a whole lot sooner than it used to be. I've never particularly enjoyed that stuffed feeling at the end of a big meal. I rarely allow myself to feel that way now.

To keep my weight in check, the scale came back when I moved to maintenance, but I still don't weigh myself frequently. Unless I'm trying to monitor occasional weight fluctuation (in which case, I might weigh once or twice a week at the gym), I usually hop on the scale every couple of weeks—sometimes only once a month.

By and large, I'm happy with the woman I'm becoming, in body—my new wardrobe is great, and I'm even comfortable on the dance floor—and in spirit. I achieved the goal I set for myself at the retreat several years ago, although I had no idea of the intense effort and immense satisfaction that would accompany its realization.

About the Calorie Analysis

When a range is listed for a yield or an ingredient, the first number is used. Optional ingredients are not included in the analysis unless otherwise noted. When more than one choice is given for an ingredient, the analysis refers to the first choice. When many choices are given, the analysis is given as an average.

STOCK UP

You may be like me. I hate rigid, boring plans and can hardly stand to eat the same thing two nights in a row. With a microwave and a well-stocked freezer, however, I can decide what I've got a taste for, and within five minutes, I'm ready to cook. And with a full fridge and pantry to supplement, I've generally got whatever I need to pull off just about anything.

You'll almost always find the following in my pantry, fridge, and freezer.

PANTRY ITEMS

Bread: Whole-grain, for morning toast.

Brown sugar: Dark brown sugar is more flavorful than white, so you can use less.

Canned beans (white, black, pinto, chickpeas, and black-eyed peas): They're a quick, healthy way to beef up a hearty main-course soup or salad.

Canned pasteurized crabmeat: Warehouse food clubs carry reasonably priced pasteurized lump crabmeat. I use crabmeat regularly to flavor soups, pastas, and quiches.

Capers: They're lower in fat than olives. I use them for pan sauces, pastas, salads, and pizzas.

Chicken broth: I keep at least 4 quarts on hand for main-course soups.

Cookies: If you allow yourself a daily sweet treat and don't make your own, you'll need a box or two of lean cookies. My favorites are vanilla wafers, chocolate wafers, gingersnaps, milk biscuits, pizzelles, and almond cookies.

Dried mushrooms: These add big flavor to pasta sauces, pan sauces, and soups.

Evaporated milk: This is great to make cream sauces or as a substitute for heavy cream in desserts like crème brûlée and panna cotta.

Extracts (vanilla, almond, coconut): These heighten flavor in smoothies, pancakes, granola, and baked goods.

Flour: I keep whole wheat flour on hand for flatbread dough and multi-grain pancakes, and white flour for making cookies and bars.

Honey: Like dark brown sugar, this is another flavorful sweetener.

Jams, preserves, and jellies: I use low-sugar fruit jam for my morning toast, but I also keep a few jars of the regular varieties, which taste and perform better in pan sauces.

Nuts: So that you don't have to keep several varieties on hand, buy roasted salted premium nuts, which usually include cashews, almonds, Brazil nuts, hazelnuts, and pecans. Then pick out the kind you need for a specific recipe. And since they're already roasted, this saves a step as well. You might also want to keep on hand shelled roasted pistachios, peanuts, walnuts, and pine nuts.

Oatmeal: Old-fashioned oats require longer cooking than the quick variety, but they've got a more satisfying texture.

Olive oil: Drizzle hearty main- or first-course salads with flavorful extra-virgin or whisk it into your favorite vinaigrette. Use pure olive oil for pan searing and sautéeing.

Olives (black, such as kalamatas, and green): Used in moderation, they add big flavor without significant calories to pizzas, salads, and pan sauces. Or nibble on them before dinner.

Pasta (linguine and other interesting shapes): Keep a few boxes of both regular and whole wheat around at all times. Since whole wheat (or whole-grain) pasta contains more fiber, you might be satisfied with smaller portions.

Rice: If you like brown rice but don't have time to cook it, Success Rice makes fully cooked brown rice that comes in two 1-cup containers. It's firmer than the minute variety.

Vinegars (balsamic, sherry, rice wine, white wine, and red wine): You'll probably be eating a lot of salad, and you'll need a variety of distinctly flavored vinegars. They're also useful for pan sauces.

PRODUCE

Bananas: Not only for a morning snack but also for smoothies and muffins.

Lemons, limes, and oranges: If a dish tastes flat or one-dimensional, reach for either salt or acid, in the form of lemons or limes (vinegar and tomatoes work as well). Hardly a day passes that I don't use a lemon to dress a salad or to perk up just about anything.

Tomatoes: Even out of season, cherry and grape tomatoes are usually excellent. They're great to munch on, toss into a salad, and roast or sauté to serve as a quick side dish. There's no prep—just dump, cook, season, and serve. Refrigerating compromises their flavor and texture.

REFRIGERATED PRODUCE

Baby greens (spring mix, arugula, spinach, and mâche): Available already washed, they make wonderfully quick, flavorful salads. With these greens in the fridge, you'll never have an excuse for not making a salad.

Romaine lettuce: Mixed with baby greens, chopped hearts of romaine make a substantial base for a hearty first- or main-course salad. Unlike other more delicate lettuces, hearts of romaine store well.

OTHER REFRIGERATED ITEMS

Cheese (Parmesan, feta, goat, blue): These are especially flavorful, so you don't need a lot for salads, pastas, and pizzas.

Chicken (boneless, skinless breasts and thighs, rotisserie chicken, and cooked chicken breast strips): Even really good chicken is relatively cheap, so buy the best you can afford. Look for words like free-range, free-roaming, and organic on the package. Rotisserie chicken and cooked strips of chicken breast (available in the supermarket refrigerator sections) are great for making quick soups, salads, and pastas, and for topping pizzas.

Dijon mustard: It offers big flavor with few calories. Use it as a "sauce" for some of the breakfast and dinner pizzas and to perk up crustless quiche. An emulsifier, it both thickens and flavors pan sauces and vinaigrettes.

Eggs and liquid egg whites: Keep a carton of each on hand for quick open-faced omelets, quiches, or salads.

Ham: Lean ham is one of my staples for soups and salads.

Light mayonnaise: One of the few "light" products that taste good. There's a significant calorie savings from regular (40 calories per tablespoon versus 90).

Prosciutto: Just a little gives great pork flavor. Use it in place of bacon or sausage to flavor soups and pastas.

Soy milk (vanilla and chocolate): Because it's sweeter than milk and has fewer calories, use it to make smoothies and Overnight Oatmeal.

Turkey breast: Great for salads. If buying slices, check the sell-by date. At a deli counter, make sure you're not buying the tail end of the hunk. Encourage the person serving you to slice from a fresh one.

Yogurt: Buy low-fat plain yogurt rather than high-sugar or artificially sweetened varieties. To sweeten it, drizzle with a little honey or lightly sprinkle with brown sugar.

FREEZER ITEMS

Fruit: If you want a quick smoothie for breakfast, you're going to need frozen fruit. Keep a variety on hand so that you're not drinking the same kind every morning.

Pizza crust: Since it's not always possible to make your own, it's nice to have a few prepared crusts in the freezer. Look for thin crusts (whole wheat, if you like).

Pork tenderloin: This makes a wonderfully quick weeknight dinner (and leftovers are great for tomorrow's lunch salad). To reduce the cooking time and keep the cut in one piece, butterfly the tenderloin by slicing it lengthwise, almost but not all the way through, then pound with your fist to a more or less even thickness.

Salmon fillets: Food warehouses sell whole sides of fresh salmon. Cut it into 5- to 6-ounce fillets and freeze, reserving the tail end for soups and pasta sauces.

Scallops (sea and bay): Seek out the untreated variety—those not tainted with the flavor-wrecking preservative called sodium tripolyphosphate. If you can't find them fresh, check the freezer section. One of my local grocery stores carries the frozen variety in both sizes—big sea scallops, perfect for searing and serving as a main course with a pan sauce or atop a large salad, and the smaller bay scallops, ideal for tossing into soups and pastas. Unlike the more common preservative-soaked varieties in many seafood cases, these scallops sear beautifully and taste fresh and sweet.

Shrimp: I recently discovered *wild*, peeled, individually quick-frozen shrimp in the grocery-store freezer case. Like all good things, wild shrimp costs a little more, but if you've lived on a steady diet of farm-raised, you'll find the wild variety's sweet, briny flavor vastly superior. Thaw only what you need. I sear (or skewer and grill) extra for dinner, then toss the leftovers into tomorrow's lunch salad or dinner pasta or even serve up a few as a predinner snack.

Turkey cutlets: Sliced from the breast, these thin, easy-to-cook cuts are a nice alternative to boneless, skinless chicken breasts. You can make your own cheaply by cutting a half turkey breast across the grain into ½-inch-thick slices.

Vegetables (spinach, green peas, okra, corn, lima beans): For soups, these particular frozen vegetables offer great quality and require no prep.

EQUIPMENT

Custard cups: Especially with dessert, it's important to take small portions. For this reason, many of the recipes in this book are baked or refrigerated in individual custard cups. Custard cups are also great for microwaving eggs.

Gas grill: Because it preheats quickly with just the turn of a knob and simultaneously cooks by direct and indirect heat, a gas grill is an efficient way to cook small cuts very quickly. If possible, park your gas grill near the kitchen—you'll be more likely to use it year-round. Look for one with a built-in thermometer (with real numbers as opposed to temperature ranges), a fuel gauge, good fat drainage, and four casters (easier to move than models with only two). Heavier grates are better and heat more evenly than thin, flexible grates. Avoid grills with lava rocks or fake coals, which absorb fat and flare up. Consider buying a grill cover, especially if the grill is fully exposed to the elements.

Microplane: An effortless way to remove zest from citrus to add intense flavor to sauces, muffins, cookies, and other desserts. If you're still scraping the zest out of a box grater, invest in one of these now.

Mini muffin tins: Just as you're probably better off ordering a couple of doughnut holes rather than a whole doughnut, make mini muffins instead of the large ones.

Salad spinner: Although I usually buy prewashed greens, it's nice to have a salad spinner for those times when you buy a whole head. Look for one with pump-action and a button brake.

Scale: It's important to know how much you're eating. Invest in a good-quality digital scale with a maximum weight reading of 10 or 11 pounds, in case you want to weigh something large, such as a roast or pumpkin.

Silicone mats: Cookies and flatbreads effortlessly slide off silicone-mat-lined cookie sheets. Cleanup is easy as well: simply sponge off the mats.

Mini springform pans: You can use a standard 9- to 10-inch springform pan for the cheesecake recipes in this book, but making them in smaller pans allows you to refrigerate one and freeze the others until you need them.

the recipes

eat (or drink) your breakfast

The evidence is overwhelming. Breakfast skippers are less efficient, more sluggish, foggier thinkers, and bigger bingers, and they have higher body mass indexes (more body fat) than those who eat breakfast. Some forgo it because they find they get hungry earlier when they eat than when they don't, but ultimately the plan backfires. Skip breakfast, your metabolism slows, and the body retreats into survival mode, burning minimal calories. Eat it, your metabolism kicks in, and the body goes to work.

And there aren't just physiological ramifications. Anybody who's ever skipped breakfast knows the head game you play the rest of the day. "Since I didn't eat breakfast, I can . . ."

But what if you're one of those people who eat breakfast and feel like raiding the pantry a couple of hours later? That was me. For years I'd eat breakfast and read the paper at 7:00 but was starving by midmorning. I used to satisfy that insatiable hunger with a large snack and then—ready or not—belly up for lunch just a few hours later. Over the years, however, I've figured out how to get my body up, running, and content. Here's what works for me.

Skip breakfast, your metabolism slows, and the body retreats into survival mode, burning minimal calories.

As soon as I get up, I drink a cup of milky tea and eat a half or whole banana. The small hit of caffeine wakes me, the little splash of milk soothes me, and the banana's carbohydrates and natural sugar energize me for my workout or run. With this snack followed by appetite-suppressing exercise, I don't eat breakfast until around 9:00, which easily keeps me going until noon.

I always take time for breakfast. Many mornings it's a couple of slices of whole-grain toast with peanut butter and low-sugar jam. When I'm heading out, it could be a quick smoothie for the road. If the fruit's ripe and especially good, I might assemble a parfait and toast. I frequently enjoy microwave-poached eggs, and love open-faced omelets too. On the weekends, I often go for whole-grain pancakes or even crustless quiche.

Whatever I eat, I know that taking time for my early-morning snack and midmorning breakfast sends a clear daily message to my body. "Don't worry. I'm paying attention, and I'm going to take care of you."

RECIPES

SMOOTHIES

Chocolate Fruit Smoothies 45
- Chocolate-Raspberry-Orange 45
- Black Forest 45

Vanilla Fruit Smoothies 46
- Raspberry-Orange 46
- Piña Colada 46
- Blueberry-Lemon 47
- Peach-Almond 47
- Mango 47
- Tropical 47

BREAKFAST PARFAITS

Fruit Parfait with Yogurt and Drizzled Honey 49
- Watermelon-Blueberry and Toasted Almond 49
- Pear-Raspberry and Toasted Hazelnut 49
- Grapefruit-Orange and Toasted Coconut 49
- Pineapple-Banana and Roasted Cashew 50
- Cantaloupe-Strawberry and Grape-Nut 50
- Honeydew-Blackberry and Granola 50
- Peach-Cherry and Toasted Pecan 50
- Apple-Grape and Toasted Walnut 50

GRANOLA

Great Granola 52
- Classic 52
- Crunchy 53
- Tropical 53

Cherries and Almond 53
Trail Mix 54
Orange-Berry with Pecans 54
Pear with Hazelnuts and Vanilla 54
Orange with Pistachios, Mangoes, and Dates 55

STICK-TO-YOUR-RIBS CEREAL

Overnight Oatmeal—Cold or Warm 57
Creamy Grits with Parmesan and Prosciutto 58

BREAKFAST PITA PIZZAS—SAVORY AND SWEET

Canadian Bacon and Cheese with Tomatoes and Basil 60
Chicken Sausage with Spinach and Feta 61
Fruit 62
Banana with Peanut Butter and Chocolate 63

PANCAKES

Multigrain Pancakes 66
Lemon–Poppy Seed 67
Orange-Cardamom 67
Gingerbread 67
Banana-Nutmeg 67
Lemon-Blueberry 67
Almond 67
Corn 68

EGGS ON THE GO

Microwave Scrambled Eggs with Scallions and Cheese 70
Microwave Poached Egg 71
Microwave "Boiled" Egg 71
Perfect Hard-Boiled Eggs 72

OMELETS

Open-Faced Omelet 74
Ham, Gruyère, and Nutmeg 74
BLT 75
Sausage, Cilantro, and Creamy Salsa Verde 75
Bacon, Watercress, and Blue Cheese 75
Tomato, Mozzarella, and Basil 75
Smoked Salmon, Cream Cheese, and Fresh Dill 76
Prosciutto, Tomato, and Fresh Goat Cheese 76
Ham, Cheddar, and Caraway 76

QUICHE

Crustless Quiche 78
Bacon, Leeks, and Goat Cheese 78
Crab, Bell Peppers, Basil, and Corn 79
Sausage, Apples, and Sage 80
Ham, Swiss Cheese, and Asparagus 80
Spinach, Mushrooms, Tomatoes, and Feta 81

a smooth start to the day

For those who need breakfast pronto, my smoothies are quick (both to make and drink), simple, and flavorful. I prefer soy milk because it is lower in calories and naturally sweeter than dairy milk.

Unsweetened cocoa powder intensifies the flavor in the chocolate smoothies, while lemon juice heightens the fruit flavor in the vanilla-based ones, both of which eliminate the need for excess sweeteners (read calories).

Whether you're making a chocolate or vanilla fruit smoothie, you'll need a frozen banana, which gives great body and subtle flavor. You'll want to keep frozen bananas on hand if you prepare smoothies regularly (or the banana muffins on page 147). Overripe ones are perfect. It's easier if you peel the bananas before freezing them, but if you don't have time, don't worry. You can remove frozen banana skins with a good vegetable peeler. Average bananas fit in a quart-sized freezer bag. Just keep adding bananas as they accumulate, and if they don't fit, simply halve them.

For those who need breakfast pronto, my smoothies are quick, simple, and flavorful.

Depending on how much you're exercising, you may want to have a piece of whole-grain toast with your smoothie.

Chocolate Fruit Smoothies

MAKES 2 CUPS, OR 1 SERVING

- 1 cup frozen fruit (strawberries, dark sweet cherries, raspberries)
- 1 medium peeled frozen banana
- 1 cup light chocolate soy milk
- 1 teaspoon unsweetened cocoa powder
- Optional flavorings (see recipes that follow)

Drop fruit of choice and banana into a blender. Whisk soy milk, cocoa powder, and optional flavorings in a 1-cup Pyrex measuring cup. With blender on high, add soy milk mixture through feeder tube, stopping and stirring as necessary, until mixture is smooth. Pour into a glass or cup and serve.

About 254 calories

Chocolate-Raspberry-Orange Smoothie

Use raspberries for fruit and whisk ¼ teaspoon finely grated orange zest into soy milk.

283 calories

Black Forest Smoothie

Use frozen cherries for fruit and whisk ½ teaspoon almond extract into soy milk.

298 calories

Vanilla Fruit Smoothies

MAKES 2 CUPS, OR 1 SERVING

- 1 cup frozen fruit (strawberries, dark sweet cherries, raspberries, blueberries, peaches, pineapple, mango)
- 1 medium peeled frozen banana
- 1 cup light vanilla soy milk
- 2 teaspoons honey
- 2 teaspoons lemon juice
- Optional flavorings (see recipes that follow)

Drop fruit of choice and banana into a blender. Whisk soy milk, honey, lemon juice, and optional flavorings in a 1-cup Pyrex measuring cup. With blender on high, add soy milk mixture through feeder tube, stopping and stirring as necessary, until mixture is smooth. Pour into a glass or cup and serve.

About 263 calories

Raspberry-Orange Smoothie

Use frozen raspberries for fruit and whisk ¼ teaspoon finely grated orange zest into soy milk.

291 calories

Piña Colada Smoothie

Use frozen pineapple for fruit and whisk ½ teaspoon coconut extract into soy milk.

291 calories

Blueberry-Lemon Smoothie

Use frozen blueberries for fruit and whisk ¼ teaspoon finely grated lemon zest into soy milk.

290 calories

Peach-Almond Smoothie

Use frozen peaches for fruit and whisk ½ teaspoon almond extract into soy milk.

297 calories

Mango Smoothie

Use frozen mango for fruit and whisk ¼ teaspoon finely grated lemon zest into soy milk.

318 calories

Tropical Smoothie

Use ½ cup each frozen pineapple and mango chunks and whisk ½ teaspoon coconut extract into soy milk.

308 calories

#1

50 WAYS TO LOSE IT

**Vow never to diet again.
Instead, prepare to change your life.**

parfait beginnings

Enjoy these attractive layered fruit cups year-round with ripe, seasonal fruit. By drizzling honey over yogurt (rather than stirring it in), you get away with using much less.

Sprinkled on in moderation, nuts, crunchy cereal, and coconut add texture. Instead of storing different bags of individual nuts, keep one can or jar of premium roasted mixed nuts in the pantry and pick out the specific variety you want as needed.

By drizzling honey over yogurt, you get away with using much less.

Fruit Parfait with Yogurt and Drizzled Honey

SERVES 1

1½ cups fruit, your choice (see below)
⅓ cup low-fat plain yogurt
2 teaspoons honey
2 tablespoons chopped toasted nuts, Grape-Nuts cereal, granola (page 52), or sweetened or unsweetened flaked coconut—your choice

Spoon half the fruit into a glass (I like a stemless wineglass) or bowl. Top with half the yogurt, drizzle with half the honey, and sprinkle with half the nuts, cereal, granola, or coconut. Repeat with remaining fruit, yogurt, honey, and nuts, cereal, granola, or coconut. Serve immediately.

About 248 calories

Watermelon-Blueberry and Toasted Almond Parfait

Use 1 cup diced watermelon and ½ cup blueberries for fruit and toasted sliced, slivered, or chopped whole almonds.

251 calories

Pear-Raspberry and Toasted Hazelnut Parfait

Use 1 cup diced pear and ½ cup raspberries for fruit and toasted chopped hazelnuts.

312 calories

Grapefruit-Orange and Toasted Coconut Parfait

Use 1 sectioned grapefruit and 1 sectioned orange for fruit and toasted flaked coconut.

280 calories

Pineapple-Banana and Roasted Cashew Parfait

Use 1 cup diced pineapple and ½ medium banana for fruit and roasted cashews.

320 calories

Cantaloupe-Strawberry and Grape-Nut Parfait

Use 1 cup diced cantaloupe and ½ cup sliced strawberries for fruit and 2 tablespoons Grape-Nuts.

227 calories

Honeydew-Blackberry and Granola Parfait

Use 1 cup diced honeydew melon and ½ cup blackberries for fruit and your favorite granola.

220 calories

Peach-Cherry and Toasted Pecan Parfait

Use 1 cup diced peach and ½ cup halved pitted dark sweet cherries for fruit and toasted pecans.

316 calories

Apple-Grape and Toasted Walnut Parfait

Use 1 cup diced apple and ½ cup halved seedless grapes for fruit and toasted walnuts.

310 calories

the best granola is homemade

This granola is chock-full of good-for-you nuts, seeds, dried fruits, zests, and spices, rather than the heavy sweeteners and fats of commercial versions.

For the best results, use old-fashioned, or rolled, oats, not quick-cooking. (Quick-cooking oats have a powdery rather than crisp texture and taste of raw starch.) Old-fashioned oats bake into crisp, golden granola. To make them clump better, add a smidgen of water. In combination with the oil and liquid sweetener, the water mixes with the wheat germ to create a delicious mortar. Squeeze the granola with your hands before baking to seal the bond and form small clumps.

This granola is chock-full of good-for-you ingredients.

I prefer to sweeten the granola with maple syrup, but you can use honey or even a combination of honey or maple syrup and molasses (as in Crunchy Granola, page 53). And don't forget salt. Just a pinch brings out the flavors. If serving the granola with milk or over plain yogurt, you may want to drizzle with a bit more sweetener. A low oven temperature helps the cereal crisp up and brown thoroughly and evenly. Adding the fruit partway through baking dries it out just enough so that it doesn't turn the granola soggy.

If you double the recipe, increase the pan size (or bake the granola in two pans), and you may need to increase the baking time. The key is to bake the granola until it's an impressive golden brown.

Great Granola

MAKES 1 QUART

- 2 cups old-fashioned oats
- ½ cup wheat germ
- ¼ teaspoon salt
- 1 cup Extra Ingredients (see below)
- ¼ cup maple syrup
- 3 tablespoons flavorless oil, such as vegetable or canola
- 2 tablespoons warm water
- Flavoring (optional; see below)

Adjust oven rack to middle position and heat oven to 275 degrees. Spray a 13-by-9-inch pan with vegetable cooking spray.

Mix oats, wheat germ, salt, and Extra Ingredients—except dried fruit—in a medium bowl. Heat syrup, oil, water, and Flavoring, if called for, to a simmer in a small saucepan over medium heat. Drizzle over oat mixture and stir to combine.

Pour mixture into prepared pan. Working a handful at a time, squeeze cereal to form small clumps. Bake for 30 minutes. Stir in dried fruit. Continue to bake until golden brown, 20 to 25 minutes longer. Let cool and serve. (Granola can be stored in an airtight tin for 1 month.)

About 121 calories per ¼ cup

Classic Granola

EXTRA INGREDIENTS:

- ⅓ cup chopped walnuts
- ⅓ cup sweetened or unsweetened flaked coconut
- ⅓ cup dark or golden raisins

FLAVORING:

- ½ teaspoon ground cinnamon

115 calories per ¼ cup

Crunchy Granola

If you like, replace the maple syrup with 2 tablespoons each maple syrup and molasses.

EXTRA INGREDIENTS:

- ¼ cup slivered almonds
- ¼ cup sunflower seeds
- 2 tablespoons sesame seeds
- 6 tablespoons dried currants

121 calories per ¼ cup

Tropical Granola

EXTRA INGREDIENTS:

- ¼ cup chopped roasted unsalted cashews
- ¼ cup sweetened or unsweetened flaked coconut
- ¼ cup chopped banana chips (add with cashews and coconut)
- ¼ cup chopped dried pineapple

FLAVORING:

- ½ teaspoon ground ginger

110 calories per ¼ cup

Cherries and Almond Granola

EXTRA INGREDIENTS:

- ⅓ cup sliced almonds
- ⅓ cup sweetened or unsweetened flaked coconut
- ⅓ cup chopped dried cherries

FLAVORING:

- ¾ teaspoon almond extract

110 calories per ¼ cup

Trail Mix Granola

EXTRA INGREDIENTS:

- ¼ cup chopped roasted unsalted peanuts
- ¼ cup sweetened or unsweetened flaked coconut
- ¼ cup dark or golden raisins
- ¼ cup mini chocolate chips (stir in after granola has completely cooled)

120 calories per ¼ cup

Orange-Berry Granola with Pecans

EXTRA INGREDIENTS:

- ½ cup chopped pecans
- ¼ cup dried cranberries
- ¼ cup dried blueberries

FLAVORING:

- ½ teaspoon finely grated orange zest

122 calories per ¼ cup

Pear Granola with Hazelnuts and Vanilla

EXTRA INGREDIENTS:

- ½ cup chopped hazelnuts
- ¼ cup chopped dried cherries
- ¼ cup chopped dried pears

FLAVORING:

- 1 teaspoon vanilla extract

119 calories per ¼ cup

Orange Granola with Pistachios, Mangoes, and Dates

EXTRA INGREDIENTS:

- ½ cup chopped roasted pistachios
- ¼ cup chopped dates
- ¼ cup chopped dried mangoes

FLAVORING:

- ½ teaspoon finely grated orange zest
- ¼ teaspoon ground allspice

119 calories per ¼ cup

#2 50 WAYS TO LOSE IT

Don't skip breakfast.

stick-to-your-ribs cereal—even when there's no time

You probably already know oatmeal's health benefits. Coupled with a diet low in saturated fat and cholesterol, this soluble-fiber-rich cereal helps lower cholesterol, which, in turn, reduces the risk of heart disease. Most of us would gladly sit down to a bowl of steaming oatmeal for breakfast—if someone else would just make it for us each morning.

So that no one has to, prepare it the night before. While someone washes the dinner dishes, simply mix oatmeal and light vanilla soy milk (lower in calories, it has all the richness and flavor of low-fat milk, and it's sweeter too). During the summer months, refrigerate the oatmeal. In cooler months, set it in a 170-degree oven. By morning, you've got instant oatmeal, but with all the texture, taste, and fiber of the real thing.

Prepare old-fashioned oatmeal the night before.

Unless grits are enriched with a generous cube of butter or a big chunk of cheese, they're undeniably bland. By flavoring them with a little minced prosciutto and a grating of lean Parmesan, however, it's possible to serve up a low-fat, high-flavor, stick-to-the-ribs hot cereal.

Overnight Oatmeal—Cold or Warm

Studded with dried fruit, this chilled oatmeal is akin to milk-moistened muesli—a wonderfully filling cereal for the warmer months.

Overnight Refrigerator Oatmeal

SERVES 4

- 2 cups old-fashioned oats
- 2 cups light vanilla soy milk
- Pinch salt
- ¼ cup dried fruit (your choice), cut into bite-sized pieces if fruit is large (optional)

Mix oats, soy milk, salt, and dried fruit of choice, if using, in a medium bowl. Cover and refrigerate overnight (oatmeal can be refrigerated for up to 4 days). Stir and serve.

About 178 calories per serving

Overnight Oven Oatmeal

Here's the perfect solution for when you don't have the drive to start from scratch. This recipe can easily be halved—use a small saucepan.

SERVES 4

- 2 cups old-fashioned oats
- 1 quart light vanilla soy milk or 2 cups 2% milk mixed with 2 cups water
- Pinch salt

Adjust oven rack to lower-middle position and heat oven to 170 degrees.

Mix oats, soy milk or milk and water, and salt in a large saucepan. Cover and set in oven until milk is absorbed and oatmeal is cooked, 4 hours minimum and up to 12 hours. Stir and serve.

208 calories per serving

Creamy Grits with Parmesan and Prosciutto

SERVES 4

- 3 cups water, measured in a microwave-safe measuring cup
- 1 teaspoon vegetable oil
- 2 ounces thin-sliced prosciutto, minced
- ¾ cup quick grits
- ¼ teaspoon salt
- ¼ cup grated Parmesan cheese, preferably Parmigiano-Reggiano
- 1 teaspoon butter
- Ground black pepper

Microwave water until it is very hot, 3 to 4 minutes. Meanwhile, heat oil in a large saucepan over medium-high heat. Add prosciutto; sauté until moisture evaporates and bits start to fry, about 3 minutes. Remove prosciutto; set aside. Add hot water to empty pan and bring to a boil. Whisk in grits and salt; simmer, uncovered, over medium-low heat until thick, about 5 minutes. Stir in prosciutto, cheese, butter, and pepper to taste. Let stand to cool and to allow flavors to blend, 2 to 3 minutes. Serve.

184 calories per serving

#3 50 WAYS TO LOSE IT

Use vanilla soy milk for smoothies and oatmeal. It's lower in calories and sweeter than milk.

breakfast pita pizzas—savory and sweet

Whether you've got a taste for savory or sweet, these breakfast pizzas are satisfying to eat and kid-simple to prepare. For a large low-cal surface on which to pile vegetables, fruits, and low-fat protein, like Canadian bacon and chicken sausages, split a whole wheat pita.

Satisfying to eat and kid-simple to prepare.

Flavor your toast sparingly with a luxurious accent—a little grated sharp cheddar or crumbled feta over a savory one or grated almond paste or even miniature chocolate chips (unless that would start you down the wrong path) over one with fruit. Without adding significant calories, small quantities of these ingredients take these toasts from tolerable to terrific.

Canadian Bacon and Cheese Pizza with Tomatoes and Basil

MAKES 2 PIZZAS

1 6- to 7-inch whole wheat pita, split into 2 thin rounds
4 teaspoons Dijon mustard
4 slices (4 ounces) Canadian bacon, cut into ½-inch dice
16 cherry tomatoes, halved and lightly salted
Generous ½ teaspoon dried basil
2 ounces shredded sharp cheddar cheese (about ½ cup)

Adjust oven rack to lowest position and heat oven to 400 degrees.

Set pita halves on a cookie sheet. Spread with mustard and top in the following order: Canadian bacon, tomatoes, basil, and cheese. Bake until pitas are crisp and cheese melts, about 10 minutes. Serve immediately.

290 calories per pizza

Chicken Sausage Pizza with Spinach and Feta

MAKES 2 PIZZAS

1 6- to 7-inch whole wheat pita, split into 2 thin rounds
1 cup baby spinach
1 teaspoon olive oil
2 fully cooked lean chicken sausages (about 1¼ ounces each), preferably Mediterranean-flavored, sliced ¼ inch thick
¼ cup crumbled feta cheese (about 1 ounce)

Adjust oven rack to center position and heat oven to 400 degrees.

Set pita halves on a cookie sheet. Toss spinach with olive oil and spread over pitas. Top with sausage and feta. Bake until pitas are crisp and golden, about 10 minutes. Serve immediately.

181 calories per pizza

Fruit Pizza

You can sprinkle these fruit pizzas with a pinch of any of the following: ground cinnamon, cloves, or ginger, or finely grated lemon or orange zest.

MAKES 2 PIZZAS

- 1 6- to 7-inch whole wheat pita, split into 2 thin rounds
- 1½ cups fresh or frozen fruit (see below)
- ¼ cup (1 ounce) coarsely grated almond paste
- 2 tablespoons finely chopped nuts (sliced or slivered almonds, pecans, walnuts, hazelnuts, pistachios)

Adjust oven rack to center position and heat oven to 400 degrees.

Set pita halves on a cookie sheet. Top with fruit and sprinkle with almond paste and nuts. Bake until pitas are crisp and golden, about 10 minutes for fresh fruit and 14 minutes for frozen. Serve immediately.

About 289 calories per pizza

FOR 2 PIZZAS, YOU'LL NEED ONE OF THE FOLLOWING:

- 1½ pears, halved, cored, and sliced thin
- 1½ peaches, halved, pitted, and sliced thin
- 3 plums, halved, pitted, and sliced thin
- 1 large apple, cored and sliced thin
- 12 medium strawberries, hulled and sliced thin
- 1½ cups fresh raspberries, blackberries, or blueberries
- 1½ cups of the following frozen fruits (do not thaw): diced peaches, blueberries, raspberries, blackberries (or mixed berries), or cherries

Banana Pizza with Peanut Butter and Chocolate

Chocolate is not a danger food for me. If it is for you though, opt for one of the savory options.

MAKES 2 PIZZAS

1 6- to 7-inch whole wheat pita, split into 2 thin rounds
2 tablespoons smooth peanut butter
1½ medium bananas, sliced ¼ inch thick
2 tablespoons semisweet chocolate mini morsels

Adjust oven rack to center position and heat oven to 400 degrees.

Set pita halves on a cookie sheet. Spread with peanut butter and top with bananas and chocolate. Bake until pitas are crisp and golden, about 10 minutes. Serve immediately.

334 calories per pizza

#4
50 WAYS TO LOSE IT

Weigh yourself and own the number.

pancakes so good you might not even need syrup

Studies show that people who eat more whole grains consistently weigh less than those who eat fewer whole grains. In fact, in the 2005 Dietary Guidelines, the U.S. government recommends that we adults eat half our grains—that's at least 3 servings a day—as whole. Made with half all-purpose flour and half whole grains, these pancakes will start you off on the right nutritional foot.

Pancakes are rare at our house during the week, but on slower-paced weekends, I frequently whip up a batch. Over the years, I've perfected my recipe and technique. These pancakes are lower in both fat and sugar than my regular pancakes, making them OK to enjoy as often as I have time to make them.

Pancake batter should pour, not glug. On the other hand, overly runny batter makes thin, odd-shaped pancakes that frequently collide on the griddle. Stir a touch more flour into thin batter. The buttermilk in this recipe gives just the right consistency. If your batter seems too thick, whisk in water, a teaspoon at a time.

The temperature of the cooking surface is also important. Too hot, and the pancakes are dark and raw. Too cool, and they're pale and hard.

For tender, golden brown pancakes, heat the pan or griddle on low during preparation. Once the batter's made, increase the heat to medium and lightly brush the pan or griddle with oil. It's ready when the oil starts to shimmer. If the pan starts to smoke, however, remove it from the burner until the smoking subsides.

Warm low-sugar jams over low heat for a low-cal syrup or serve the pancakes with apple or pumpkin butter. Many of the pancake variations are so delicious you may find that you don't need syrup at all.

These pancakes will start you off on the right nutritional foot.

Multigrain Pancakes

MAKES SIXTEEN 4-INCH PANCAKES

- 1 cup bleached all-purpose flour
- ⅓ cup each cornmeal, whole wheat flour, and old-fashioned oats (for 1 cup total)
- 4 teaspoons sugar
- 1 teaspoon salt
- 1 teaspoon baking powder
- ½ teaspoon baking soda
- 1½ cups low-fat buttermilk
- ½ cup low-fat milk
- 2 large eggs
- 2 tablespoons vegetable oil
- 1 teaspoon vanilla extract
- Vegetable oil for brushing griddle

Heat a large nonstick skillet or griddle over low heat while preparing batter.

Mix flour, cornmeal, whole wheat flour, oats, sugar, salt, baking powder, and baking soda in a medium bowl. Microwave buttermilk and milk together in a 1-quart Pyrex measuring cup to room temperature, 20 to 30 seconds. Whisk eggs, oil, and vanilla into the buttermilk and milk. Pour wet ingredients into dry ingredients and whisk until just mixed. Return batter to measuring cup, stirring in a teaspoon or so of water, if necessary, to make a thick but pourable batter.

Increase heat to medium and lightly brush skillet or griddle with oil. When oil starts to spread out but before it starts to smoke, pour in batter, about ¼ cup at a time, working in batches, if necessary, to avoid overcrowding. When pancake bottoms are golden brown and tops start to bubble, 2 to 3 minutes, flip pancakes and cook until golden brown on remaining side. Repeat, brushing skillet or griddle with oil as needed. Serve hot.

94 calories per pancake

Lemon–Poppy Seed Multigrain Pancakes

Whisk 1 teaspoon finely grated lemon zest and 1 teaspoon poppy seeds into dry ingredients.

95 calories per pancake

Orange-Cardamom Multigrain Pancakes

Whisk 1 teaspoon finely grated orange zest and ¼ teaspoon ground cardamom into dry ingredients.

94 calories per pancake

Gingerbread Multigrain Pancakes

Omit sugar and add 4 teaspoons molasses to wet ingredients. Whisk ½ teaspoon ground cinnamon, ½ teaspoon ground ginger, and ⅛ teaspoon ground cloves into dry ingredients.

95 calories per pancake

Banana-Nutmeg Multigrain Pancakes

Whisk ½ teaspoon ground nutmeg into dry ingredients. While cooking the first side, drop 5 or 6 thin slices of banana (2 small bananas total) on each pancake as it cooks, then turn and cook other side.

106 calories per pancake

Lemon-Blueberry Multigrain Pancakes

Whisk 1 teaspoon finely grated lemon zest into dry ingredients. Sprinkle about 2 tablespoons frozen blueberries (about 1 cup total) over each pancake as it cooks, then turn and cook other side.

100 calories per pancake

Almond Multigrain Pancakes

Substitute 1 teaspoon almond extract for vanilla extract.

94 calories per pancake

Corn Multigrain Pancakes

Sprinkle about 2 tablespoons frozen corn (about 1 cup total) over each pancake as it cooks, then turn and cook other side.

104 calories per pancake

#5

50 WAYS TO LOSE IT

Warm low-sugar jams over low heat for a flavorful low-cal syrup.

eggs on the go

If you eat eggs often, you probably already know how to scramble or poach your favorite style on the stovetop. I know from experience, however, that time and a dirty skillet or pot can keep me from a warm, nourishing egg breakfast. For this reason, I offer recipes for super-quick, perfectly cooked, microwave scrambled and poached eggs. Following either of these methods, you can be sitting down to a hearty, nutritious breakfast in just a couple of minutes.

There's an art to a perfectly boiled egg.

Since boiled eggs are such a regular part of my diet, I frequently cook up a batch and store them in the fridge (marked with a big black X). When I want one, I simply peel it (and, if I want it warm, microwave it for a few seconds). There's an art to a perfectly boiled egg—and a big difference in taste between an egg with a tender white and bright yellow yolk and one that's rubbery hard with a sulfurous green ring. For times when you're desperate for a faux boiled egg to toss into an impromptu salad or put on toast, I offer a 4-minute microwave method as well.

Microwave Scrambled Eggs with Scallions and Cheese

A touch of buttermilk both moistens and adds a subtle pleasant tang to the eggs.

SERVES 1

2 large eggs
2 tablespoons low-fat buttermilk
1 scallion, sliced thin
Scant ¼ teaspoon salt and a couple of grinds of black pepper
2 tablespoons grated cheese (your choice)

Spray a small microwave-safe cereal bowl (about 10-ounce capacity) with vegetable cooking spray. Add eggs, buttermilk, scallion, salt, and pepper and whisk until beaten well. Microwave on high power until partially set, about 1 minute. Scramble with a fork, then continue to microwave until mostly set, about 45 seconds more. Scramble again, stirring in cheese. Cover with a plate and let stand until eggs are soft but set, about 1 minute. Serve.

If you want only 1 scrambled egg, halve the recipe and decrease the first microwaving time to 35 seconds and the second microwaving time to 15 seconds, and the rest time to 30 seconds.

About 222 calories

Microwave Poached Egg

SERVES 1

- ½ cup water
- ¼ teaspoon vinegar (your choice)
- ¼ teaspoon salt
- 1 large egg

Coat a 2-cup Pyrex measuring cup with vegetable cooking spray. Mix water, vinegar, and salt in measuring cup. Crack egg into water. Microwave on high power for 2 minutes 15 seconds for a runny yolk and 2 minutes 30 seconds for a soft yolk. Remove from microwave and let stand for 1 minute.

For 2 poached eggs, add another egg to measuring cup and increase microwave time to 2 minutes 45 seconds for runny yolks and 3 minutes for soft yolks.

71 calories

Microwave "Boiled" Egg

SERVES 1

- 1 large egg

Spray a small cereal bowl with vegetable cooking spray. Crack egg into bowl. Carefully pierce yolk with a fork 2 or 3 times. Cover with a saucer and microwave on defrost for 3 minutes. Let stand for 1 minute. At this point, egg white and yolk should be fully cooked.

71 calories

Perfect Hard-Boiled Eggs

SERVES 6

6 large eggs

Place eggs in a single layer in a medium saucepan. Cover with water, then pan lid, and bring to a full boil over medium-high heat. Remove from heat and let stand, covered, for 10 minutes. Drain water and run cold water over eggs until saucepan has completely cooled. Add 1 quart ice cubes to water to cool eggs as quickly as possible.

71 calories per egg

#6

50 WAYS TO LOSE IT

Look your best five days a week. (We all deserve a couple of days off.)

omelets with more filling, less hassle

Omelets may seem like a breakfast extravagance, but by pairing an egg with liquid egg whites, you get all the flavor of a real two-egg omelet without the extra calories.

Rather than folding the omelet around the filling ingredients, leave it open. It's easier, plus the omelet looks big, colorful, and attractive.

If you've got 10 minutes, most of these omelets are simple enough to prepare for a weekday breakfast. They're equally perfect for a weeknight supper or weekend breakfast, brunch, or even lunch.

An open-faced omelet is easier, plus it looks big, colorful, and attractive.

Open-Faced Omelet

SERVES 1

- 1 teaspoon oil
- 1 large egg
- ¼ cup liquid 100% egg whites
- Generous sprinkling of salt and ground black pepper
- Optional toppings (see recipes that follow)

Heat oil in an 8-inch nonstick skillet over low heat. Beat egg and egg whites in a small bowl along with salt and pepper.

A couple of minutes before cooking, increase temperature under skillet to medium-high. When wisps of smoke start to rise from pan, swirl oil to completely coat.

Add eggs. Using a plastic or wooden spatula to push back eggs that have set, tilt pan so that uncooked eggs run into empty portion of skillet. Continue pushing back cooked eggs and tilting pan until omelet top is wet but not runny. Turn heat to low and sprinkle toppings, if using, over eggs. Cover and cook until cheese melts and/or herbs or greens wilt, about 2 minutes.

About 144 calories

Ham, Gruyère, and Nutmeg Omelet

- ⅛ teaspoon ground nutmeg
- 1 slice (1 ounce) Canadian bacon, cut into small dice (scant ¼ cup)
- ½ ounce grated Gruyère cheese (2 tablespoons)

Whisk nutmeg in with salt and pepper. Top cooked eggs with Canadian bacon and cheese.

235 calories

BLT Omelet

1 tablespoon crumbled fried bacon (about 1 slice)
6 grape or cherry tomatoes, halved and lightly salted
¼ cup packed chopped arugula

Top cooked eggs with bacon, tomatoes, and arugula.

195 calories

Sausage, Cilantro, and Creamy Salsa Verde Omelet

You can substitute regular salsa for the salsa verde, if you like.

2 tablespoons light sour cream
2 tablespoons store-bought salsa verde
½ fully cooked lean turkey sausage (2 ounces), sliced thin
2 tablespoons chopped fresh cilantro leaves

Whisk sour cream and salsa verde in a small bowl. Top cooked eggs with sausage, salsa verde mixture, and cilantro.

266 calories

Bacon, Watercress, and Blue Cheese Omelet

1 tablespoon crumbled fried bacon (about 1 slice)
½ ounce crumbled blue cheese (scant 2 tablespoons)
¼ cup packed chopped watercress leaves

Top cooked eggs with bacon, blue cheese, and watercress.

230 calories

Tomato, Mozzarella, and Basil Omelet

1 ounce part-skim mozzarella, cut into small dice (scant ¼ cup)
6 grape or cherry tomatoes, halved and lightly salted
2 tablespoons torn fresh basil leaves

Top cooked eggs with cheese, tomatoes, and basil.

233 calories

Smoked Salmon, Cream Cheese, and Fresh Dill Omelet

1 ounce smoked salmon, cut into small dice (scant ¼ cup)
1 ounce light Neufchatel cream cheese, pinched into small chunks (2 tablespoons)
2 tablespoons chopped fresh dill

Top cooked eggs with salmon, cream cheese, and dill.

249 calories

Prosciutto, Tomato, and Fresh Goat Cheese Omelet

1 thin slice (about ½ ounce) prosciutto
6 grape or cherry tomatoes, halved and lightly salted
½ ounce crumbled fresh goat cheese (scant 2 tablespoons)
2 tablespoons torn fresh basil leaves

Top cooked eggs with prosciutto, tomatoes, goat cheese, and basil.

247 calories

Ham, Cheddar, and Caraway Omelet

¼ teaspoon caraway seeds
1 slice (1 ounce) Canadian bacon, cut into small dice (scant ¼ cup)
1 ounce cheddar cheese, grated (¼ cup)

Toast caraway seeds in an 8-inch nonstick skillet over low heat while preparing omelet ingredients. Transfer caraway seeds to small cup. Using same skillet, add oil and proceed with recipe. Top cooked eggs with Canadian bacon, cheese, and caraway seeds.

291 calories

quiche for the twenty-first century

With its rich crust and cream-based custard, conventional quiche will never make it onto a list of the most healthy dishes. But take away the crust (it's usually soggy anyway), stretch the eggs with lower-calorie liquid eggs or whites, and substitute intensely flavored but lower-calorie evaporated milk for the cream, and you've got a perfect breakfast, brunch, or supper main course. Fill the custard with highly flavorful ingredients and season it generously.

Take away the usual crust, and you've got a perfectly healthy brunch.

Crustless Quiche

SERVES 6

- Filling ingredients of choice (see recipes that follow)
- 2 large eggs
- ½ cup liquid eggs or egg whites
- 1 small can (5 ounces) evaporated milk
- 2 teaspoons Dijon mustard
- ½ teaspoon salt
- ¼ teaspoon ground black pepper
- Dried herb of choice (see recipes that follow)
- Cheese of choice (see recipes that follow)

Adjust oven rack to center position and heat oven to 400 degrees. Grease a 9-inch Pyrex pie plate.

Prepare filling ingredients and set aside.

Whisk eggs, milk, mustard, salt, and pepper in a medium bowl. Stir in herb, cheese, and filling ingredients.

Pour mixture into pie plate and bake until just set, 25 to 30 minutes. Remove from oven and let rest 5 minutes. Cut into 6 wedges and serve.

About 67 calories per serving (without cheese)

Quiche with Bacon, Leeks, and Goat Cheese

FILLING INGREDIENTS:

- 6 ounces sliced bacon, cut into 1-inch pieces
- 1 large leek (8–10 ounces), darkest green section trimmed, light green and white section quartered lengthwise, sliced thin, and washed thoroughly

DRIED HERB:

- Scant ¼ teaspoon dried thyme leaves

CHEESE:

4 ounces crumbled fresh goat cheese (scant 1 cup)

Heat a large skillet over medium-high heat. Add bacon; fry until brown and crisp, 5 to 6 minutes. Drain bacon in a small colander set over a bowl to catch drippings. Return 2 teaspoons of the drippings to skillet. Add leek, sauté until tender, 5 to 6 minutes, and add to colander with bacon.

Add thyme, cheese, and filling ingredients to egg mixture.

222 calories per serving

Quiche with Crab, Bell Peppers, Basil, and Corn

FILLING INGREDIENTS:

2 teaspoons olive oil
½ small bell pepper, cut into small dice
1 cup frozen corn, thawed and drained
8 ounces pasteurized lump crabmeat, drained, picked over, and patted dry
2 scallions, sliced thin

DRIED HERB:

¼ teaspoon dried basil

CHEESE:

3 ounces grated pepper Jack cheese (about ¾ cup)

Heat oil in a large skillet over medium-high heat. Add pepper; sauté until just tender, 2 to 3 minutes. Add corn; sauté to heat through. Stir in crab and scallions; remove from heat.

Add basil, cheese, and filling ingredients to egg mixture.

208 calories per serving

Quiche with Sausage, Apples, and Sage

FILLING INGREDIENTS:

- 2 teaspoons vegetable oil
- 1 large Granny Smith apple, cored and cut into medium dice
- 6 ounces fully cooked lean chicken sausages, quartered lengthwise and cut into medium dice

DRIED HERB:

- ¼ teaspoon dried rubbed sage

CHEESE:

- 3 ounces grated sharp cheddar cheese (about ¾ cup)

Heat oil in a large skillet over medium-high heat. Add apple; sauté until caramel brown, about 4 minutes. Add sausages; sauté until golden brown, about 2 minutes longer.

Add sage, cheese, and filling ingredients to egg mixture.

192 calories per serving

Quiche with Ham, Swiss Cheese, and Asparagus

FILLING INGREDIENTS:

- 1 teaspoon olive oil
- 8 ounces asparagus, tough ends snapped, cut into 1-inch lengths
- 3 tablespoons water
- 1 6-ounce chunk ham, cut into medium dice

DRIED HERB:

- ¼ teaspoon dried tarragon

CHEESE:

- 3 ounces grated part-skim Jarlsberg cheese (about ¾ cup)

Place oil, asparagus, and water in a large skillet. Cover and place over high heat. Cook until asparagus is bright green and just tender, 3 to 4 minutes. Add ham and sauté until well browned, 2 to 3 minutes longer.

Add tarragon, cheese, and filling ingredients to egg mixture.

160 calories per serving

Quiche with Spinach, Mushrooms, Tomatoes, and Feta

FILLING INGREDIENTS:

- 1½ tablespoons olive oil
- 1 package (10 ounces) sliced domestic white or baby bella mushrooms
- Salt and ground black pepper
- 1 box (10 ounces) frozen spinach, thawed and squeezed dry
- 12 cherry or grape tomatoes, halved and lightly salted
- 2 scallions, sliced thin

DRIED HERB:

- ¼ teaspoon dried oregano

CHEESE:

- 4 ounces crumbled feta cheese (about ¾ cup)

Heat 1 tablespoon oil in a large skillet over medium-high heat. Add mushrooms and sauté, seasoning lightly with salt and pepper, until golden brown, about 5 minutes. Transfer to a medium bowl. Add remaining ½ tablespoon oil, along with spinach and tomatoes. Sauté, seasoning lightly with salt and pepper, to evaporate some of the tomato liquid, 2 to 3 minutes. Stir in scallions.

Add oregano, feta, and filling ingredients to egg mixture.

180 calories per serving

#7

50 WAYS TO LOSE IT

Use liquid egg whites and a whole egg for 2-egg dishes.

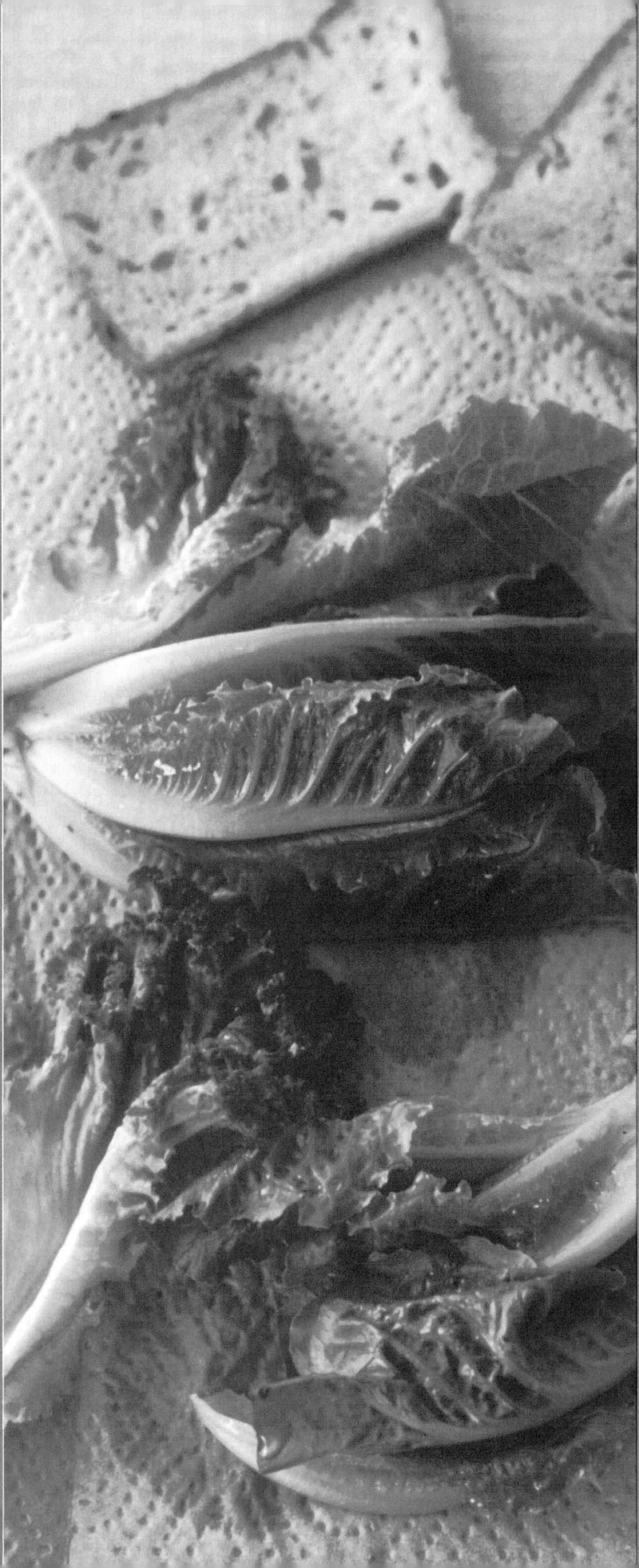

big lunch in a bowl

With a good breakfast under my belt, my hunger's under control until 12:30, which is when I usually eat lunch. Although it's not always possible to eat on a schedule, the more regular you are, the more your body starts to trust that you're going to treat it right, and there'll be less ravenous between-meal hunger. If you can't eat lunch at a consistent time, it may be worth asking why. I did, and here's what I learned about myself.

Because our house is so close to my husband's work, we're able to eat lunch together several times a week. For years I'd have lunch ready around 12:30. Sometimes he'd arrive on time, but often he was in the middle of something really important and he'd forget to call. If he wasn't home by 1:00, I'd start huffing. By 1:30, I'd cave in and make the angry phone call. As much as I'd complain, it never seemed to get better.

If you can't eat lunch at a consistent time, it may be worth asking why.

And because I was never sure what time I'd be eating lunch, I'd devour a big midmorning snack just to make sure I was covered until he arrived. If he showed up on time, I'd eat, even though I wasn't hungry. (I didn't want to own up to my snacking.)

Now we have a plan. Lunch is at 12:30. If my husband's running late, he calls. If he's tied up for a few extra minutes, I wait. If it's longer, I decide whether I want to dine alone (and that's OK too) or hold out for lunch for two.

Although there are no strict rules about lunch, I tend toward main-course salads in the warmer months and hearty soups when it's cool. Any of these soups or salads are perfect for dinner as well.

Since they're so satisfying and complete (and because teatime is just a few hours away), I don't usually need anything else.

RECIPES

MEAL-IN-A-BOWL SALADS

Meal-in-a-Bowl Salad 92
- Olive Oil–Vinegar Drizzle 93
- Low-Fat Creamy Herb and Parmesan Dressing 96
- Low-Fat Balsamic Vinaigrette 96
- Sweet-and-Sour Orange Dressing 96
- Chicken, Tomato, Black Bean, and Corn 97
- Chicken, Apricot, Chickpea, and Red Onion 97
- Ham, Pear, Hazelnut, and Goat Cheese 98
- Sausage, Roasted Pepper, Olive, and Feta 98
- Tuna, White Bean, Olive, and Tomato 99
- Smoked Salmon and Trimmings 99
- Seared Scallop, Black Bean, Orange, and Avocado 100
- Seared Turkey Burger with Blue Cheese and Red Onion 100
- Chicken, Grape, Walnut, and Blue Cheese 101
- Asian Chicken 101
- Crab, Corn, Roasted Pepper, and Avocado 102
- Sliced Pork Tenderloin, Orange, Dried Cranberry, and Pecan 102
- Pork Tenderloin, Plum, Cashew, and Cilantro 103
- Shrimp, Bacon, Cherry Tomato, and Feta 103
- Seared Tuna, Mushroom, Artichoke Heart, and Shaved Parmesan 104
- Seared Salmon, Egg, Sun-Dried Tomato, and Melba Croutons 104

Seared Sea Scallops 105

Seared or Grilled Salmon 106

Light Crab Cakes 107

Seared Turkey Burgers 108

MEAL-IN-A-BOWL SOUPS

Meal-in-a-Bowl Soup 111

- Chicken with Lima Beans and Corn 112
- Brazilian Ham and Black Bean 112
- Mexican Chicken and Hominy (or Black Bean) 113
- Shrimp and Sausage Gumbo 114
- Spicy Sausage and White Bean with Winter Squash and Broccoli Rabe 114
- Lemon Chicken and Orzo with Spinach 115
- Ham and White Bean with Cabbage, Carrots, and Caraway 116
- Pork and Hoppin' John with Collards and Peppers 117
- Scallop and Rice with Tomato 118
- Summer Crab and Corn 118
- Italian Turkey Meatball 119
- Fish with Bok Choy, Mushrooms, and Cilantro 120

Creamy Soups 124

- Quick Cream of Tomato 125
- Cream of Asparagus 126
- Cream of Mushroom 127

Hearty Almost-Homemade Soups 128

- Creamy Black Bean with Cumin and Salsa Verde 129
- Creamy Chickpea with Garam Masala and Cilantro 130
- Creamy White Bean with Rosemary and Basil 131
- Quick Garlic Croutons 131
- Ham and Lentil with Tomatoes and Arugula 133
- Moroccan Lentil 134
- Tomato-Tortellini with Spinach and Italian Spices 135
- Creamy Chili-Corn with Chicken and Black Beans 136
- Asian Chicken Noodle 137

create your own meal-in-a-bowl salad

Making a main-course salad used to be a big deal. Before you could spear the first bite, you had to wash, dry, and tear lettuce, cook meat, chop vegetables or fruit, roast nuts, and grate cheese. By then, it almost seemed time for the next meal!

Now making a salad is a breeze. Lettuces come prewashed and dried, cabbage already shredded. You can get roast chicken and pork and boiled and peeled shrimp and eggs. You have your choice of raw or toasted nuts of all kinds and of shredded, sliced, or crumbled cheese.

As you let the oil drizzle over the salad, keep in mind there are 120 calories in that tablespoon.

Lettuce is the foundation. Since it gives the salad bulk (plus it has few calories), allow yourself a generous packed two cups. For textural, visual, and flavor interest, use a mix of greens. Start with chopped hearts of romaine, for example, to give the salad weight. Add a handful of baby greens—spinach, spring mix, arugula, watercress, or mâche—or mix in coleslaw mix or shredded purple cabbage. Packaged whole-leaf greens are a wonderful convenience, but avoid the bagged chopped salad mixes, which smell and taste like a cheap salad bar. When possible, stick with romaine, mesclun, or slaws, or if you have time, buy whole heads to wash, spin dry, and chop or tear yourself.

Choose your protein first. Whether it's seafood or shellfish, lean pork or poultry, protein defines the salad and determines the other ingredients you'll add. There are lots of possibilities. It all depends on what you have time for and what's around.

If you need lunch to be quick, choose ingredients you can just dump into a bowl and toss: cooked shrimp, chicken strips, pasteurized crabmeat, canned tuna, or smoked salmon. If there's a minute more, reach for Canadian bacon for julienning or cubing, lean cooked chicken sausage for slicing, or rotisserie chicken for shredding. When time is not an issue or you want something fancier, sear (or grill) chicken breasts, salmon, pork tenderloin, or a turkey burger or crab cake. It's a whole lot easier to make a mixed green salad with pork tenderloin, apples, celery, and walnuts if there are leftovers from last night's dinner, so when cooking, always be thinking about preparing the next meal.

Once you've decided on the protein, the rest of the ingredients naturally start to fall into place. Choose smoked salmon, for example, and you'll probably think of fresh dill or capers, while chicken sausage pairs up beautifully with roasted red peppers and feta cheese.

Since most vegetables are relatively low in calories, choose at least a couple from this category. Think out of the bag: red onion, scallions, celery or fennel for crunch without calories, mushrooms for earthy substance, avocados for richness. And don't forget seasonal fruit, which distinguishes a salad without adding lots of calories.

For richness, you can add just about any cheese, but Parmesan, feta, goat, and blue are my top picks. They're so highly flavored that you don't need much, and the first three are relatively low in fat. They're also easy to distribute evenly throughout the salad. Nuts, used sparingly, stick with you long after the lettuce and celery have burned off. Similarly, a little bit of bacon is a protein that goes a long way. And for the crunch and flavor of croutons without the added fat, try Melba toast.

Because your salad is chock-full of flavorful ingredients, you can dress it simply with extra-virgin olive oil, a sprinkling of salt and pepper, and a splash of vinegar or lemon juice. The key is to go easy on the olive oil.

Drizzle each salad portion with a tablespoon of extra-virgin olive oil (which is more full-flavored than regular, so you can get away with less), sprinkle with a generous pinch of salt and a few grinds of black pepper, and toss, using spring-action tongs or a similar utensil, to coat evenly. As you let the oil drizzle over the salad, keep in mind there are 120 calories in that tablespoon. When dressing a large salad with a small amount of oil, it's important to be equally stingy with the acid ingredient, or the salad will taste unpleasantly sharp. Start by sprinkling the oil-dressed salad with a couple of teaspoons of red wine vinegar, rice wine vinegar, sherry vinegar, balsamic vinegar, or fresh lemon juice and toss again to coat.

More important than picking the right vinegar is using the right amount. Mild rice wine vinegar is the most all-purpose of the lot. Sweeter, thicker balsamic vinegar pairs well with fruits, pork, and chicken. Sharper sherry vinegar and red wine vinegar are naturals with rustic, savory Mediterranean-style salads. Lemon juice is well suited for salads with fresh fruit and seafood.

When was the last time you called someone to the salad bar because you couldn't decide what went together and how much you needed?

Taste a lettuce leaf or two and adjust the flavorings. You'll probably need another hit of vinegar or lemon juice and another pinch of salt, but it's easier to add a little more at the end than to balance the flavor if you add too much up front.

For those occasions when you want something a bit different from the usual oil and vinegar or when you have a little more time, I offer three sensational low-fat salad dressings I've developed over the years: balsamic vinaigrette, herb and Parmesan, and sweet-and-sour orange.

The following recipes are just guides. After all, when was the last time you called someone to the salad bar because you couldn't decide what went together and how much you needed?

Meal-in-a-Bowl Salad

For a first-course dinner salad, halve the recipe and omit the protein.

MAKES 1 MAIN-COURSE SALAD

Salad base (2 heaping cups—a mix of the following):

Hearts of romaine, quartered lengthwise, cored, and cut into bite-sized pieces

Prewashed lettuces: spring mix, spinach, arugula, baby romaine, mâche, watercress

Coleslaw mix and packaged shredded purple cabbage

Belgian endive, quartered lengthwise, cored, and cut into bite-sized pieces

Radicchio, halved, cored, and cut into bite-sized pieces

Protein (add 3 ounces cooked or 4–5 ounces precooked):

Packaged cooked chicken breast strips (available in most supermarkets with the other cooked meats) or other cooked boneless, skinless chicken

Cooked shrimp

Smoked salmon

Fully cooked lean chicken sausage

Canadian bacon or other lean ham

Canned tuna

Pasteurized lump crabmeat

½ cup drained canned beans (black, white, pinto, black-eyed peas, or chickpeas)

Seared Sea Scallops (page 105)

Seared (see page 227) or grilled shrimp

Light Crab Cakes (page 107)

Seared or Grilled Salmon (page 106)

Seared Turkey Burgers (page 108)

Seared (see page 222 or 224) or grilled boneless, skinless chicken breasts or thighs

Seared (see page 225 or 226) or grilled pork tenderloin or pork loin chops

Vegetables (choose at least 1 or 2 kinds):

- 1/8 red onion, sliced thin
- 1–2 scallions, trimmed and sliced thin
- 6 cherry tomatoes, halved and lightly salted (technically fruit, but savory like a vegetable)
- 1 large carrot, peeled and coarsely grated
- 1 medium celery stalk, sliced thin
- ½ medium fennel, halved, cored, and sliced thin
- ¼ yellow, red, orange, or green bell pepper, cut into short, thin strips
- 1 cup thin-sliced mushrooms
- ½ cup thin-sliced English (seedless) cucumber
- ¼ avocado cut into medium dice
- ½ cup cooked thin-sliced or julienned beets

Possible add-ins (pages 94–95)

Dressing:

OLIVE OIL–VINEGAR DRIZZLE

- 1 tablespoon extra-virgin olive oil
- Generous pinch salt and a few grinds black pepper
- 2 teaspoons balsamic vinegar, red wine vinegar, rice wine vinegar, sherry vinegar, or fresh lemon juice

or

Low-Fat Creamy Herb and Parmesan Dressing (page 96), Low-Fat Balsamic Vinaigrette (page 96), Sweet-and-Sour Orange Dressing (page 96), or other dressing of choice

Place salad ingredients in a bowl.

If using Olive Oil–Vinegar Drizzle, drizzle oil over salad and sprinkle with salt and pepper, then toss, using spring-action tongs or a similar utensil, to coat evenly. Add vinegar or lemon juice and toss again to coat. Taste salad and adjust flavorings, adding more vinegar or lemon juice, salt or pepper, as needed.

Or toss salad with other dressing of choice.

About 360 calories (includes salad base, 3 ounces protein, 2 vegetables, and olive oil drizzle). Olive Oil–Vinegar Drizzle: 128 calories

Fruit:

- ½ medium apple, halved, cored, and sliced thin or cut into medium dice
- ½ medium pear, halved, cored, and sliced thin or cut into medium dice
- ½ orange, peeled and sectioned, or ½ cup drained mandarin oranges
- ½ grapefruit, peeled and sectioned
- ½ peach or nectarine, pitted and sliced thin or cut into medium dice
- 1 plum, pitted and sliced thin
- 2 fresh figs, quartered
- 1 apricot, pitted and sliced thin
- 10 seedless red or green grapes, halved
- 1 cup strawberries, hulled and sliced thin
- ½ cup blueberries, raspberries, or blackberries

Dried fruit—good with pork and chicken (use 2 tablespoons per salad):

- Dried cranberries
- Dried cherries
- Raisins or dried currants
- Dried apricots, peaches, plums (prunes), or pears, cut into small dice

Cheese:

- Feta cheese, crumbled (¼ cup)
- Blue cheese, crumbled (2 tablespoons)
- Fresh goat cheese, crumbled (scant ¼ cup)
- Parmesan cheese, preferably Parmigiano-Reggiano, grated or shaved with a vegetable peeler (¼ cup)

Toasted nuts (use 1 tablespoon per salad):

Almonds, sliced, slivered, or coarsely chopped
Cashews, coarsely chopped
Walnuts, coarsely chopped
Pecans, coarsely chopped
Hazelnuts, coarsely chopped
Pistachios, coarsely chopped
Pine nuts

Other flavorings:

1 hard-boiled large egg (see page 72), diced
2 tablespoons crumbled fried bacon
¼ cup thawed frozen corn
¼ cup drained canned beans (black, white, pinto, black-eyed peas, or chickpeas)
2 tablespoons drained capers
2 tablespoons pitted, coarsely chopped pungent black olives (about 6 kalamatas)
2 tablespoons pitted, coarsely chopped green olives
2 tablespoons drained, coarsely chopped sun-dried tomatoes packed in oil
2 canned artichoke hearts, cut into sixths
7 cornichons (1 ounce), sliced thin
5 round Melba toasts, crumbled

Fresh or dried herbs, spices, and other flavorings:

¼ cup chopped fresh cilantro leaves
¼ cup torn fresh basil leaves
2 tablespoons chopped fresh dill
Pinch cumin
Pinch dried oregano
1 teaspoon low-sodium soy sauce

#8

50 WAYS TO LOSE IT

Keep a stash of hard-boiled eggs in the fridge, marked with a big black X.

Low-Fat Creamy Herb and Parmesan Dressing

MAKES ABOUT 1½ CUPS, SERVING 12

- 1 large garlic clove, minced
- ⅓ cup light mayonnaise
- ⅓ cup light sour cream
- ⅔ cup low-fat buttermilk
- 2 tablespoons rice wine vinegar
- ¼ teaspoon each salt, ground black pepper, dried basil, dried tarragon, and dried dill
- 2 tablespoons finely grated Parmesan cheese, preferably Parmigiano-Reggiano

Whisk all ingredients in a medium bowl. (Dressing can be refrigerated in an airtight container for up to 3 weeks.)

41 calories per 2-tablespoon serving

Low-Fat Balsamic Vinaigrette

MAKES 1 CUP, SERVING 8

- 1 large garlic clove, minced
- ⅓ cup balsamic vinegar
- 2 tablespoons Dijon mustard
- ¼ teaspoon each salt and ground black pepper
- ½ cup extra-virgin olive oil

Whisk garlic, vinegar, mustard, salt, and pepper in a 2-cup Pyrex measuring cup. Slowly whisk in oil until you reach the 1-cup mark. (Dressing can be stored at room temperature in an airtight container for up to 1 week.)

134 calories per 2-tablespoon serving

Sweet-and-Sour Orange Dressing

This dressing is particularly good for salads containing fresh or dried fruit.

MAKES 1½ CUPS, SERVING 12

- ½ cup frozen orange juice concentrate (no need to thaw)
- ½ cup rice wine vinegar
- ½ cup olive oil

Whisk all ingredients in a medium bowl. (Dressing can be refrigerated in an airtight container for up to 3 weeks.)

98 calories per 2-tablespoon serving

Chicken, Tomato, Black Bean, and Corn Salad

MAKES 1 SALAD

2 heaping cups salad greens (chopped romaine hearts and spring mix)
3 ounces cooked chicken breast strips (available in most supermarkets with the other cooked meats)
¼ cup thawed frozen corn
¼ cup drained canned black beans
2 scallions, sliced thin
6 cherry tomatoes, halved and lightly salted
¼ cup chopped fresh cilantro leaves
Olive Oil–Vinegar Drizzle (page 93), Low-Fat Creamy Herb and Parmesan Dressing (page 96), or Low-Fat Balsamic Vinaigrette (page 96)

Follow directions for Meal-in-a-Bowl Salad (page 92).

About 430 calories

Chicken, Apricot, Chickpea, and Red Onion Salad

MAKES 1 SALAD

2 heaping cups salad greens (chopped romaine hearts and spring mix or watercress)
3 ounces cooked chicken breast strips (available in most supermarkets with the other cooked meats)
¼ cup drained canned chickpeas
2 tablespoons finely chopped dried apricots
⅛ red onion, sliced thin
¼ red bell pepper, cut into short, thin strips
1 celery stalk, sliced thin
¼ cup chopped fresh cilantro leaves
Pinch ground cumin (optional)
Olive Oil–Vinegar Drizzle (page 93), Low-Fat Creamy Herb and Parmesan Dressing (page 96), or Sweet-and-Sour Orange Dressing (page 96)

Follow directions for Meal-in-a-Bowl Salad (page 92).

About 411 calories

Ham, Pear, Hazelnut, and Goat Cheese Salad

MAKES 1 SALAD

- 2 heaping cups salad greens (chopped romaine hearts and baby spinach or arugula)
- 3 ounces sliced Canadian bacon or other lean ham, cut into thin strips
- ½ ripe pear, cored and cut into medium dice
- Scant ¼ cup crumbled fresh goat cheese
- 1 tablespoon chopped toasted hazelnuts
- 1 celery stalk, sliced thin
- Olive Oil–Vinegar Drizzle (page 93), Low-Fat Creamy Herb and Parmesan Dressing (page 96), or Sweet-and-Sour Orange Dressing (page 96)

Follow directions for Meal-in-a-Bowl Salad (page 92).

About 447 calories

Sausage, Roasted Pepper, Olive, and Feta Salad

MAKES 1 SALAD

- 2 heaping cups salad greens (chopped romaine hearts and shredded purple cabbage)
- 1 fully cooked lean chicken sausage, preferably Mediterranean-flavored
- ¼ cup chopped roasted red pepper
- ⅛ red onion, sliced thin
- 1 large carrot, peeled and coarsely grated
- 2 tablespoons pitted, coarsely chopped kalamata olives
- ¼ cup crumbled feta cheese (about 1 ounce)
- Pinch dried oregano (optional)
- Olive Oil–Vinegar Drizzle (page 93), Low-Fat Creamy Herb and Parmesan Dressing (page 96), or Low-Fat Balsamic Vinaigrette (page 96)

Follow directions for Meal-in-a-Bowl Salad (page 92).

About 387 calories

Tuna, White Bean, Olive, and Tomato Salad

MAKES 1 SALAD

- 2 heaping cups salad greens (chopped romaine hearts and baby field greens)
- ½ 6-ounce can white albacore tuna packed in water, drained
- ¼ cup drained canned white beans
- ¼ cup thin-sliced yellow bell pepper
- 6 cherry tomatoes, halved and lightly salted
- 2 tablespoons pitted, coarsely chopped kalamata olives
- ⅛ red onion, sliced thin
- Olive Oil–Vinegar Drizzle (page 93), Low-Fat Creamy Herb and Parmesan Dressing (page 96), or Low-Fat Balsamic Vinaigrette (page 96)

Follow directions for Meal-in-a-Bowl Salad (page 92).

About 377 calories

Smoked Salmon and Trimmings Salad

MAKES 1 SALAD

- 2 heaping cups salad greens (chopped romaine hearts and watercress)
- 2 ounces smoked salmon, cut into bite-sized pieces
- 1 hard-boiled large egg (see page 72), diced
- 2 tablespoons drained capers
- ⅛ red onion, sliced thin
- 5 round Melba toasts, crumbled
- 2 tablespoons packed chopped fresh dill (optional)
- Olive Oil–Vinegar Drizzle (page 93), Low-Fat Creamy Herb and Parmesan Dressing (page 96), or Low-Fat Balsamic Vinaigrette (page 96)

Follow directions for Meal-in-a-Bowl Salad (page 92).

About 398 calories

Seared Scallop, Black Bean, Orange, and Avocado Salad

MAKES 1 SALAD

- 3 Seared Sea Scallops (page 105)
- 2 heaping cups salad greens (chopped romaine hearts and watercress)
- ¼ cup drained canned black beans
- ¼ avocado, cut into medium dice
- ½ cup drained mandarin oranges, or ½ large orange, peeled and sectioned
- 1 celery stalk, sliced thin
- 2 scallions, sliced thin
- ¼ cup packed fresh cilantro leaves
- Olive Oil–Vinegar Drizzle (page 93), Low-Fat Creamy Herb and Parmesan Dressing (page 96), or Sweet-and-Sour Orange Dressing (page 96)

Follow directions for Meal-in-a-Bowl Salad (page 92).

About 495 calories

Seared Turkey Burger Salad with Blue Cheese and Red Onion

MAKES 1 SALAD

- 1 4-ounce Seared Turkey Burger (page 108)
- 2 heaping cups salad greens (chopped romaine hearts and purple cabbage)
- 7 cornichons (1 ounce), sliced thin
- 6 cherry tomatoes, halved and lightly salted
- ⅛ red onion, sliced thin
- 2 tablespoons crumbled blue cheese (½ ounce)
- Olive Oil–Vinegar Drizzle (page 93), Low-Fat Creamy Herb and Parmesan Dressing (page 96), or Low-Fat Balsamic Vinaigrette (page 96)

Follow directions for Meal-in-a-Bowl Salad (page 92).

About 402 calories

Chicken, Grape, Walnut, and Blue Cheese Salad

MAKES 1 SALAD

- 2 heaping cups salad greens (chopped romaine hearts and purple cabbage)
- 3 ounces cooked boneless, skinless chicken breast
- 10 seedless red grapes, halved
- ⅛ red onion, sliced thin
- 2 tablespoons toasted chopped walnuts or pecans
- 2 tablespoons crumbled blue cheese (½ ounce)
- Olive Oil–Vinegar Drizzle (page 93), Low-Fat Creamy Herb and Parmesan Dressing (page 96), or Sweet-and-Sour Orange Dressing (page 96)

Follow directions for Meal-in-a-Bowl Salad (page 92).

About 496 calories

Asian Chicken Salad

MAKES 1 SALAD

- 2 heaping cups salad greens (chopped spinach and purple cabbage)
- 3 ounces cooked boneless, skinless chicken breast
- 1 large carrot, peeled and coarsely grated
- ½ cup thin-sliced seedless (English) cucumber
- 2 scallions, sliced thin
- ¼ cup packed fresh cilantro leaves
- 2 tablespoons coarsely chopped roasted peanuts
- Olive Oil–Vinegar Drizzle (page 93) made with rice wine vinegar
- 1 teaspoon soy sauce
- 1 teaspoon sugar

Follow directions for Meal-in-a-Bowl Salad (page 92).

482 calories

Crab, Corn, Roasted Pepper, and Avocado Salad

If you like, cut back on the salt and sprinkle the salad with Old Bay Seasoning.

MAKES 1 SALAD

- 2 heaping cups salad greens (chopped spinach and purple cabbage)
- 3 ounces pasteurized lump crabmeat (½ packed cup), picked over and patted dry
- ½ cup thawed frozen corn
- 1 celery stalk, sliced thin
- ¼ cup chopped roasted red pepper
- 2 scallions, sliced thin
- ¼ avocado, cut into small dice
- Olive Oil–Vinegar Drizzle (page 93), Low-Fat Creamy Herb and Parmesan Dressing (page 96), or Low-Fat Balsamic Vinaigrette (page 96)

Follow directions for Meal-in-a-Bowl Salad (page 92).

About 436 calories

Sliced Pork Tenderloin, Orange, Dried Cranberry, and Pecan Salad

MAKES 1 SALAD

- 2 heaping cups salad greens (chopped spinach and purple cabbage)
- 3 ounces seared pork tenderloin (see page 225), sliced
- ⅛ red onion, sliced thin
- ½ cup drained mandarin oranges, or ½ large orange, peeled and sectioned
- 2 tablespoons dried cranberries
- 2 tablespoons chopped toasted pecans
- Olive Oil–Vinegar Drizzle (page 93), Low-Fat Creamy Herb and Parmesan Dressing (page 96), or Sweet-and-Sour Orange Dressing (page 96)

Follow directions for Meal-in-a-Bowl Salad (page 92).

About 486 calories

Pork Tenderloin, Plum, Cashew, and Cilantro Salad

MAKES 1 SALAD

- 2 heaping cups salad greens (chopped romaine hearts and slaw mix)
- 3 ounces seared pork tenderloin (see page 225), sliced thin
- 1 large carrot, peeled and coarsely grated
- ¼ red bell pepper, cut into short, thin strips
- 2 scallions, sliced thin
- 1 plum, halved, pitted, and sliced thin
- 2 tablespoons chopped roasted cashews
- 1 tablespoon chopped fresh cilantro leaves
- Olive Oil–Vinegar Drizzle (page 93), Low-Fat Balsamic Vinaigrette (page 96), or Sweet-and-Sour Orange Dressing (page 96)

Follow directions for Meal-in-a-Bowl Salad (page 92).

About 477 calories

Shrimp, Bacon, Cherry Tomato, and Feta Salad

MAKES 1 SALAD

- 2 heaping cups salad greens (chopped romaine hearts and spinach)
- 3 ounces cooked shrimp, halved lengthwise
- 1 celery stalk, sliced thin
- ¼ yellow bell pepper, cut into short, thin strips
- 6 cherry tomatoes, halved and lightly salted
- ⅛ red onion, sliced thin
- ¼ cup crumbled feta cheese (about 1 ounce)
- 2 tablespoons crumbled fried bacon
- Olive Oil–Vinegar Drizzle (page 93), Low-Fat Creamy Herb and Parmesan Dressing (page 96), or Low-Fat Balsamic Vinaigrette (page 96)

Follow directions for Meal-in-a-Bowl Salad (page 92).

About 387 calories

Seared Tuna, Mushroom, Artichoke Heart, and Shaved Parmesan Salad

MAKES 1 SALAD

- 2 heaping cups salad greens (chopped romaine hearts and arugula)
- 3 ounces seared tuna (see headnote, page 229)
- ¼ cup drained canned white beans
- 1 cup thin-sliced white mushrooms
- 1 celery stalk, sliced thin
- ⅛ red onion, sliced thin
- 2 canned artichoke hearts (not marinated), cut into sixths
- ¼ cup shaved Parmesan, preferably Parmigiano-Reggiano
- Olive Oil–Vinegar Drizzle (page 93), Low-Fat Creamy Herb and Parmesan Dressing (page 96), or Low-Fat Balsamic Vinaigrette (page 96)

Follow directions for Meal-in-a-Bowl Salad (page 92).

About 482 calories

Seared Salmon, Egg, Sun-Dried Tomato, and Melba Crouton Salad

MAKES 1 SALAD

- 2 heaping cups salad greens (chopped romaine hearts and watercress)
- 3 ounces Seared or Grilled Salmon (page 106)
- 1 hard-boiled large egg (page 72), chopped
- 2 tablespoons drained finely chopped sun-dried tomatoes packed in oil
- 2 tablespoons drained capers
- 5 round Melba toasts, crumbled
- 2 scallions, sliced thin
- 2 tablespoons packed chopped fresh dill
- Olive Oil–Vinegar Drizzle (page 93), Low-Fat Creamy Herb and Parmesan Dressing (page 96), or Low-Fat Balsamic Vinaigrette (page 96)

Follow directions for Meal-in-a-Bowl Salad (page 92).

About 452 calories

Seared Sea Scallops

FOR 1 SALAD

- 3 large sea scallops (about 5 ounces), preferably dry-packed and untreated (see page 31)
- ½ teaspoon vegetable oil
- Salt and ground black or white pepper

Heat a small skillet over medium heat. Coat scallops with oil and season both sides with salt and pepper. A couple of minutes before cooking, turn on exhaust fan and increase heat to high.

Add scallops to hot skillet; cook, turning only once, until they develop a rich brown crust, 4 to 5 minutes. Transfer to a plate and let rest for a couple of minutes. Serve over salad.

145 calories (does not include salad)

For 2:

Increase scallop quantity to 6, oil to 1 teaspoon, and skillet size to medium (10 inches).

For 4:

Increase scallop quantity to 12, oil to 2 teaspoons, and skillet size to large (12 inches).

#9
50 WAYS TO LOSE IT

Eat five or six times a day: three small meals and two or three snacks.

Seared or Grilled Salmon

FOR 1 OR 2 SALADS

1–2 center-cut skinned salmon fillets (about 5 ounces each)
½–1 teaspoon vegetable oil
Salt and ground black or white pepper

Heat a small skillet over medium heat. Coat each salmon fillet with ½ teaspoon oil and season both sides with salt and pepper. A couple of minutes before cooking, turn on exhaust fan and increase heat to high.

Add salmon to hot skillet; cook, turning only once, until it develops a rich brown crust on both sides, about 6 minutes for medium-rare, 7 minutes for medium, and 8 minutes for medium-well. Transfer to a plate, let rest for a couple of minutes, and serve over salad.

For 3 or 4 salads:

Increase fillets to 3 or 4, oil to 1½–2 teaspoons (½ teaspoon per fillet), and increase skillet size to medium (10 inches).

For 5 or 6 salads:

Increase salmon fillets to 5 or 6, oil to 2½–3 teaspoons (½ teaspoon per fillet), and skillet size to large (12 inches).

To grill salmon, heat gas grill, igniting all burners on high for at least 10 minutes. Clean hot grill rack with a wire brush, then, using spring-action tongs, rub rack with a vegetable-oil-soaked rag to keep salmon from sticking.

Place desired number of salmon fillets on hot grate; grill, turning only once, until both sides have developed grill marks, about 4 minutes for medium-rare, 5 minutes for medium, and 6 minutes for medium-well. Remove from grill, let rest for 5 minutes, and serve over salad.

200 calories per serving (does not include salad)

Light Crab Cakes

If serving over salad, make the 6 large cakes as suggested. If serving as a main course, use a ⅓-cup measure to make 8 cakes.

FOR 6 SALADS, OR SERVES 4 AS A MAIN COURSE

- 2 large egg whites, or ¼ cup liquid 100% egg whites
- 2 tablespoons light mayonnaise
- 2 tablespoons chopped scallion greens
- ¼ teaspoon Old Bay Seasoning
- ¼ teaspoon hot red pepper sauce, preferably Tabasco
- 1 pound pasteurized lump crabmeat, drained, picked over, and patted dry
- 4 teaspoons low-fat milk
- 10 saltine crackers, crushed
- 2 tablespoons olive oil
- Lemon wedges

Mix egg whites, mayonnaise, scallions, seasoning, and hot red pepper sauce in a small bowl.

Mix crabmeat and milk in a medium bowl. Add crackers and toss to combine. Add egg mixture and toss to combine again. Divide mixture into six ½-cup portions, pressing on the mixture to form a tight, compact patty.

Heat oil in a large (12-inch) skillet over medium heat. Add crab cakes and cook, turning only once, until golden brown on both sides and cooked through, about 6 minutes. Transfer to a paper-towel-lined plate. (Crab cakes can be transferred to a wire rack and kept warm in a 200-degree oven for up to 30 minutes.) Serve with lemon wedges.

169 calories per serving (does not include salad)

Seared Turkey Burgers

If serving as a main course, form the ground meat mixture into 4 patties. If serving over a salad, you may want to make 5 patties.

SERVES 4 OR 5

- 1¼ pounds 93% ground turkey
- ½ teaspoon salt
- ½ teaspoon ground black pepper
- 2 teaspoons Dijon mustard
- 2 teaspoons Worcestershire sauce

Heat a large (12-inch) skillet over low heat while making patties. Place ground turkey in a medium bowl. Add salt, pepper, mustard, and Worcestershire; mix lightly with a fork to distribute seasonings evenly. Divide mixture into 4 or 5 portions (see headnote) and form each into a thin patty.

A couple of minutes before cooking, increase heat to medium-high. Add patties and cook, turning only once, until seared on both sides and cooked through, about 10 minutes. Serve over salad, if desired.

193 calories per serving (does not include salad)

#10

50 WAYS TO LOSE IT

Toss crumbled low-calorie Melba toasts on salads instead of croutons.

deep-bowl satisfaction in minutes

If you think thick, hearty soups are too labor-intensive and long-simmering to make regularly, read on.

Using my formula as a guide, you can mix up a pot of flavorful, low-calorie soup in about 30 minutes. To make great soup quickly, however, requires efficiency, so before you pull out your knife and cutting board or even open the fridge, start by heating a quart of chicken broth and a can of tomatoes in the microwave and a little oil in a soup kettle. Taking a moment for these steps now will shave several minutes off the cooking time later.

Using my formula as a guide, you can make a pot of flavorful, low-calorie soup in about 30 minutes.

- Don't wait until all the ingredients are prepared before starting the soup.
- Chop the onion first and drop it into the hot oil.
- While it sautés, prepare the remaining ingredients. When the onion has softened, add the remaining ingredients (unless you're using scallops or shrimp, which are added at the end). If you're not finished prepping the ingredients when the onion is ready,

add what you've got, along with the hot chicken broth and tomatoes. Toss in the remaining ingredients as you prepare them.

- Since the broth and tomatoes are already hot, the soup simmers almost immediately. In just 20 minutes, it's done.

If you've stocked up on lean protein—shredded cooked chicken, ham, lean sausage, shrimp, lump crabmeat, or pork, for example—you're just about there. If you've got a pound of seasonal vegetables in the fridge or a box or two of standbys in the freezer, you're set. All you need is a little starch, and who doesn't have a handful of pasta or red potatoes, a can of beans, a box of frozen corn, or ¼ cup of rice?

Just about anything goes: fish, potatoes, and cabbage; chicken, okra, lima beans, and corn; ham, white beans, and kale; scallops, carrots, and fennel. Substitute fish for ham, scallops for chicken, and you'll still have a delicious soup.

After making a few of the soups that follow, you'll get the hang of it and quickly develop the confidence to create your own.

Meal-in-a-Bowl Soup

MAKES ABOUT 2 QUARTS, SERVING 4 TO 6

1 quart chicken broth
1 can (14.5 ounces) petite diced tomatoes
2 teaspoons vegetable oil
1 medium-large onion, cut into medium dice
Dried herbs/spices (optional; see page 121)
12 ounces meat, poultry, or seafood (see page 121)
1 pound vegetables (see page 122)
Starch (see page 122)
Fresh herbs and/or other flavorings (optional; see page 123)

Microwave broth and tomatoes in a 2-quart Pyrex measuring cup or similar-sized microwave-safe container on high power until steamy hot, about 5 minutes.

Meanwhile, heat oil in a Dutch oven or small soup kettle over medium-high heat. Add onion and sauté until soft and golden brown, about 5 minutes. Add dried herbs or spices, if using, and sauté until fragrant, 1 to 2 minutes. Add meat or poultry (hold seafood until later), vegetables, and starch of choice, along with hot broth mixture. Bring to a simmer, reduce heat to low, and simmer, partially covered, until vegetables are tender and flavors have blended, about 20 minutes. Turn off heat. Stir in fresh herbs and other flavorings, if using (as well as seafood); cover and let stand to allow flavors to blend (or until seafood is opaque), about 5 minutes. Adjust seasonings. Serve.

About 352 calories per serving

Chicken Soup with Lima Beans and Corn

MAKES ABOUT 2 QUARTS, SERVING 4 TO 6

1 quart chicken broth
1 can (14.5 ounces) petite diced tomatoes
2 teaspoons vegetable oil
1 medium-large onion, cut into medium dice

DRIED HERBS/SPICES:

2 bay leaves

MEAT, POULTRY, OR SEAFOOD:

12 ounces shredded cooked chicken

VEGETABLES:

10 ounces frozen okra
2 medium carrots, peeled and sliced thin
1 medium celery stalk, sliced thin

STARCH:

8 ounces each frozen corn and frozen lima beans

OTHER FLAVORINGS:

¼ cup ketchup
1 teaspoon (or more) hot red pepper sauce, preferably Tabasco

Follow directions for Meal-in-a-Bowl Soup (page 111).

About 388 calories per 2-cup serving

Brazilian Ham and Black Bean Soup

MAKES ABOUT 2 QUARTS, SERVING 4 TO 6

1 quart chicken broth
1 can (14.5 ounces) petite diced tomatoes
2 teaspoons vegetable oil
1 medium-large onion, cut into medium dice

MEAT, POULTRY, OR SEAFOOD:

12 ounces diced ham

VEGETABLES/FRUIT:

1 red bell pepper, stemmed, seeded, and cut into medium dice
1 mango, peeled, pitted, and cut into medium dice
2 medium carrots, peeled and sliced thin

STARCH:

8 ounces sweet potato, peeled and cut into medium dice
1 can (15.5 ounces) black beans, drained

FRESH HERBS:

¼ cup (or more) chopped fresh cilantro

Follow directions for Meal-in-a-Bowl Soup (page 111).

About 408 calories per 2-cup serving

Mexican Chicken and Hominy (or Black Bean) Soup

MAKES ABOUT 2 QUARTS, SERVING 4 TO 6

1 quart chicken broth
1 can (14.5 ounces) petite diced tomatoes
2 teaspoons vegetable oil
1 medium-large onion, cut into medium dice

DRIED HERBS/SPICES:

1 tablespoon chili powder
1 teaspoon dried oregano

MEAT, POULTRY, OR SEAFOOD:

12 ounces shredded cooked chicken

VEGETABLES:

1 can (4 ounces) diced green chiles
2 medium carrots, peeled and sliced thin
1 medium zucchini, quartered lengthwise and cut into medium dice

STARCH:

8 ounces frozen corn
1 can (15.5 ounces) hominy or black beans, drained

FRESH HERBS AND OTHER FLAVORINGS:

½ cup chopped fresh cilantro leaves
2 tablespoons fresh lime juice

Follow directions for Meal-in-a-Bowl Soup (page 111).

About 413 calories per 2-cup serving

Shrimp and Sausage Gumbo

MAKES ABOUT 2 QUARTS, SERVING 4 TO 6

1 quart chicken broth
1 can (14.5 ounces) petite diced tomatoes
2 teaspoons vegetable oil
1 medium-large onion, cut into medium dice

DRIED HERBS/SPICES:

½ teaspoon dried thyme leaves
¼ teaspoon cayenne pepper

MEAT, POULTRY, OR SEAFOOD:

6 ounces cooked lean chicken sausage, sliced thin
6 ounces medium peeled and deveined shrimp, halved lengthwise

VEGETABLES:

1 medium yellow bell pepper, stemmed, seeded, and cut into medium dice
1 celery stalk, cut into small dice
6 ounces frozen okra

STARCH:

¼ cup long-grain white rice

OTHER FLAVORINGS:

1 teaspoon hot red pepper sauce, preferably Tabasco (optional)

Follow directions for Meal-in-a-Bowl Soup (page 111).

About 229 calories per 2-cup serving

Spicy Sausage and White Bean Soup with Winter Squash and Broccoli Rabe

Some produce departments carry winter squash that is already peeled, seeded, and diced. You can also save time by using lean cooked kielbasa.

MAKES ABOUT 2 QUARTS, SERVING 4 TO 6

1 quart chicken broth
1 can (14.5 ounces) petite diced tomatoes
2 teaspoons vegetable oil
1 medium-large onion, cut into medium dice

DRIED HERBS/SPICES:

½ teaspoon hot red pepper flakes
½ teaspoon dried rubbed sage

MEAT, POULTRY, OR SEAFOOD:

12 ounces cooked Italian sausage (from 1 pound raw), sliced into bite-sized rounds

VEGETABLES:

8 ounces broccoli rabe, chopped (about 6 cups)
8 ounces butternut or other winter squash, peeled, seeded, and cut into medium dice (about 1½ cups)

STARCH:

2 cans (15.5 ounces each) white beans, drained

Follow directions for Meal-in-a-Bowl Soup (page 111).

About 365 calories per 2-cup serving

Lemon Chicken and Orzo Soup with Spinach

MAKES ABOUT 2 QUARTS, SERVING 4 TO 6

1 quart chicken broth
1 can (14.5 ounces) petite diced tomatoes
2 teaspoons vegetable oil
1 medium-large onion, cut into medium dice

MEAT, POULTRY, OR SEAFOOD:

12 ounces shredded cooked chicken

VEGETABLES:

1 package (7–9 ounces) prewashed spinach
1 medium zucchini, quartered lengthwise and cut into medium dice
3 ounces (about ¾ cup) frozen green peas

STARCH:

- 1/3 cup orzo

FRESH HERBS AND OTHER FLAVORINGS:

- 1/4 cup chopped fresh dill
- 2 tablespoons fresh lemon juice

Follow directions for Meal-in-a-Bowl Soup (page 111).

About 310 calories per 2-cup serving

Ham and White Bean Soup with Cabbage, Carrots, and Caraway

MAKES ABOUT 2 QUARTS, SERVING 4 TO 6

- 1 quart chicken broth
- 1 can (14.5 ounces) petite diced tomatoes
- 2 teaspoons vegetable oil
- 1 medium-large onion, cut into medium dice

DRIED HERBS/SPICES:

- 1/2 teaspoon caraway seeds

MEAT, POULTRY, OR SEAFOOD:

- 12 ounces lean ham or Canadian bacon, cut into medium dice

VEGETABLES:

- 2 medium carrots, peeled and cut into medium dice
- 2 medium celery stalks, cut into medium dice
- 1/2 small cabbage, cored and shredded (about 4 cups)

STARCH:

- 2 cans (15.5 ounces each) white beans, drained

OTHER FLAVORINGS:

- 1 tablespoon Worcestershire sauce

Follow directions for Meal-in-a-Bowl Soup (page 111).

About 385 calories per 2-cup serving

Pork and Hoppin' John Soup with Collards and Peppers

Down south, we call black-eyed peas and rice Hoppin' John. Add a little pork and greens for a satisfying pot of soup.

If your grocery store doesn't sell prepared pulled pork, substitute shredded cooked chicken and add ¼ cup barbecue sauce along with the pickled jalapeño juice.

MAKES ABOUT 2 QUARTS, SERVING 4 TO 6

1 quart chicken broth
1 can (14.5 ounces) petite diced tomatoes
2 teaspoons vegetable oil
1 medium-large onion, cut into medium dice

MEAT, POULTRY, OR SEAFOOD:

12 ounces (1 package) barbecued pulled pork

VEGETABLES:

1 medium red bell pepper, stemmed, seeded, and cut into medium dice
8 ounces collard greens, stemmed and coarsely chopped (about 8 cups)

STARCH:

1 can (15.5 ounces) black-eyed peas, drained
2 tablespoons long-grain white rice

OTHER FLAVORINGS:

2 tablespoons jarred pickled jalapeño juice; pickled jalapeño slices to pass separately

Follow directions for Meal-in-a-Bowl Soup (page 111).

About 349 calories per 2-cup serving

Scallop and Rice Soup with Tomato

MAKES ABOUT 2 QUARTS, SERVING 4 TO 6

1 quart chicken broth
1 can (14.5 ounces) petite diced tomatoes
2 teaspoons vegetable oil
1 medium-large onion, cut into medium dice

DRIED HERBS/SPICES:

2 teaspoons dried basil

MEAT, POULTRY, OR SEAFOOD:

12 ounces bay scallops, preferably dry-packed and untreated (see page 31)

VEGETABLES:

1 medium orange bell pepper, stemmed, seeded, and cut into medium dice
2 medium celery stalks, cut into medium dice
8 ounces asparagus, tough ends snapped, cut into 1-inch lengths (about 2 cups)

STARCH:

¼ cup long-grain white rice

OTHER FLAVORINGS:

1 teaspoon finely grated orange zest

Follow directions for Meal-in-a-Bowl Soup (page 111).

About 218 calories per 2-cup serving

Summer Crab and Corn Soup

MAKES ABOUT 2 QUARTS, SERVING 4 TO 6

1 quart chicken broth
1 can (14.5 ounces) petite diced tomatoes
2 teaspoons vegetable oil
1 medium-large onion, cut into medium dice

DRIED HERBS/SPICES:

1 tablespoon Old Bay Seasoning

MEAT, POULTRY, OR SEAFOOD:

12 ounces pasteurized lump crabmeat, drained, picked over, and patted dry

VEGETABLES:

1 medium yellow bell pepper, stemmed, seeded, and cut into medium dice
1 medium carrot, peeled and sliced thin
8 ounces trimmed green beans, cut into 1-inch lengths (about 2 cups)

STARCH:

8 ounces red boiling potatoes, cut into medium dice
8 ounces frozen or fresh corn kernels

FRESH HERBS:

½ cup chopped fresh basil leaves

Follow directions for Meal-in-a-Bowl Soup (page 111).

About 300 calories per 2-cup serving

Italian Turkey Meatball Soup

MAKES ABOUT 2 QUARTS, SERVING 4 TO 6

1 quart chicken broth
1 can (14.5 ounces) petite diced tomatoes
2 teaspoons vegetable oil
1 medium-large onion, cut into medium dice

DRIED HERBS/SPICES:

2 teaspoons dried basil
1 teaspoon dried oregano

MEAT, POULTRY, OR SEAFOOD:

12 ounces (1 package) cooked turkey meatballs (available in most supermarkets with the other cooked meats), quartered

VEGETABLES:

1 medium carrot, peeled and sliced thin
1 medium zucchini, quartered lengthwise and cut into medium dice
8 ounces cauliflower, trimmed and cut into florets (about 2 cups)

STARCH:

1 scant cup dried bite-sized pasta, such as ditalini, farfalle (bow ties), fusilli (corkscrews), elbow macaroni, rotelle (wagon wheels), or penne

FRESH HERBS:

¼ cup chopped fresh parsley leaves (optional)

Follow directions for Meal-in-a-Bowl Soup (page 111).

About 343 calories per 2-cup serving

Fish Soup with Bok Choy, Mushrooms, and Cilantro

MAKES ABOUT 2 QUARTS, SERVING 4 TO 6

1 quart chicken broth
1 can (14.5 ounces) petite diced tomatoes
2 teaspoons vegetable oil
1 medium-large onion, cut into medium dice

MEAT, POULTRY, OR SEAFOOD:

12 ounces white fish fillet, such as cod, snapper, grouper, or tilapia

VEGETABLES:

12 ounces bok choy, stemmed and coarsely chopped (about 4 cups)
4 ounces mushrooms, sliced

STARCH:

¼ cup long-grain white rice

FRESH HERBS AND OTHER FLAVORINGS:

¼ cup chopped fresh cilantro leaves
1 tablespoon soy sauce

Follow directions for Meal-in-a-Bowl Soup (page 111).

About 201 calories per 2-cup serving

Create-Your-Own-Soup Combos

Dried herbs/spices (optional):

1 tablespoon chili powder
1 tablespoon Old Bay Seasoning
1 tablespoon curry powder
1 tablespoon garam masala
2 teaspoons dried basil
1 teaspoon dried oregano
1 teaspoon ground cumin
1 teaspoon ground coriander
½ teaspoon dried thyme leaves
½ teaspoon dried rubbed sage
½ teaspoon caraway seeds
½ teaspoon hot red pepper flakes
½ teaspoon dried dill
½ teaspoon dried tarragon
½ teaspoon cayenne pepper

Meat/poultry/seafood (use 12 ounces, or 6 ounces of each of 2 kinds):

Shredded cooked chicken breast or thighs (heaping 2 cups)

Packaged turkey meatballs (available in most supermarkets with the other cooked meats), quartered

Fully cooked lean chicken sausage and lean kielbasa, sliced thin

Cooked Italian sausage (turkey or chicken), sliced thin

Pulled pork (available in most supermarkets with the other cooked meats)

Spiral-cut ham, Canadian bacon, or other lean ham, cut into small dice

Flaky fish, such as cod, haddock, snapper, grouper, or salmon (add near end of cooking)

Pasteurized lump crabmeat, drained, picked over, and patted dry (add at end of cooking)

Peeled salad shrimp (add at end of cooking)

Bay scallops, preferably dry-packed and untreated (see page 31; add at end of cooking)

Vegetables (add 1 pound total of any combination of the following):

Celery stalks, cut into small dice

Fennel, halved (or quartered, if large) and sliced thin

Carrots, peeled (halved if large) and sliced thin

Bell peppers, stemmed, seeded, and cut into small dice (or one 4-ounce can diced green chiles)

Zucchini and yellow squash, quartered lengthwise and cut into medium dice

Mushrooms, sliced thin

Asparagus, tough ends snapped, cut into 1-inch lengths

Green beans, trimmed and cut into 1-inch lengths

Broccoli, trimmed and cut into small florets

Cauliflower, trimmed and cut into small florets

Tough and tender greens (spinach, arugula, beet greens, Swiss chard, escarole, curly endive, turnip greens, mustard greens, collards, kale, and broccoli rabe), stemmed, washed, and coarsely chopped

Cabbage, halved, cored, and shredded (or coleslaw mix)

Winter squash, peeled, seeded, and cut into medium dice

Frozen okra, green peas, green beans

Frozen spinach (drained weight from a 10-ounce box is 4 ounces)

Starch (choose 1 of the following or half portions of 2):

1 pound red boiling potatoes, cut into medium dice

1 pound sweet potatoes, peeled and cut into medium dice

1 pound frozen corn

1 pound frozen lima beans

2 cans (15.5 ounces each) black beans, white beans, pinto beans, chickpeas, black-eyed peas, or hominy, drained

4 ounces dried bite-sized pasta (about 1 cup), or ⅓ cup orzo

¼ cup long-grain white rice

Fresh herbs and/or other flavorings (optional):

½ cup chopped fresh basil leaves

¼ cup chopped fresh parsley leaves

¼ cup chopped fresh cilantro leaves

¼ cup chopped fresh dill

¼ cup ketchup or barbecue sauce

2 tablespoons fresh lemon or lime juice

2 tablespoons jarred pickled jalapeño juice

1 tablespoon soy sauce

1 tablespoon Worcestershire sauce

1 teaspoon hot red pepper sauce, preferably Tabasco

1 teaspoon finely grated orange or lemon zest

#11

50 WAYS TO LOSE IT

Use high-flavor cheeses (feta, Parmesan, blue, and fresh goat cheese).

soup with creamy comfort—and less fat

Although I frequently serve a pureed vegetable soup as a first course, it's usually not satisfying enough as a main. There are, however, exceptions to that rule.

My Quick Cream of Tomato Soup gets its richness from evaporated milk, which doesn't have the calorie count of cream. The baking soda prevents the tomatoes' acid from curdling the milk. The secret to the Cream of Asparagus Soup and Cream of Mushroom Soup is instant rice, which, when pureed, makes the soups taste sumptuous. Because the rice cooks so quickly, the soups are done and ready for the blender in under 15 minutes.

My soups are ready for the blender in 15 minutes or less.

Pureed beans give Creamy Black Bean Soup with Cumin and Salsa Verde, Creamy Chickpea Soup with Garam Masala and Cilantro, and Creamy White Bean Soup with Rosemary and Basil a naturally creamy consistency, and the chickpea soup benefits from light coconut milk as well.

Quick Cream of Tomato Soup

MAKES 6 CUPS, SERVING 6 AS A FIRST COURSE OR 4 AS A MAIN COURSE

- 1 tablespoon olive oil
- 1 medium-large onion, chopped
- 1 tablespoon curry powder
- 1 can (28 ounces) crushed tomatoes
- ½ teaspoon baking soda
- 1 cup 1% milk
- 1 can (5 ounces) evaporated milk
- Salt and ground black pepper

Heat oil in a Dutch oven over medium-high heat. Add onion and sauté until tender, about 5 minutes. Stir in curry powder and cook until fragrant, less than 1 minute. Add tomatoes and baking soda and bring to a simmer. Reduce heat to low and simmer, partially covered, to blend flavors, about 5 minutes.

Stir in milk and evaporated milk. Pour soup into a blender and puree, venting the blender by removing the pop-out center and draping a kitchen towel over the top, until soup is creamy smooth, 30 to 60 seconds. Return to pot; reheat to a simmer and season with salt and pepper to taste. Ladle into soup bowls and serve.

125 calories per cup

#12

50 WAYS TO LOSE IT

Eat only at scheduled times. Your next meal should never be more than three waking hours away.

Cream of Asparagus Soup

To save calories, squeeze a little lemon juice into the soup rather than serving it with a dollop of sour cream.

MAKES 6 CUPS, SERVING 6 AS A FIRST COURSE OR 4 AS A MAIN COURSE

- 6 cups chicken broth
- 2 teaspoons olive oil or butter
- 1 medium onion, cut into small dice
- ½ teaspoon dried tarragon
- ⅔ cup instant rice
- 2 pounds asparagus, tough ends snapped, stalks cut into 1-inch pieces (about 1 pound trimmed)
- Salt and ground black pepper
- ¼ cup light sour cream (see headnote)

Microwave broth in a 2-quart Pyrex measuring cup until steamy hot; set aside. Meanwhile, heat oil or butter in a Dutch oven over medium-high heat. Add onion and sauté until tender, about 4 minutes. Stir in tarragon and rice, then add asparagus and broth. Bring to a boil, reduce heat to low, and simmer, partially covered, until asparagus and rice are just tender, 6 to 7 minutes.

Pour soup into a blender and puree, in batches if necessary, venting the blender by removing the pop-out center and draping a kitchen towel over the top, until soup is creamy smooth. Return to pot and heat through. Add salt and pepper to taste. Ladle into soup bowls, top with sour cream, and serve.

114 calories per cup

Cream of Mushroom Soup

To save calories, squeeze a little lemon juice into the soup rather than serving it with sour cream.

MAKES 6 CUPS, SERVING 6 AS A FIRST COURSE OR 4 AS A MAIN COURSE

- 6 cups chicken broth
- 1 ounce dried mushrooms
- 2 teaspoons olive oil or butter
- 1 medium-large onion, cut into medium dice
- 2/3 cup instant rice
- 1 teaspoon dried thyme leaves
- Salt and ground black pepper
- 1/4 cup light sour cream (see headnote)

Place broth and mushrooms in a microwave-safe bowl and microwave on high power until steamy hot, about 5 minutes. Meanwhile, heat oil or butter in a Dutch oven over medium-high heat. Add onion and sauté until tender, 4 to 5 minutes. Stir in rice and thyme, then broth mixture. Bring to a boil, reduce heat to low, and simmer, partially covered, until rice and mushrooms are tender, about 10 minutes.

Pour soup into a blender and puree, in batches if necessary, venting the blender by removing the pop-out center and draping a kitchen towel over the top, until soup is creamy smooth. Return to pot and heat through. Add salt and pepper to taste. Ladle into soup bowls, top with sour cream, and serve.

91 calories per cup

#13
50 WAYS TO LOSE IT

Use pureed instant rice in soups in place of heavy cream.

hearty soups that taste homemade

I don't like the flavor of most canned soups, and since I can make a pot so quickly and simply, I don't see the point of buying them.

However, I'm not a total purist. If I'm in a real hurry, I can doctor certain canned soups and other convenience products to look and taste homemade. Better to have a few soups you can throw together quickly than to eat something you shouldn't because you couldn't wait.

The next several recipes reflect this approach: using ingredients like canned beans, tomatoes, lentil soup, creamed corn, green chiles, jarred salsa, and ramen noodles (minus the flavoring packet) and freshening them with herbs and spices to make quick "homemade" soups.

Creamy Black Bean Soup with Cumin and Salsa Verde

MAKES ABOUT 6 CUPS, SERVING 6 AS A FIRST COURSE OR 4 AS A MAIN COURSE

2 cans (15.5 ounces each) black beans, drained
1½ cups chicken broth
1 cup store-bought salsa verde
¼ cup packed fresh cilantro leaves, plus extra sprigs for garnish (optional)
1 teaspoon ground cumin
¼ cup light sour cream

Puree beans, broth, salsa verde, cilantro, and cumin in a blender until smooth. Pour into a large saucepan or Dutch oven and bring to a simmer. Simmer, partially covered and stirring frequently to blend flavors, for 4 to 5 minutes. Ladle into soup bowls, garnish with sour cream and cilantro sprigs, if using, and serve.

160 calories per 1-cup serving

#14
50 WAYS TO LOSE IT

No eating between meals (that goes for celery and carrots too).

Creamy Chickpea Soup with Garam Masala and Cilantro

There's no doubt about the Indian inspiration for this soup. Almost as widely available as curry powder, garam masala is an Indian spice blend. The most popular brand is McCormick.

MAKES ABOUT 6 CUPS, SERVING 6 AS A FIRST COURSE OR 4 AS A MAIN COURSE

- 2 cans (15.5 ounces each) chickpeas, drained
- 1 can (14 ounces) light unsweetened coconut milk
- 1 cup chicken broth
- ½ cup store-bought salsa
- 1½ teaspoons garam masala
- 1 teaspoon ground ginger
- 2 tablespoons apple juice concentrate
- ¼ cup packed fresh cilantro leaves
- ¼ cup low-fat plain yogurt for garnish
- ¼ cup thin-sliced scallion greens for garnish

Puree all ingredients, except yogurt and scallions, in a blender until smooth. Pour into a large saucepan or Dutch oven and bring to a simmer. Simmer, partially covered and stirring frequently to blend flavors, for 4 to 5 minutes. Ladle into soup bowls, garnish with yogurt and scallions, and serve.

184 calories per 1-cup serving

Creamy White Bean Soup with Rosemary and Basil

MAKES ABOUT 6 CUPS, SERVING 6 AS A FIRST COURSE OR 4 AS A MAIN COURSE

2 cans (15.5 ounces each) white beans, drained
2 cups chicken broth
1 cup store-bought marinara sauce
2 large garlic cloves
¼ cup packed fresh basil leaves, or 1 teaspoon dried
1 teaspoon minced fresh rosemary leaves
¼ teaspoon hot red pepper flakes
Quick Garlic Croutons (see below) for garnish (optional)

Puree all ingredients, except croutons, in a blender until smooth. Pour into a large saucepan or Dutch oven and bring to a simmer. Simmer, partially covered and stirring frequently to blend flavors, for 4 to 5 minutes. Ladle into soup bowls, garnish with croutons, if using, and serve.

144 calories per 1-cup serving

Quick Garlic Croutons

These croutons can be stored in an airtight container for up to 1 week—just be sure you cook them until they're totally crisp throughout. If you double the recipe, use a 10-inch skillet.

MAKES ¾ CUP

1 cup ½-inch bread cubes from good-quality French or Italian loaf
2 teaspoons olive oil
⅛ teaspoon garlic powder
Pinch salt

Heat a small skillet over low heat while preparing bread. A minute or so before cooking, increase heat to medium. In a medium bowl, toss bread cubes with oil, garlic powder, and salt. Add bread to skillet and cook, stirring frequently for even browning, until golden brown and crisp, 7 to 8 minutes.

About 47 calories per 3 tablespoons

#15
50 WAYS TO LOSE IT

When you travel, check the weather at your destination and pack appropriate exercise clothes.

Ham and Lentil Soup with Tomatoes and Arugula

MAKES ABOUT 2 QUARTS, SERVING 4

2 teaspoons olive oil
4 large garlic cloves, minced
1 package (8 ounces) ham, diced
1½ teaspoons Italian seasoning
2 cans (19 ounces each) lentil soup (I use Progresso)
1 can (14.5 ounces) petite diced tomatoes
1 can (14.5 ounces) chicken broth
4 cups (about 4 ounces) prewashed arugula
Salt and ground black pepper

In a Dutch oven or soup kettle, heat oil and garlic over medium-high heat until garlic begins to sizzle. Add ham and sauté until ham starts to turn golden, about 5 minutes. Add Italian seasoning, then soup, tomatoes, and broth. Bring to a simmer. Add arugula and continue to simmer until it wilts, 2 to 3 minutes longer. Add salt and pepper to taste and serve.

281 calories per 2-cup serving

Moroccan Lentil Soup

A spice blend, garam masala is available in the spice section of most decently stocked grocery stores.

MAKES ABOUT 2 QUARTS, SERVING 4

2 teaspoons olive oil
4 large garlic cloves, minced
1 tablespoon garam masala
1 teaspoon ground ginger
2 cans (19 ounces each) lentil soup (I use Progresso)
1 can (15.5 ounces) chickpeas, drained
1 can (14.5 ounces) petite diced tomatoes
1 can (14.5 ounces) chicken broth
4 cups (about 4 ounces) prewashed spinach
Salt and ground black pepper

In a Dutch oven or soup kettle, heat oil and garlic over medium-high heat until garlic starts to sizzle. Add garam masala and ginger; sauté until fragrant, about 30 seconds. Add soup, chickpeas, tomatoes, and broth. Bring to a simmer. Add spinach and continue to simmer until it wilts, 2 to 3 minutes longer. Add salt and pepper to taste and serve.

287 calories per 2-cup serving

#16
50 WAYS TO LOSE IT

Take care of yourself first. (You'll better care for others.)

Tomato-Tortellini Soup with Spinach and Italian Spices

If you like, sprinkle each serving with a little freshly grated Parmesan cheese.

MAKES 2 QUARTS, SERVING 4

- 2 teaspoons olive oil
- 4 large garlic cloves, minced
- 1½ teaspoons Italian seasoning
- 1 can (28 ounces) crushed tomatoes
- 1 quart chicken broth
- ½ teaspoon baking soda
- 2½ cups dried cheese and spinach tortellini from a 13-ounce bag
- 6 ounces (about 4 cups packed) prewashed spinach
- Salt and ground black pepper

In a Dutch oven or soup kettle, heat oil and garlic over medium-high heat until garlic starts to sizzle. Add Italian seasoning, tomatoes, broth, and baking soda and bring to a boil. Add tortellini and return to a boil, then reduce heat to low and simmer, partially covered, until almost tender, about 10 minutes. Add spinach and simmer until spinach has wilted and tortellini is tender, 2 to 3 minutes longer. Add salt and pepper to taste and serve.

291 calories per 2-cup serving

Creamy Chili-Corn Soup with Chicken and Black Beans

MAKES 2 QUARTS, SERVING 4

- 2 teaspoons vegetable or olive oil
- 4 large garlic cloves, minced
- 2 tablespoons chili powder
- 1 teaspoon ground cumin
- 2 cans (14.5 ounces each) creamed corn
- 1 can (14.5 ounces) petite diced tomatoes
- 1 can (14.5 ounces) chicken broth
- 1 can (15.5 ounces) black beans, drained
- 1 can (4 ounces) diced green chiles
- 1 cup shredded cooked chicken
- ¼ cup chopped fresh cilantro leaves
- Salt and ground black pepper

In a Dutch oven or soup kettle, heat oil and garlic over medium-high heat until garlic starts to sizzle. Add chili powder and cumin and sauté until fragrant, about 30 seconds. Add corn, tomatoes, broth, beans, chiles, and chicken. Bring to a boil, reduce heat to low, and simmer, partially covered, to blend flavors, about 5 minutes. Stir in cilantro, add salt and pepper to taste, and serve.

377 calories per 2-cup serving

Asian Chicken Noodle Soup

MAKES ABOUT 2 QUARTS, SERVING 4

- 1½ quarts (6 cups) low-sodium chicken broth
- 4 large garlic cloves, minced
- 1 tablespoon minced fresh ginger, or 1 teaspoon ground
- ¼ cup low-sodium soy sauce
- 2 cups shredded cooked chicken
- 2 packages (3 ounces each) ramen noodles, flavor packets discarded
- 2 cups fresh bean sprouts
- 4 scallions, white and green parts, sliced thin
- ¼ cup chopped fresh cilantro leaves
- 1 lime, quartered

In a Dutch oven or soup kettle, bring broth, garlic, ginger, soy sauce, and chicken to a boil. Add noodles; return to a boil and cook until tender, about 3 minutes. Add bean sprouts, scallions, and cilantro and ladle into soup bowls immediately. Serve with a lime wedge on the side.

282 calories per 2-cup serving

#17

50 WAYS TO LOSE IT

Season your food—the more flavorful it is, the more satisfying.

time for tea

When we visited our older daughter in England, where she was studying, pots of hot tea and plates of scones contented us after a long day of touring, refreshed us for the drive back to our rented cottage, and sustained us until dinner. At home, I find that taking time to sit and have a cup of tea soothes me—just a few minutes is like a mini retreat—and energizes me for the final push as I wrap up the day's work.

This ritual is good for me—the few calories I spend here save hundreds later in the day. I don't need a rich scone or a mall-sized cookie. A good cup of tea, along with a splash of 2% milk (16 calories for 2 tablespoons), a small sweet treat, and a moment to relax suffice. These few minutes give me pleasure and a little sustenance and keep me from predinner starvation—in under 150 calories.

Teatime sends me a clear message that I'm not dieting. By giving myself a little treat each day, I never feel deprived. Take away all its pleasures, and the body will bite back—hard. Pull its carbs for a couple of weeks, and it might insist on an entire cheese pizza in one sitting. Withhold a reasonable sweet, and it might beg for a quart of premium ice cream or a bag of M&M's.

Teatime sends me a clear message that I'm not dieting.

Since tea is a part of my daily routine, I try to have it wherever I am. If I'm out shopping, I can feel myself getting cranky around 4:00. I used to press on miserably, but no more. Whether I'm alone or with one of my daughters or a friend, I always stop for tea. If the coffee shop sweets are unusually large, I split one with my companion or, if I'm alone, I pick up a low-cal biscotti.

If I'm at the airport in the late afternoon, I start looking for tea and a small cookie, or I buy something before boarding and enjoy tea on the plane. When I'm in a hotel, I use teatime as an opportunity to get out for some fresh air.

At home I usually have quick homemade treats on hand. I pull an apricot-cherry bar or a few biscotti from the tin or thaw a couple of whole wheat pumpkin or banana muffins in the microwave.

When there's nothing homemade, I reach for a couple of low-fat store-bought wafers or cookies that I spread with a smidgen of low-sugar jam, lemon curd, fruit butter, or Nutella. The key to teatime goodies is to keep them small and flavorful. The more pronounced the flavor, the more pleasant the experience, the more satisfied you'll be, and the less likely you are to cheat.

With body relaxed and mind rejuvenated, who cares that dinner is still a couple of hours away?

#18
50 WAYS TO LOSE IT

Sprinkle or drizzle sweeteners on top rather than stirring them in. (You won't need as much.)

RECIPES

MINI WHOLE WHEAT MUFFINS

Pumpkin Muffins with Orange Drizzle 145
Apple Muffins with Cinnamon Glaze 146
Banana Muffins with Nutmeg Glaze 147

COOKIES AND BARS

All-Purpose Slice-and-Bake Butter Cookies 150
- Cardamom Pistachio 151
- Lemon Pistachio 151
- Banana Peanut 152
- Chocolate Hazelnut 152
- Lime Coconut 152
- Ginger Sesame 152
- Cranberry-Orange Walnut 152
- Cherry Almond 153
- Orange Pecan 153
- Cinnamon Cashew 153
- Rosemary with Almonds and Currants 153
- Anise with Pine Nuts 154

Chocolate-Coconut "Cookies" 155
Miniature Apricot-Cherry Bars with Oatmeal Crumble Topping 156
Gingerbread Straws 158
Simplest Fruit Bars 160
- Peach Pecan 161
- Strawberry Almond 161
- Apricot Pistachio 161
- Lemon Coconut 161

My Favorite Biscotti 162
- Orange (or Lemon) Pistachio 163
- Cherry Almond 163
- Cranberry Orange (or Lemon) 163
- Spiced Raisin 163

Mini Whole Wheat Pumpkin Muffins with Orange Drizzle

As tender and flavorful as these muffins are, you'd never guess they were made with whole wheat flour. Since the muffins are drizzled with the sweet glaze, you don't need lots of sugar in the batter. Simmering the puree with the spices eliminates the tinny taste of the pumpkin and intensifies the flavors.

MAKES 2 DOZEN MUFFINS

- 1 can (15 ounces) 100% pure pumpkin
- 1½ teaspoons ground ginger
- 1 teaspoon ground cinnamon
- ¼ teaspoon ground cloves
- ¾ cup dark brown sugar
- ½ cup flavorless oil, such as vegetable or canola
- 2 large eggs, lightly beaten
- 1 cup whole wheat flour
- 2 tablespoons cornstarch
- 2 teaspoons baking powder
- ¼ teaspoon baking soda
- ½ teaspoon salt

ORANGE GLAZE (OPTIONAL)

- ¼ cup confectioners' sugar
- ¼ teaspoon finely grated orange zest
- 2 teaspoons orange juice

Adjust oven rack to center position and heat oven to 425 degrees. Spray 24 mini muffin cups with vegetable cooking spray.

Place pumpkin, ginger, cinnamon, and cloves in a small nonstick skillet over medium heat. Bring to a simmer and cook, stirring, to blend flavors, about 3 minutes. Pour hot puree into a medium bowl. Whisk in brown sugar and oil, then slowly beat in eggs.

Whisk flour, cornstarch, baking powder, baking soda, and salt in a medium bowl. Whisk pumpkin mixture into flour mixture until just combined.

Divide batter among muffin cups (a 2-tablespoon spring-action ice-cream scoop works well) and bake until golden and cooked through, 10 to 12 minutes. Let muffins stand for a couple of minutes, then remove from the cups and place on a wire rack to cool.

ORANGE GLAZE (OPTIONAL):

Whisk ingredients together in a small bowl. Drizzle over warm muffins.

99 calories per unglazed muffin; 104 calories glazed

Mini Whole Wheat Apple Muffins with Cinnamon Glaze

Follow directions for Mini Whole Wheat Pumpkin Muffins (page 145) but substitute 1½ cups *no-sugar-added* apple butter, 2 teaspoons ground cinnamon, and ¼ teaspoon ground cloves for the cooked spiced pumpkin puree (do not cook apple butter mixture) and reduce brown sugar to 2 tablespoons.

CINNAMON GLAZE (OPTIONAL):

In a small bowl, whisk ¼ cup confectioners' sugar, ⅛ teaspoon ground cinnamon, 1½ teaspoons milk, and a few drops of lemon juice to taste. Drizzle over warm muffins.

103 calories per unglazed muffin; 108 calories glazed

Mini Whole Wheat Banana Muffins with Nutmeg Glaze

Follow directions for Mini Whole Wheat Pumpkin Muffins (page 145) but substitute 3 medium very ripe mashed bananas (about 1½ cups) for the cooked spiced pumpkin puree (do not cook bananas) and reduce brown sugar to ½ cup.

NUTMEG GLAZE (OPTIONAL):

In a small bowl, whisk ¼ cup confectioners' sugar, ⅛ teaspoon ground nutmeg, 1½ teaspoons milk, and a few drops of lemon juice to taste. Drizzle over warm muffins.

97 calories per unglazed muffin; 102 calories glazed

#19
50 WAYS TO LOSE IT

Freeze overripe bananas for breakfast smoothies and tea muffins.

one dough, one dozen very different, very easy cookies

If you love to bake cookies but are afraid you'll be tempted to eat the whole batch, then these slice-and-bake, or icebox, cookies are perfect for you.

With just one batch of dough, you can make two (or even four) very different looking and tasting batches of cookies. Simply halve (or quarter) the dough, stir a different flavoring into each portion—lime zest in one, miniature chocolate chips in another, for example, or crystallized ginger in one, almond extract in the other—then form each portion of dough into a log.

> If you love to bake cookies but are afraid you'll be tempted to eat the whole batch, icebox cookies are perfect for you.

You can also change the look of the cookies. For rounds and ovals, roll the dough into a round log, cutting the ovals on a slight angle. For squares and diamonds, form the dough into a square log, cutting the diamond shapes on a slight angle.

You can roll the differently flavored doughs in the same coating or vary it. A cookie rolled in chopped walnuts or pistachios looks very different from a cookie rolled in coconut or sesame seeds or peanuts.

After making and shaping the dough and chilling it, slice off and bake what you need. Freeze the remaining dough logs, slicing and baking the frozen slices as you need fresh cookies.

The technique is old and practical, but the flavors are raise-your-eyebrows new.

All-Purpose Slice-and-Bake Butter Cookies

If you're pressed for time or just want to enjoy these cookies plain, skip the extra flavorings and coating.

MAKES ABOUT 6 DOZEN COOKIES

- 1 large egg, plus 1 yolk
- 1 teaspoon vanilla extract
- ½ teaspoon salt
- 2 sticks (½ pound) unsalted butter, softened to a cool room temperature
- 1 cup sugar
- 2½ cups all-purpose flour

Mix egg, yolk, vanilla, and salt in a small bowl. Beat butter and sugar with an electric mixer on medium speed or process in a food processor until well mixed and smooth. Add egg mixture; blend on low speed or pulse until well incorporated. Add flour and mix on low speed (or pulse) until a smooth dough forms.

Divide dough in half. Stir flavoring of choice (recipes follow) into each portion of dough.

Line a work surface with plastic wrap. Scrape 1 portion of dough onto plastic wrap. With floured hands, form dough into a 9-inch-long round or square log. Spread coating next to dough log on plastic wrap. Using plastic wrap to handle dough, roll log in coating to cover all around, lightly pressing on coating so that it adheres to dough. Using a second coating, repeat with remaining portion of dough. Wrap tightly in the plastic wrap and refrigerate until solid, at least 30 minutes. (Dough can be double-wrapped and frozen for up to 2 months.)

Adjust oven racks to upper-middle and lower-middle positions and heat oven to 375 degrees. Line two cookie sheets with parchment paper or silicone mats. Unwrap dough logs but leave on plastic wrap. Slice dough ¼ inch thick and place slices about ½ inch apart on cookie sheets.

Bake, rotating each sheet from front to back and from upper to lower positions after 6 minutes, until cookies are golden brown, 12 to 14 minutes total. Transfer to a wire rack and allow to cool completely. (Cookies can be stored in an airtight container for up to 2 weeks.)

51 calories per cookie

The following cookies taste better when rolled in *toasted* coatings. Of course, some nuts, like pistachios, peanuts, and cashews, are often sold already toasted. For those that aren't—and for coconut and sesame seeds—toast in a 325-degree oven until fragrant and slightly darker in color, 5 to 10 minutes. In addition to the nuts you'll need for coating, allow ½ cup for garnish and toast them too. In some cases, you'll have a little more than you need, but it never hurts to have toasted nuts in the cupboard to toss into salads, cereals, or muffins.

Cardamom Pistachio Cookies

Stir ½ teaspoon ground cardamom into 1 portion of dough. Roll dough log in ½ cup coarsely chopped roasted pistachios. Garnish each cookie with half a roasted pistachio and bake as directed.

56 calories per cookie

Lemon Pistachio Cookies

Stir 1 teaspoon finely grated lemon zest into 1 portion of dough. Roll 1 dough log in ½ cup coarsely chopped roasted pistachios. Garnish each cookie with half a roasted pistachio and bake as directed.

56 calories per cookie

Banana Peanut Cookies

Roll 1 dough log in ½ cup coarsely chopped roasted unsalted peanuts. Garnish each cookie with 2 overlapping banana-chip halves. You'll need a heaping ½ cup banana chips. Bake as directed.

58 calories per cookie

Chocolate Hazelnut Cookies

Stir ½ cup mini chocolate chips into 1 portion of dough. Roll 1 dough log in ½ cup coarsely chopped toasted hazelnuts. Garnish each cookie with 3 toasted hazelnut halves and bake as directed.

65 calories per cookie

Lime Coconut Cookies

Stir 1 teaspoon finely grated lime zest into 1 portion of dough. Roll 1 dough log in toasted coconut. Garnish each cookie with a pinch of additional toasted coconut and bake as directed.

54 calories per cookie

Ginger Sesame Cookies

Stir ½ teaspoon ground ginger and 3 tablespoons minced crystallized ginger into 1 portion of dough. Roll 1 dough log in ¼ cup toasted sesame seeds. Garnish each cookie with additional crystallized ginger cut into thin strips and bake as directed.

56 calories per cookie

Cranberry-Orange Walnut Cookies

Stir ½ teaspoon finely grated orange zest and ½ cup dried cranberries into 1 portion of dough. Roll 1 dough log in ½ cup coarsely chopped toasted walnuts. Bake as directed.

59 calories per cookie

Cherry Almond Cookies

Stir ¼ teaspoon almond extract and ½ cup dried cherries into 1 portion of dough. Roll 1 dough log in ¾ cup toasted slivered almonds. Garnish each cookie with 3 toasted almond slivers and bake as directed.

62 calories per cookie

Orange Pecan Cookies

Stir ½ teaspoon finely grated orange zest into 1 portion of dough. Roll 1 dough log in ½ cup coarsely chopped toasted pecans. Garnish each cookie with a toasted pecan piece and bake as directed.

56 calories per cookie

Cinnamon Cashew Cookies

Mix 1 teaspoon ground cinnamon into 1 portion of dough, leaving cinnamon swirls. Roll 1 dough log in ½ cup coarsely chopped roasted salted or unsalted cashews. Garnish each cookie with 3 cashew halves arranged in a pinwheel design and bake as directed.

58 calories per cookie

Rosemary Cookies with Almonds and Currants

Stir ½ cup dried currants and 2 teaspoons minced fresh rosemary leaves into 1 portion of dough. Roll 1 dough log in ¾ cup toasted slivered almonds. Garnish each cookie with 3 toasted almond slivers and bake as directed.

61 calories per cookie

Anise Cookies with Pine Nuts

In a small skillet over medium heat, heat 1 teaspoon aniseed, stirring occasionally, until fragrant, 2 to 3 minutes. Use a rolling pin to crush seeds to a coarse powder and stir into 1 portion of dough. Garnish each cookie with 3 toasted pine nuts and bake as directed.

55 calories per cookie

#20 50 WAYS TO LOSE IT

Arrange tea snacks or cookies on a small plate, then put the box away.

Chocolate-Coconut "Cookies"

Since they're bigger, the Nestlé Chocolatier Dark Chocolate Morsels make a more impressive chocolate center. If you can't find them, use two regular chocolate chips.

MAKES 30 COOKIES

- 1 bag (14 ounces) sweetened or unsweetened flaked coconut
- 1 can (14 ounces) sweetened condensed milk
- 2 teaspoons vanilla extract
- 30 chocolate chips (preferably Nestlé Chocolatier; see headnote), about 1½ tablespoons

Adjust oven racks to lower-middle and upper-middle positions and heat oven to 350 degrees. Line two cookie sheets with foil and spray with vegetable cooking spray, or line with silicone mats.

Mix coconut, condensed milk, and vanilla in a medium bowl. Using a 2-tablespoon measure (a standard coffee scoop works well), drop coconut mixture onto cookie sheets and top each with a chocolate chip.

Bake, rotating each sheet from front to back and from upper to lower positions after 7 minutes, until cookies are golden brown and cooked through, 12 to 14 minutes total. Transfer to a wire rack and allow to cool to room temperature. (Cookies can be stored in an airtight container for up to 2 weeks.)

110 calories per cookie

Miniature Apricot-Cherry Bars with Oatmeal Crumble Topping

Although on the caloric side, these bars are mostly filled with good-for-you dried fruit and nuts, and I find that one small square is usually enough to satisfy. It's a pain to have half a can of condensed milk left over, so if you've got a few extra minutes, make a half batch of Chocolate-Coconut "Cookies" (page 155).

MAKES ABOUT 54 BITE-SIZED BARS

- 1 cup all-purpose flour
- 1 cup old-fashioned oats
- ¾ cup light brown sugar
- ¼ teaspoon salt
- 1 stick (8 tablespoons) unsalted butter, melted
- 2 cups sweetened or unsweetened flaked coconut
- 2 cups sliced almonds
- 2 cups coarsely chopped dried cherries (about 10 ounces)
- 2 cups coarsely chopped dried apricots (about 16 ounces)
- 1½ cans (14 ounces each) sweetened condensed milk

Adjust oven rack to lower-middle position and heat oven to 325 degrees. Coat a 13-by-9-inch Pyrex baking pan with vegetable cooking spray. Line with heavy-duty foil, leaving an overhang on two sides to facilitate removal of bar from pan. Coat with vegetable cooking spray.

Mix flour, oats, brown sugar, and salt in a medium bowl. Add melted butter, stirring with a fork until well mixed and clumps form.

Spread 1½ packed cups oatmeal mixture over pan bottom, pressing into a thin crust. Mix coconut, almonds, cherries, apricots, and condensed milk in a large bowl. Pour over oatmeal crust, using a rubber spatula to distribute mixture evenly in pan and press it in place. Sprinkle remaining ¾ cup oatmeal mixture on top.

Bake until lightly golden, about 30 minutes. Set on a wire rack and allow to cool to room temperature. (Bar can be double-wrapped and frozen for several months or stored in an airtight container for up to 2 weeks.) Use foil "handles" to remove bar from pan. Cut into approximately 1½-inch squares and serve.

144 calories per square

#21

50 WAYS TO LOSE IT

To taste as you're cooking, don't stand at the counter or stove and graze. Spoon a two- or three-bite portion into a small ramekin or onto a saucer.

Gingerbread Straws

I love everything about these cookies—their intense ginger flavor, their long, slender shape, and their impressive calorie count. If you prefer wafers, you can use a cookie cutter to shape cookies.

MAKES 56 COOKIES

3¾ cups all-purpose flour
1 tablespoon ground ginger
2 teaspoons ground cinnamon
1 teaspoon ground cloves
1 teaspoon ground nutmeg
¾ teaspoon salt
¾ teaspoon baking soda
¾ cup molasses
¼ cup water
1½ sticks (12 tablespoons) unsalted butter, softened
1 cup light or dark brown sugar
4 tablespoons sugar

Mix flour, ginger, cinnamon, cloves, nutmeg, salt, and baking soda in a medium bowl. In a small bowl, mix molasses and water.

In a large bowl, beat butter and brown sugar with a hand mixer until light and fluffy. Beat in molasses mixture, then dry ingredients to form a stiff dough, adding up to ¼ cup extra flour if dough is sticky. Divide dough into quarters, forming each portion into a disk. Wrap in plastic wrap and refrigerate until firm, about 1 hour. (Dough can be refrigerated for up to 1 week or frozen for up to 1 month.)

Adjust oven racks to lower-middle and upper-middle positions and heat oven to 350 degrees. Line two cookie sheets with parchment paper or silicone mats.

Working with 1 portion of dough at a time on a heavily floured work surface, roll into a 9-by-7-inch rectangle. Sprinkle with 1 tablespoon sugar and press sugar into dough with a rolling pin. Use a pastry wheel (preferably with a fluted edge) to cut dough into approximately 9-by-½-inch sticks. Place sticks about ½ inch apart on cookie sheets.

Bake, rotating each sheet from back to front and from upper to lower positions after 10 minutes, until straws are fragrant and crisp, 18 to 22 minutes total. Transfer to a wire rack and allow to cool to room temperature. (Straws can be stored in an airtight container for up to 2 weeks.)

84 calories per cookie

#22

50 WAYS TO LOSE IT

Buy low-calorie treats (gingersnaps, biscotti, chocolate wafers, ladyfingers, graham crackers, milk biscuits) for quick tea snacks. Smear with low-sugar jam.

Simplest Fruit Bars

You can create whatever flavor fruit bar you've got a taste for with this recipe. For best results, use real jam—not the low- or no-sugar kind. Lemon curd is more caloric than jam, but when divided over 16 bars, it's only slightly more, and it's my favorite.

MAKES 16 BARS

- ¼ cup sweetened or unsweetened flaked coconut, sliced almonds, or chopped pecans, walnuts, or pistachios
- 1 cup all-purpose flour
- ¼ cup confectioners' sugar
- ¼ teaspoon salt
- ½ stick (4 tablespoons) unsalted butter, melted
- 1 cup prepared lemon curd or your favorite jam

Adjust oven rack to lower-middle position and heat oven to 350 degrees. Line an 8-inch square baking pan (disposable is fine) with heavy-duty foil, leaving an overhang on two sides to facilitate removal of bar from pan. Coat with vegetable cooking spray.

Scatter coconut or nut of choice in a small shallow baking pan and set aside.

Mix flour, sugar, and salt in a medium bowl. Stir in butter with a fork, then switch to hands and continue to mix until dough is crumbly and sticks together when squeezed. Press dough into the bottom of prepared pan.

Place pan in oven, along with pan of coconut or nuts. Bake coconut for 7 minutes (almonds for 5 minutes, chopped nuts for 9 to 10 minutes), until golden. Bake bars until golden brown, about 20 minutes.

Remove crust from oven. Spread curd or jam over crust, then sprinkle with the toasted coconut or nuts.

Return to oven and bake until bubbly, about 20 minutes. Let cool for 5 minutes. Using foil "handles," lift bar from pan. Let cool to room temperature, then cut into 2-inch squares and serve. (Bars can be double-wrapped and frozen for 3 months, covered with foil and refrigerated for 1 week, or stored at room temperature for several days.)

About 100 calories per square

Peach Pecan Bars

Use peach jam and chopped pecans.

124 calories per square

Strawberry Almond Bars

Use strawberry jam and sliced almonds.

119 calories per square

Apricot Pistachio Bars

Use apricot jam and chopped pistachios.

121 calories per square

Lemon Coconut Bars

Use lemon curd and toasted sweetened or unsweetened flaked coconut.

100 calories per square

#23
50 WAYS TO LOSE IT

Decide what you need (and don't need) to eat to be happy.

My Favorite Biscotti

Biscotti are among my favorite tea sweets. As cookies go, they're lean, yet flavorful and satisfying, and the dough is simple to make and bake. The baking time is slow and the oven temperature is low, making it almost impossible to burn biscotti. After forming the dough into two logs, pop them into the oven for the first baking. There's plenty of time for a nice walk, and when you get back, the baked logs are ready to slice. Return the sliced cookies to the oven for the second baking. As soon as they crisp up and turn golden, they're done. Now you've got enough treats for many cups of late-afternoon tea or coffee.

MAKES ABOUT 4 DOZEN BISCOTTI

- 3 large eggs
- 1 teaspoon vanilla extract
- Other flavorings (optional; recipes follow)
- 2 cups all-purpose flour
- 1 cup minus 2 tablespoons sugar
- 2 teaspoons baking powder
- ¼ teaspoon salt
- 1 cup almonds, pistachios, pine nuts, dried cherries, dried cranberries, raisins, or dried currants

Adjust oven rack to center position and heat oven to 300 degrees. Line a cookie sheet with parchment paper or a silicone mat.

Mix eggs, vanilla, and other flavorings in a small bowl. Mix flour, sugar, baking powder, and salt in a medium bowl. Stir egg mixture into dry ingredients, first with a rubber spatula, then with your hands, to form a smooth, sticky dough. Stir in nuts or dried fruit until evenly distributed. Halve dough and transfer to a floured surface. With floured hands, roll each portion of dough into a 12-inch-long log and place on cookie sheet. Bake until golden brown, about 50 minutes. Transfer logs to a wire rack and allow to cool for 5 minutes.

Adjust oven racks to lower-middle and upper-middle positions and lower oven temperature to 275 degrees. Line two cookie sheets with parchment paper or silicone mats.

Working with 1 log at a time, place on a cutting board and, using a serrated knife, slice diagonally into ½-inch-thick slices. Place biscotti on cookie sheets. Bake until golden brown and almost crisp throughout, 25 to 30 minutes. Transfer to a wire rack to cool and dry. (Biscotti can be stored in an airtight container for up to 1 month.)

About 48 calories per biscotti

Orange (or Lemon) Pistachio Biscotti

Follow directions for My Favorite Biscotti, using 2 tablespoons finely grated orange or lemon zest and 1 cup roasted pistachios.

53 calories per biscotti

Cherry Almond Biscotti

Follow directions for My Favorite Biscotti, using 2 teaspoons almond extract and 1 cup dried cherries.

48 calories per biscotti

Cranberry Orange (or Lemon) Biscotti

Follow directions for My Favorite Biscotti, using 2 tablespoons finely grated orange or lemon zest and 1 cup dried cranberries.

46 calories per biscotti

Spiced Raisin Biscotti

Follow directions for My Favorite Biscotti, using 2 teaspoons ground cinnamon, 1 teaspoon ground nutmeg, ¼ teaspoon ground cloves, and 1 cup golden or dark raisins.

49 calories per biscotti

before-dinner nibbles

You may not need a before-dinner nibble, but I do. My usual snack is a couple tablespoons of flavored nuts or spiced pumpkin seeds that I measure into a small ramekin and enjoy with a glass of white wine. Roasted nuts are salty, savory, and caloric, but unlike potato chips, they don't contain "empty calories" and are good for you.

Since we're paying attention to calories, you might question the wisdom of having this high-calorie treat (100 to 150 calories for a mere 2 tablespoons of nuts or seeds and 70 for a scant half-cup of wine) on a regular basis when you're trying to lose weight.

This snack keeps me from thoughtless picking while I cook dinner and excess eating when I'm at the table.

You'll have to decide whether a snack is right for you, but for me a glass of wine and a simple hors d'oeuvre is an important nightly ritual. Just as tea and a cookie offer that end-of-the-day energy boost, wine and a little nibble signal that the day is winding down and it's time to relax. This pleasurable moment keeps me from thoughtless picking while I cook dinner and excess eating when I'm at the table. In fact, with my appetite quieted, it's not unusual for me to leave food on my dinner plate—something that would have been unheard of until just a few years ago.

After I have dinner at around 6:30, I'm finished eating for the night. Since I'm an early riser, I'm not up late enough to face the midnight munchies. If you are, you may want to exchange teatime or a predinner nibble for a midevening snack. Be careful, however: the later you eat, the less time your body has to burn off the calories (and post-dinner eating can be notoriously decadent). But if you've chosen the foods you need to be healthy and happy all day long, then trust yourself. If you listen, your body will tell you what it needs.

For those who don't drink but like the idea of this moment, sip on something nonalcoholic. Have an herbal or decaffeinated tea. Or, for a wonderfully refreshing low-calorie drink, mix sparkling water with ¼ cup orange juice—just 25 calories—or another fruit juice. If diet soda is on your "gotta-have" list, pour one for yourself and slowly sip it. If there's time to sit for a moment, that's even better. You're calm and satisfied, and you won't need an over-the-top dinner portion.

#24
50 WAYS TO LOSE IT

Pack healthy snacks before you travel.

RECIPES

Seasoned Roasted Peanuts 170
Roasted Pumpkin Seeds 171
with Chili and Lime 171
with Curry and Cayenne 171

Bar Nuts à la Union Square Cafe 172
I Can't Believe They're Not Fried Tortilla Chips 173
Pita Crisps 174
Curried 174
Caraway and Mustard Seed 174
Pecorino, Pepper, and Oregano 175
Cumin and Coriander 175
"Everything" 175

Wine Biscuits with Cracked Black Pepper 176
Smoked Salmon Tartare 177
Classic Texas Caviar 178
Deviled Eggs for Two 179

Seasoned Roasted Peanuts

MAKES HEAPING 3 CUPS

- 1 jar (16 ounces) dry-roasted unsalted peanuts (heaping 3 cups)
- 2 tablespoons fresh lime juice
- ⅓ cup Old Bay Seasoning

Adjust oven rack to center position and heat oven to 350 degrees.

In a 13-by-9-inch metal baking pan, toss nuts with lime juice and seasoning. Roast nuts, stirring occasionally, until very hot and fragrant, about 10 minutes. Set aside to cool. Serve warm or at room temperature. (Nuts can be stored in a sealed tin or jar for up to 1 month.)

111 calories per 2-tablespoon serving

#25

50 WAYS TO LOSE IT

Nibble on a small handful of nuts before dinner to curb your appetite.

Roasted Pumpkin Seeds with Chili and Lime

MAKES 1 CUP

- 1 cup roasted salted pumpkin seeds
- 2 teaspoons fresh lime juice
- 1½ teaspoons chili powder
- ⅛ teaspoon cayenne pepper
- Kosher salt (optional)

Adjust oven rack to middle position and heat oven to 350 degrees.

In a medium bowl, toss pumpkin seeds with lime juice, chili powder, and cayenne. Transfer to an 8- or 9-inch square baking pan. Bake, stirring occasionally, until golden brown and fragrant, about 10 minutes. Taste, sprinkling lightly with kosher salt, if you like. Let cool slightly and serve. (Seeds can be stored in a airtight container for up to 2 weeks.)

96 calories per 2-tablespoon serving

Roasted Pumpkin Seeds with Curry and Cayenne

Substitute 1½ teaspoons curry powder for chili powder.

96 calories per 2-tablespoon serving

Bar Nuts à la Union Square Cafe

I buy the 2.5-pound size of Extra Fancy Mixed Nuts—cashews, almonds, pecans, hazelnuts, and Brazil nuts—at Costco, skim off a few, add a handful of pistachios, and roast a large quantity at one time.

The recipe is adapted from the recipe for Union Square Cafe Bar Nuts that appears in The Union Square Cafe Cookbook. *I start with easy-to-find roasted salted nuts, add pistachios, cut back on the salt, and lower the oven temperature. I enjoy these roasted nuts with a glass of wine, and I also chop them to add to salads.*

The recipe easily halves.

MAKES A HEAPING 6 CUPS

- **2 pounds (about 6 cups) premium roasted salted mixed nuts**
- **8 ounces (about 1⅔ cups) roasted salted pistachios**
- **1 tablespoon butter**
- **¼ cup minced fresh rosemary leaves**
- **½ teaspoon cayenne pepper**
- **2 teaspoons dark brown sugar**
- **1 teaspoon kosher salt**

Adjust oven rack to middle position and heat oven to 325 degrees.

Spread nuts on a large (18-by-12-inch) baking sheet in a single layer. Roast, stirring occasionally, until fragrant and very hot, about 10 minutes.

Meanwhile, microwave butter in a medium microwave-safe bowl until melted. Stir in rosemary, cayenne, sugar, and salt. Pour hot nuts into a large bowl. Add rosemary mixture and stir until completely coated. Pour nuts back onto baking sheet and spread in a single layer to cool. Serve warm or at room temperature. (Nuts can be stored in an airtight container for about 1 month.)

146 calories per 2-tablespoon serving

I Can't Believe They're Not Fried Tortilla Chips

Tossed with a minimal amount of oil, these chips taste fried, even though they're baked.

SERVES 12

12 corn tortillas from an 11-ounce package
3 tablespoons olive oil
Kosher salt

Adjust oven racks to upper-middle and lower-middle positions and heat oven to 400 degrees.

Leaving tortillas in a stack, cut into 6 wedges. Toss tortilla wedges in the oil and arrange in a single layer on two cookie sheets. Bake, rotating each sheet from front to back and from upper to lower positions after 8 minutes, until crisp and golden brown, about 12 minutes total. Season hot chips with salt and serve.

61 calories per 6 wedges

#26

50 WAYS TO LOSE IT

Buy a few basic clothes at each smaller size when you are losing weight.

Pita Crisps

SERVES 4

- 2 whole wheat pitas, split to make 4 rounds
- 4 teaspoons vegetable or olive oil
- Choice of seasoning mixture (see below)
- ¼ teaspoon kosher salt
- ½ teaspoon ground black pepper

Adjust oven rack to center position and heat oven to 350 degrees.

Place pitas on a baking sheet large enough to hold them in a single layer. Drizzle oil over pitas and spread with a dull knife. Mix seasoning with salt and pepper and sprinkle evenly over pitas. Bake until crisp and golden brown, 8 to 10 minutes. If pitas are brown but not completely crisp, turn off oven, open oven door, and allow to stand for 5 minutes.

122 calories per round

Curried Pita Crisps

- 1½ teaspoons curry powder
- 1 teaspoon mustard seeds

Mix curry and mustard seeds with salt and pepper and sprinkle over each pita.

128 calories per round

Caraway and Mustard Seed Pita Crisps

- 1 teaspoon caraway seeds
- 1 teaspoon mustard seeds

Mix caraway and mustard seeds with salt and pepper and sprinkle over each pita.

127 calories per round

Pecorino, Pepper, and Oregano Pita Crisps

¼ cup finely grated Pecorino Romano or Parmigiano-Reggiano cheese

1 teaspoon dried oregano

Because the cheese is salted, omit salt here. Mix cheese and oregano with pepper and sprinkle over each pita.

136 calories per round

Cumin and Coriander Pita Crisps

1½ teaspoons ground coriander

1½ teaspoons cumin seeds

Mix coriander and cumin with salt and pepper and sprinkle over each pita.

127 calories per round

"Everything" Pita Crisps

1 teaspoon poppy seeds

1 teaspoon sesame seeds

1 teaspoon dried minced garlic

Mix poppy seeds, sesame seeds, and garlic with salt and pepper and sprinkle over each pita.

132 calories per round

Wine Biscuits with Cracked Black Pepper

Here's the recipe for those crackers that sell in specialty shops for $6.99 for two dozen. Serve them unadorned or with a smidgen of goat cheese.

MAKES 3 DOZEN BISCUITS

- ½ cup dry red wine
- 1 cup bread flour
- 3 tablespoons sugar
- 1 teaspoon cracked black pepper
- 1 teaspoon minced fresh rosemary or thyme leaves
- ½ teaspoon salt
- ½ teaspoon baking powder
- 3 tablespoons extra-virgin olive oil

In a small saucepan over medium-high heat, bring wine to a boil. Continue to boil until reduced by half, 2 to 3 minutes.

Meanwhile, adjust oven racks to lower-middle and upper-middle positions and heat oven to 325 degrees. Line two cookie sheets with parchment paper or silicone mats.

Process flour, sugar, pepper, rosemary or thyme, salt, and baking powder in a food processor to combine.

Mix wine and oil and add to dry ingredients. Process until dough just comes together. Turn out onto a lightly floured work surface and roll out to a little more than ⅛ inch thick. Using a 1½-inch cookie cutter (or a screw-cap lid from a vegetable-oil or similar-sized bottle), cut out dough rounds and place on cookie sheets. Roll scraps once or twice to make 3 dozen rounds.

Bake until golden and crisp, about 30 minutes. Transfer to a wire rack and allow to cool. (Biscuits can be stored in an airtight container for up to 1 month.)

29 calories per biscuit

Smoked Salmon Tartare

If you don't want the added calories of a cracker, serve a small mound of the tartare in teaspoons. Whether you enjoy this hors d'oeuvre on a cracker or from a spoon, you can top each bite with a small piece of very thinly sliced lemon, rind and all.

MAKES ABOUT 1⅓ CUPS, SERVING ABOUT 14

- ¼ cup drained capers
- 8 ounces smoked salmon
- 2 tablespoons chopped fresh dill
- 2 tablespoons extra-virgin olive oil
- ½ teaspoon finely grated lemon zest
- ¼ cup finely diced red onion

Pulse capers in a food processor until coarsely chopped. Add salmon, dill, oil, and lemon zest and pulse until salmon is finely chopped and tartare is well mixed. Transfer to a small bowl, stir in red onion, and serve.

38 calories per serving (4–5 teaspoons)

#27

50 WAYS TO LOSE IT

Use a butter knife rather than a pastry brush for spreading oil so that you don't lose it in the bristles.

Classic Texas Caviar

A batch of this spread keeps for weeks in the refrigerator. Use it as a quick weeknight hors d'oeuvre with I Can't Believe They're Not Fried Tortilla Chips (page 173) or as a salad flavoring and dressing. For a first-course salad, allow about ¼ cup per serving; for a main-course salad, about ½ cup per serving.

MAKES 1 QUART

- 2 cans (15.5 ounces each) black-eyed peas, drained
- 1 can (14.5 ounces) petite diced tomatoes, drained
- 2 medium jalapeño peppers, stemmed, seeded, and minced
- 1 small yellow onion, cut into small dice
- ½ yellow bell pepper, cut into small dice
- ¼ cup chopped fresh cilantro leaves
- 6 tablespoons red wine vinegar
- 6 tablespoons olive oil (not extra-virgin)
- ½ teaspoon each salt and ground black pepper
- ½ teaspoon garlic powder
- 1 teaspoon dried oregano
- 1½ teaspoons ground cumin

Mix all ingredients in a medium bowl. Cover and refrigerate for 2 hours or up to 2 days. Before serving, taste and add more vinegar, salt, or pepper, if needed. Transfer to a serving bowl.

99 calories per ¼-cup serving

Deviled Eggs for Two

If making deviled eggs for a special occasion, I use real mayo, but for a weeknight predinner nibble, these eggs suit me just fine.

SERVES 2

2 hard-boiled eggs (see page 72)
Salt and ground black pepper

SALSA, RELISH, OR OTHER FLAVORING (CHOOSE 1 OF THE FOLLOWING):

2 tablespoons of your favorite prepared salsa (I like Pace brand)

2 tablespoons dill pickle relish

1 tablespoon salsa verde

1 tablespoon sweet pickle relish, preferably Claussen brand (found in the refrigerated section), mixed with 2 teaspoons Dijon mustard

1 tablespoon drained prepared horseradish mixed with 1 tablespoon light mayonnaise

1 tablespoon drained capers mixed with 1 tablespoon light mayonnaise

Peel eggs and halve them crosswise (not lengthwise). Remove yolks and transfer to a small plate. Slice a tiny piece of white off bottom of each egg half so that eggs will sit upright. Using a fork, mash yolks with salt and pepper and salsa, relish, or other flavoring until smooth. Spoon filling into egg halves and serve.

77 calories per egg

dinners—fast and faster

Dinner at our house is light. I usually start off with a first-course salad, flavoring it with seasonal ingredients. For the main course, we often enjoy pasta, but instead of cooking half a box for my husband and me, as I used to, I weigh out six ounces. As long as the crust is thin and the rich ingredients sparse, flatbread pizza is frequent in my world. I occasionally get a taste for the familiar tomato-sauce variety, but seeing the crust as nothing more than a piece of thin, crisp bread, I've developed several quick, intriguing variations as well.

Until I took charge of my diet, I used to let others influence how much I ate—especially at dinner.

At least one night a week, I make pan-seared pork, poultry, or seafood with one of the interchangeable pan sauces. Or I might assemble one of the foil packs described on page 243. These little pouches are sophisticated, flavorful, and complete, and they cook in just 15 minutes, giving you enough time to prepare and enjoy a salad.

If we eat meat, fish, or poultry as the main course, I generally skip the starch and serve grilled, roasted, or steam-sautéed vegetables. If we eat pasta or pizza, I dramatically reduce (or drop) the meat.

I grill a lot in the warm months, but since my gas grill is right off the kitchen, I cook outside regularly in the dead of winter as well. I tend to stick with small, lean, boneless cuts, such as pork chops, chicken breasts and thighs, and sturdy fish steaks. Unlike pan searing, grilling produces no drippings from which to make a sauce, so I normally season the cuts liberally with a flavorful spice rub and, if there's time, serve them with a quick-from-scratch sauce or fruit salsa.

Until I took charge of my diet, I used to let others influence how much I ate—especially at dinner. If people at the table had bread with their salad, I'd pick up a slice too. If they didn't, I might not. If they finished their meal, I'd clean my plate. If they left food, I did as well.

Here was my rationale: if the people weighed more than I did, I thought I could afford to eat more. If my dinner companions weighed less, I figured they knew what they were doing and followed accordingly.

As they reached for the butter, enjoyed seconds, or indulged in a decadent dessert, I failed to see it as a snapshot moment. What had these people eaten last night or this morning? How would they exercise tomorrow? I now know that these svelte people weren't just eating mindlessly. They likely worked hard to earn those extra treats. Maybe he had worked out for an hour that (and every) morning. Perhaps she had eaten only fruit for lunch, or she may have allowed herself one dessert a week, and this was it.

Some people may lead you to believe that looking fit is easy, that they eat like horses and don't exercise, but it's not true. Very few are blessed with a high metabolism. Every fit person I know has developed his or her own way to maintain weight. It doesn't just happen.

By the time I've enjoyed two meals, teatime, a predinner nibble with a glass of wine, and a first-course salad, I'm quite satisfied. I serve myself a modest portion, and regardless of what others at the table do, I frequently leave food on my dinner plate.

RECIPES

PIZZA

Quick Flatbread Dough 191
White Whole-Wheat 191
Whole Wheat 192

Fresh Tomato Flatbread with Arugula and Prosciutto 193
Sausage and Caramelized Onion Flatbread with Kale and Parmesan 194
Greek Flatbread with Spinach, Feta, and Olives 195
Flatbread d'Alsace 196
Chicken Flatbread with Salsa Verde, White Beans, and Corn 197
Thai Chicken Flatbread with Carrots and Cilantro 198
Curried Chicken Flatbread with Chutney and Yogurt Drizzle 199
Slaw-Topped Mexican Flatbread with Refried Beans and Pepper Jack 200
Chicken and Cranberry Flatbread with Caramelized Onions and Goat Cheese 201
Barbecue Chicken Flatbread 202
Reuben Flatbread 203
Flatbread with Smoked Salmon and All the Trimmings 204

PASTA

Creamy Light Pasta 206
Salmon, Asparagus, and Dill 208
Shrimp, Spinach, and Oregano 208
Scallops, Peas, and Saffron 209
Crab and Roasted Peppers 209
Clams, Italian Herbs, and Parsley 209
Spicy Chicken, Broccoli, and Basil 210
Mushroom-Flavored with Ham and Rosemary 210

Pasta with Just-Right Red Sauce 213
- Shrimp, Spinach, and Lemon Zest 215
- Crab, Mushrooms, and Basil 215
- Scallops, Asparagus, and Orange Zest 216
- Tuna, Onions, and Kalamata Olives 216
- White Beans, Kale, and Rosemary 216
- Chicken, Broccoli, and Sun-Dried Tomatoes 217
- Sausage, Broccoli Rabe, and Red Pepper 217

SEAR-AND-SAUCE SUPPERS

Chicken Cutlets 222
Chicken Thighs 224
Pork Tenderloin 225
Pork Loin Chops 226
Shrimp 227
Sea Scallops 228
Salmon Fillets 229
White Wine Cream Sauce with Chives 230
Salsa Verde Cream Sauce with Cilantro 230
Mushroom-Thyme Cream Sauce 231
Mustard Cream Sauce with Tarragon 231
Light Tomato Sauce with Vinegar and Basil 231
Orange-Dijon Pan Sauce 232
Apricot Pan Sauce with Pistachios and Cumin 232
Prune Pan Sauce with Warm Spices 233
Marsala Pan Sauce with Raisins or Prunes 233
Cherry-Balsamic Pan Sauce with Toasted Almonds 233
Red Wine Pan Sauce with Garlic, Olives, and Oregano 234
Apple-Ginger Pan Sauce 234

BAKED FISH AND VEGETABLES

Asparagus, Lemon, and Fresh Herbs 236
Oven-Sautéed Tomatoes, Basil, and Garlic 237
Green Beans and Capers 238
Mushrooms and Thyme 239
Spinach and Asian Drizzle 240

MIX-AND-MATCH FOIL PACKETS

Chicken breasts, pork tenderloin, shrimp, scallops, or salmon with vegetables and:
Lemon Dill 243
Barbecue 243
Tarragon Mustard Cream 244
Soy Sesame 244
Tomato, Italian Herbs, and Capers 244
Tomato, Orange, and Saffron 244

FROM THE GRILL

Spiced-Up Grilled Boneless Pork, Poultry, or Salmon 248
Spicy Grilled Shrimp 250
Simple Spice Rubs and Pastes 251
Basic Paprika Garlic Spice Rub 251
Fennel Garlic Spice Rub 251
Cumin and Coriander Spice Rub 251
Warm Spice Rub 252
Spicy Rosemary Rub 252
Garlicky Chinese Five-Spice Rub 252
Caribbean Spice Paste 253
Tandoori Paste 253
Grilled Swordfish or Tuna Steaks 254
Seared Steak with Rosemary and Garlic 255

Create-Your-Own Fruit Salsa 256
Pineapple Salsa with Radishes, Peppers, and Cilantro 257
Green Grape Salsa with Scallions and Mint 257
Mango Peanut Salsa 258
Cherry Tomato Relish with Capers and Green Olives 258

VEGETABLES

Grilled Vegetables 261
Grilled Fruit 263
Roasted Fall/Winter Vegetables 265
Roasted Spring Vegetables 266
Roasted Summer Vegetables 267
Roasted Green Beans with Cherry Tomatoes and Oregano 268
Roasted Buttered Brussels Sprouts with Dijon and Lemon 269
Roasted Mushrooms with Garlic and Thyme 270
Steam-Sautéed Vegetables 272
Quick Tomato-Stewed Zucchini with Basil and Garlic 274
Rich and Creamy Cauliflower Puree 275

pizza light for a busy night

No matter how you look at it—through the carb, fat, or calories lens—your typical slice of greasy, thick-crusted pepperoni and four-cheese pizza isn't going to make the healthy-lifestyle cut. But if you start with a thin crust, top it generously with lean, highly flavored ingredients, and accent it sparingly with rich ones, you've got a fun, satisfying meal that won't break the calorie bank.

> My flatbreads are designed for weeknight suppers. You can make the yeastless dough in the food processor in under a minute.

At first you may be surprised by the similar calorie counts between the average commercial pizza and the ones in this chapter. The difference, however, lies in the portion sizes. A slice of pepperoni and cheese from a 16-inch take-out pizza might be only 340 calories. Not bad, until you realize the calories are based on a mere one twelfth of the pizza. Can you imagine ordering one large pizza for twelve people? On the other hand, if you make my Quick Flatbread Dough, you can have your very own 12-by-4-inch pizza for approximately the same number of calories. And if you opt for a 12-inch store-bought thin crust, you get one fifth of the pie.

The following flatbread pizzas are designed for weeknight suppers. You can make the yeastless dough in the food processor in under a minute. No yeast means the dough can be rolled immediately. Most of these pizzas, including the dough, can be ready in about 30 minutes. If you start with a prepared crust, you can be eating even sooner.

The key is to follow the order of instructions. It can take up to 10 minutes for the oven to reach 500 degrees, so start by preheating it. Unless you've selected a topping that requires cooking (only a few call for caramelizing onions), make and roll the dough next (or simply use a packaged 12-inch thin pizza crust).

Finally, prepare the toppings. Since most of the flatbreads are topped twice—before and after baking—prepare the prebake toppings first. When the flatbread pizzas go into the oven, prepare the post-bake toppings—chop the herbs, toss the slaw, grate the cheese.

If you're in the mood for a more familiar combination, smear the dough with a friendly tomato sauce, top it with your favorite vegetables or lean meat, and bake. Shower it with Parmesan as it emerges from the oven.

Quick Flatbread Dough

This yeastless dough bakes into a flatter, more crisp crust than traditional pizza crust, but you don't have to plan ahead to enjoy this from-scratch weeknight treat.

MAKES 4 FLATBREAD PIZZAS

- **1 cup bread flour, plus extra for dusting**
- **½ teaspoon salt**
- **⅓ cup warm water, plus extra if necessary**
- **1 teaspoon extra-virgin olive oil**

Mix flour and salt in a food processor. Mix water and oil and pour over flour mixture; process to form a soft dough ball. If dough is too stiff (hard-clay texture), process in another tablespoon of warm water. Continue to process until dough is well kneaded, about 15 seconds.

With floured hands, turn dough out onto a lightly floured surface and cut into quarters. Working with one quarter at a time, roll dough out to about a 12-by-4-inch rectangle, dusting with flour and turning as necessary to keep it from sticking.

Line a large cookie sheet with parchment paper or a silicone mat. (All 4 flatbreads should fit crosswise on the same sheet.) To top and bake, see following recipes.

110 calories per crust

Quick White Whole-Wheat Flatbread Dough

White whole-wheat flour delivers the appealing flavor of white flour with all the nutrition of whole wheat and is available under the King Arthur brand. You may find it in the baking aisle of your grocery store. If not, you can order it online at www.kingarthurflour.com.

Substitute 1 cup white whole-wheat flour for bread flour. This dough is stiffer and takes longer to form a ball.

110 calories per crust

Quick Whole Wheat Flatbread Dough

Although not as crisp, flatbreads made with whole wheat flour are still delicious.

Reduce bread flour to ½ cup and add ½ cup whole wheat flour with bread flour.

111 calories per crust

#28

50 WAYS TO LOSE IT

Eat fiber-rich whole grains. (You'll be satisfied with smaller portions.)

Fresh Tomato Flatbread with Arugula and Prosciutto

MAKES 4 INDIVIDUAL FLATBREAD PIZZAS,
OR ONE 12-INCH THIN PIZZA, SERVING 5

Quick Flatbread Dough (pages 191–192), or 1 packaged 12-inch thin pizza crust
1 pound fresh tomatoes, sliced thin
Salt
1 teaspoon dried basil
2 large garlic cloves, minced
1 tablespoon plus 2 teaspoons extra-virgin olive oil
4 cups (about 4 ounces) prewashed arugula
6 paper-thin slices prosciutto
2 ounces Parmesan cheese, preferably Parmigiano-Reggiano, shaved with a vegetable peeler (scant loosely packed cup)

Adjust oven rack to lowest position and heat oven to 500 degrees for flatbread dough or 450 degrees for packaged pizza crust.

Place flatbread dough or pizza crust on a cookie sheet. Arrange tomatoes over dough. Season with salt and sprinkle with basil. In a small bowl, mix garlic and 1 tablespoon oil. Drizzle over tomatoes.

Bake until crust is crisp and golden and tomatoes are cooked, 10 to 12 minutes.

Meanwhile, toss arugula with remaining 2 teaspoons oil and salt to taste. Remove pizza from oven, top with prosciutto, arugula, and Parmesan. Serve individual flatbreads or cut pizza into serving portions.

301 calories per serving

Sausage and Caramelized Onion Flatbread with Kale and Parmesan

MAKES 4 INDIVIDUAL FLATBREAD PIZZAS,
OR ONE 12-INCH THIN PIZZA, SERVING 5

- 1½ tablespoons olive oil
- 2 medium-large onions, halved and sliced thin
- Quick Flatbread Dough (pages 191–192), or 1 packaged 12-inch thin pizza crust
- ½ cup (no sugar added) apple butter
- 3 cups chopped fresh kale
- Salt and ground black pepper
- 2 6-ounce fully cooked chicken or turkey sausages, sliced thin
- 2 ounces Parmesan cheese, preferably Parmigiano-Reggiano, shaved with a vegetable peeler (a scant loosely packed cup)

Adjust oven rack to lowest position and heat oven to 500 degrees for flatbread dough or 450 degrees for packaged pizza crust.

Heat 1 tablespoon oil in a large skillet over medium-high heat while slicing onions. When wisps of smoke start to rise from pan, add onions and sauté, stirring infrequently at first and more toward the end, until they turn a rich brown color, 7 to 8 minutes.

Meanwhile, place flatbread dough or pizza crust on a cookie sheet and spread with apple butter. In a large bowl, toss kale with remaining 1½ teaspoons oil and a sprinkling of salt and pepper. Top flatbreads or pizza crust with caramelized onions, kale, then sausage.

Bake until spotty brown, 10 to 12 minutes. Remove from oven and scatter cheese over top. Serve individual flatbreads or cut pizza into serving portions.

404 calories per serving

Greek Flatbread with Spinach, Feta, and Olives

MAKES 4 INDIVIDUAL FLATBREAD PIZZAS, OR ONE 12-INCH THIN PIZZA, SERVING 5

- ½ cup light mayonnaise
- 4 garlic cloves, minced
- ¾ cup crumbled feta cheese (about 4 ounces)
- Quick Flatbread Dough (pages 191–192), or 1 packaged 12-inch thin pizza crust
- ½ cup coarsely chopped drained sun-dried tomatoes packed in oil, plus 1 teaspoon of the oil
- ¼ cup pitted kalamata olives, chopped coarsely
- 1 teaspoon dried oregano
- 2 cups baby spinach leaves
- ½ small red onion, halved and sliced thin

Adjust oven rack to lowest position and heat oven to 500 degrees for flatbread dough or 450 degrees for packaged pizza crust.

Mix mayonnaise, garlic, and half the feta in a medium bowl. Place flatbread dough or pizza crust on a cookie sheet and spread with mayonnaise mixture. Top with tomatoes and olives and sprinkle with oregano.

Bake until heated through and crisp, about 10 minutes. Meanwhile, in a medium bowl, toss spinach and onion with tomato oil. Top hot pizza with spinach mixture and remaining feta and return to oven until spinach wilts, about 2 minutes longer. Serve individual flatbreads or cut pizza into serving portions.

358 calories per serving

Flatbread d'Alsace

MAKES 4 INDIVIDUAL FLATBREAD PIZZAS,
OR ONE 12-INCH THIN PIZZA, SERVING 5

- 1 tablespoon olive oil
- 2 medium-large onions, halved and sliced thin
- 2 teaspoons chopped fresh thyme leaves, or ½ teaspoon dried
- Quick Flatbread Dough (pages 191–192), or 1 packaged 12-inch thin pizza crust
- 3 tablespoons brown mustard
- 1 package (6 ounces) sliced Canadian bacon
- 6 thin slices (3 ounces) Swiss cheese
- 3 tablespoons light sour cream, thinned with 1½ tablespoons water

Adjust oven rack to lowest position and heat oven to 500 degrees for flatbread dough or 450 degrees for packaged pizza crust.

Heat oil in a large skillet over medium-high heat while slicing onions. When wisps of smoke start to rise from pan, add onions and sauté, stirring infrequently at first and more toward the end, until they turn a rich brown color, 7 to 8 minutes. Stir in thyme, remove from heat, and set aside.

Meanwhile, place flatbread dough or pizza crust on a cookie sheet and spread with mustard. Top with Canadian bacon and caramelized onions. Bake until crust is golden brown, 10 to 12 minutes. Top hot pizza with cheese and return to oven until cheese melts, 1 to 2 minutes longer. Drizzle with sour cream and serve individual flatbreads or cut pizza into serving portions.

324 calories per serving

Chicken Flatbread with Salsa Verde, White Beans, and Corn

MAKES 4 INDIVIDUAL FLATBREAD PIZZAS,
OR ONE 12-INCH THIN PIZZA, SERVING 5

Quick Flatbread Dough (pages 191–192), or 1 packaged 12-inch thin pizza crust
1 cup drained white beans (from a 15.5-ounce can), mashed
1 cup store-bought salsa verde
2 cups shredded cooked chicken breast
1 cup frozen corn (no need to thaw)
1 cup shredded Monterey or pepper Jack cheese (3 ounces)
3 medium scallions, sliced thin
2 tablespoons chopped fresh cilantro leaves

Adjust oven rack to lowest position and heat oven to 500 degrees for flatbread dough or 450 degrees for packaged pizza crust.

Place flatbread dough or pizza crust on a cookie sheet. In a small bowl, mix together beans and ½ cup of the salsa; spread over dough. In a medium bowl, toss remaining ½ cup salsa with chicken and corn. Top pizza with chicken mixture.

Bake until spotty brown, 10 to 14 minutes. Top hot pizza with cheese, scallions, and cilantro, return to oven, and bake until cheese melts, about 2 minutes longer. Serve individual flatbreads or cut pizza into serving portions.

415 calories per serving

#29
50 WAYS TO LOSE IT

Vow to walk three times a week.

Thai Chicken Flatbread with Carrots and Cilantro

MAKES 4 INDIVIDUAL FLATBREAD PIZZAS, OR ONE 12-INCH THIN PIZZA, SERVING 5

Quick Flatbread Dough (pages 191–192), or 1 packaged 12-inch thin pizza crust
6 tablespoons store-bought Thai peanut sauce
2 tablespoons peanut butter
2 cups shredded cooked chicken breast
2 medium carrots, peeled and grated
3 scallions, sliced thin
¼ cup chopped roasted peanuts
¼ cup chopped fresh cilantro

Adjust oven rack to lowest position and heat oven to 500 degrees for flatbread dough or 450 degrees for packaged pizza crust.

Place flatbread dough or pizza crust on a cookie sheet. Mix peanut sauce and peanut butter in a small bowl. Spread two thirds of sauce over dough. In a medium bowl, toss remaining one third of sauce with chicken; spread chicken over pizza.

Bake until crust is crisp and golden, 10 to 12 minutes. Remove from oven and top pizza with carrots, scallions, peanuts, and cilantro. Serve individual flatbreads or cut pizza into serving portions.

420 calories per serving

#30

50 WAYS TO LOSE IT

Exercise more during the weight loss phase (two or three short sessions a day, whenever possible).

Curried Chicken Flatbread with Chutney and Yogurt Drizzle

MAKES 4 INDIVIDUAL FLATBREAD PIZZAS, OR ONE 12-INCH THIN PIZZA, SERVING 5

- 1/3 cup Major Grey's chutney
- 1 tablespoon rice wine vinegar
- 1 teaspoon curry powder
- 2 cups shredded cooked chicken breast
- Quick Flatbread Dough (pages 191–192), or 1 packaged 12-inch thin pizza crust
- 1 container (6 ounces) low-fat plain yogurt, whisked to loosen
- 6 tablespoons thin-sliced scallions
- 6 tablespoons chopped fresh cilantro leaves
- 1 medium jalapeño pepper, stemmed, seeded, and sliced thin

Adjust oven rack to lowest position and heat oven to 500 degrees for flatbread dough or 450 degrees for packaged pizza crust.

Mix chutney, vinegar, and curry powder in a small bowl. Place chicken in a medium bowl, add a heaping tablespoon of chutney mixture, and toss to coat. Place flatbread dough or pizza crust on a cookie sheet. Spread remaining chutney mixture over dough, then top with chicken.

Bake until crust is golden brown, 10 to 12 minutes. Remove from oven and drizzle hot pizza with yogurt, then top with scallions, cilantro, and jalapeño. Serve individual flatbreads or cut pizza into serving portions.

322 calories per serving

Slaw-Topped Mexican Flatbread with Refried Beans and Pepper Jack

If you can't find the spicy variety, use traditional refried beans and add 1 teaspoon chili powder.

MAKES 4 INDIVIDUAL FLATBREAD PIZZAS, OR ONE 12-INCH THIN PIZZA, SERVING 5

- ½ 16-ounce can (1 scant cup) spicy fat-free refried beans
- 1 cup store-bought salsa
- Quick Flatbread Dough (pages 191–192), or 1 packaged 12-inch thin pizza crust
- 2 tablespoons light mayonnaise
- 2 cups coleslaw mix (from an 8-ounce bag)
- 2 medium scallions, sliced thin
- 2 tablespoons chopped fresh cilantro leaves
- 3 ounces shredded pepper Jack cheese (1 heaping cup)

Adjust oven rack to lowest position and heat oven to 500 degrees for flatbread dough or 450 degrees for packaged pizza crust.

Mix beans and ½ cup salsa in a medium bowl. Place flatbread dough or pizza crust on a cookie sheet and spread with bean mixture. Bake until crisp and spotty brown, 10 to 14 minutes.

Meanwhile, in a medium bowl, whisk remaining ½ cup salsa with mayonnaise, then add coleslaw mix, scallions, and cilantro and toss together. Top hot pizza with slaw mixture, sprinkle with cheese, and return to oven until cheese melts, 1 to 2 minutes longer. Serve individual flatbreads or cut pizza into serving portions.

297 calories per serving

Chicken and Cranberry Flatbread with Caramelized Onions and Goat Cheese

MAKES 4 INDIVIDUAL FLATBREAD PIZZAS, OR ONE 12-INCH THIN PIZZA, SERVING 5

1 tablespoon olive oil
2 medium-large onions, halved and sliced thin
Quick Flatbread Dough (pages 191–192), or 1 packaged 12-inch thin pizza crust
1 cup whole-berry cranberry sauce (from a 16-ounce can)
2 cups shredded cooked chicken breast
2 teaspoons chopped fresh thyme leaves
2 ounces crumbled fresh goat cheese (about ½ cup)

Adjust oven rack to lowest position and heat oven to 500 degrees for flatbread dough or 450 degrees for packaged pizza crust.

Heat oil in a large skillet over medium-high heat while slicing onions. When wisps of smoke start to rise from pan, add onions and sauté, stirring infrequently at first and more toward the end, until they turn a rich brown color, 7 to 8 minutes.

Meanwhile, place flatbread dough or pizza crust on a cookie sheet and spread with ½ cup cranberry sauce. In a medium bowl, toss remaining ½ cup cranberry sauce with chicken. Sprinkle pizza with chicken, caramelized onions, thyme, and cheese.

Bake until crust is crisp and cheese melts, 10 to 12 minutes. Serve individual flatbreads or cut pizza into serving portions.

443 calories per serving

Barbecue Chicken Flatbread

MAKES 4 INDIVIDUAL FLATBREAD PIZZAS,
OR ONE 12-INCH THIN PIZZA, SERVING 5

Quick Flatbread Dough (pages 191–192), or 1 packaged 12-inch thin pizza crust
¾ cup barbecue sauce, preferably Cattlemen's Original
2 cups shredded cooked chicken breast
3 cups coleslaw mix (from an 8-ounce bag)
2 medium scallions, sliced thin
3 tablespoons light mayonnaise
1½ teaspoons cider vinegar
Salt and ground black pepper
3 ounces shredded pepper Jack cheese (1 cup)

Adjust oven rack to lowest position and heat oven to 500 degrees for flatbread dough or 450 degrees for packaged pizza crust.

Place flatbread dough or pizza crust on a cookie sheet and spread with ½ cup barbecue sauce. In a medium bowl, toss remaining ¼ cup barbecue sauce with chicken and scatter over dough. Bake until crisp and spotty brown, 10 to 12 minutes.

Meanwhile, in a medium bowl, toss coleslaw mix with scallions, mayonnaise, vinegar, and salt and pepper to taste. Top hot pizza with slaw mixture, sprinkle with cheese, and return to oven until cheese melts, about 2 minutes longer. Serve individual flatbreads or cut pizza into serving portions.

445 calories per serving

Reuben Flatbread

MAKES 4 INDIVIDUAL FLATBREAD PIZZAS,
OR ONE 12-INCH THIN PIZZA, SERVING 5

- 1 teaspoon caraway seeds
- Quick Flatbread Dough (pages 191–192), or 1 packaged 12-inch thin pizza crust
- 3 tablespoons brown mustard
- 1 package (6 ounces) sliced Canadian bacon
- 8 ounces (1 cup) drained refrigerated sauerkraut
- 6 thin slices (3 ounces) Swiss cheese
- 2 tablespoons light mayonnaise
- 1 tablespoon ketchup
- About 1 tablespoon water

Adjust oven rack to lowest position and heat oven to 500 degrees for flatbread dough or 450 degrees for packaged pizza crust.

Heat caraway seeds in a small skillet over medium heat until they are fragrant and starting to pop, 3 to 4 minutes. Transfer to a cutting board and mince; set aside.

Place flatbread dough or pizza crust on a cookie sheet and spread with mustard. Top with Canadian bacon, sauerkraut, and caraway seeds.

Bake until crust is golden brown, 10 to 12 minutes. Top hot pizza with cheese and return to oven until cheese melts, 1 to 2 minutes longer.

Meanwhile, in a small bowl, mix mayonnaise, ketchup, and just enough water to make a pourable sauce. Drizzle over hot pizza. Serve individual flatbreads or cut pizza into serving portions.

288 calories per serving

Flatbread with Smoked Salmon and All the Trimmings

If the lemon's pith is thick, use a vegetable peeler to remove some of it before slicing the lemon.

MAKES 4 INDIVIDUAL FLATBREAD PIZZAS, OR ONE 12-INCH THIN PIZZA, SERVING 5

- Quick Flatbread Dough (pages 191–192), or 1 packaged 12-inch thin pizza crust
- ½ cup whipped cream cheese
- 1 teaspoon finely grated lemon zest
- 2 tablespoons chopped fresh dill
- 3 tablespoons drained capers
- ½ small red onion, sliced paper thin
- 8 ounces thin-sliced smoked salmon
- 1 lemon, sliced very thin

Adjust oven rack to lowest position and heat oven to 500 degrees for flatbread dough or 450 degrees for packaged pizza crust.

Place flatbread dough or pizza crust on a cookie sheet and bake until spotty brown and crisp, about 10 minutes.

Meanwhile, in a small bowl, mix cream cheese, lemon zest, and 1 tablespoon of the dill. Remove flatbreads or pizza crust from oven. Spread with cream cheese mixture and top with capers, then with onion, smoked salmon, and lemon slices. Sprinkle with remaining 1 tablespoon dill. Serve individual flatbreads or cut pizza into serving portions.

257 calories per serving

alfredo sauce for everyone

I love pasta (and pizza) too much to give them up or to feel guilty when I eat them. Creamy foods run a close second for my affection, so one of the first challenges in my new life was to develop a satisfying creamy pasta with reasonable nutritional stats.

Low-fat evaporated milk diluted with rich chicken broth, flavored with garlic and Parmesan, and thickened with a little butter and flour produces a full-bodied sauce. These recipes also satisfy another one of my requirements: they're not complicated.

One of my first challenges was to develop a satisfying creamy pasta with reasonable nutritional stats.

When I make pasta, I'm willing to pull out only two pots—one for the pasta and one for the sauce. In my recipes, vegetables like asparagus and broccoli cook with the pasta. Frozen peas, spinach, and artichoke hearts, jarred roasted red peppers, or dried mushrooms can be added directly to the cream sauce, saving both time and the fat that would normally be used in sautéing.

Creamy Light Pasta is not only light in calories but light in feel. It lends itself well to seafood, chicken, or the occasional bit of ham. Or you can just make the simple sauce, toss it with the pasta, and dig in.

Creamy Light Pasta

SERVES 5 OR 6

- Salt
- 1 pound dried pasta
- Fresh vegetable (optional; see recipes that follow or page 211)
- 1 cup chicken broth
- 1 cup 2% evaporated milk
- 2 large garlic cloves, minced
- 1½ tablespoons butter
- 3 tablespoons all-purpose flour
- ¼ cup Parmesan cheese, preferably Parmigiano-Reggiano, plus extra for sprinkling
- Frozen, jarred, or dried vegetable (optional; see recipes that follow or page 211)
- Chicken, seafood, or ham (optional; see recipes that follow or page 211)
- Herbs and/or flavorings (optional; see recipes that follow or page 211)
- Ground black pepper

Bring 2 quarts water and 1 tablespoon salt to a boil in a large soup kettle. Add pasta and, using the time given on the package as a guide, cook, partially covered and stirring frequently at first to prevent sticking, until just tender. If using a fresh vegetable, add during last 4 to 5 minutes of cooking.

Meanwhile, microwave broth, milk, and garlic in a 1-quart Pyrex measuring cup or small microwave-safe bowl until steamy hot, 3 to 4 minutes; let stand for a couple of minutes.

Place butter in a Dutch oven or large saucepan over low heat. When butter melts, whisk in flour, then hot milk mixture all at once, whisking constantly until sauce thickens, 1 to 2 minutes. Stir in Parmesan, along with frozen vegetable, chicken, seafood, or ham, and herbs and/or flavorings, if using. Add salt and pepper to taste and simmer to blend flavors, about 5 minutes.

Drain pasta, reserving 1 cup pasta cooking liquid. Return pasta to pot.

Pour cream sauce over pasta, adding enough reserved cooking liquid to moisten. Toss and serve immediately with a light sprinkling of Parmesan.

If you have any leftover pasta, pour it onto a baking sheet to cool quickly, then refrigerate. Save any remaining pasta cooking liquid to toss with pasta when reheating. (Leftover pasta can be refrigerated for up to 4 days. To reheat, microwave on high or warm over low heat, stirring in enough water or reserved pasta cooking liquid to make it creamy again.)

About 453 calories per serving

#31

50 WAYS TO LOSE IT

When boiling pasta, reserve a little of the starch-rich cooking liquid. It comes in handy as a low-cal, full-bodied thinner for the sauce and pasta.

Creamy Pasta with Salmon, Asparagus, and Dill

If you buy a whole side of salmon, cut it into fillets, reserving the thin tail end for pasta dishes just like this one.

SERVES 6

- Creamy Light Pasta (page 206)
- 3 cups asparagus, tough ends snapped, spears cut into 1-inch pieces
- 12 ounces salmon, cut into 2-inch chunks
- 1 teaspoon finely grated lemon zest
- ¼ cup chopped fresh dill

Add asparagus to boiling pasta during last 5 minutes of cooking. Add salmon, lemon zest, and dill to simmering sauce. (Salmon will flake into bite-sized pieces as it cooks.)

460 calories per serving

Creamy Pasta with Shrimp, Spinach, and Oregano

SERVES 4 OR 5

- Creamy Light Pasta (page 206)
- 12 ounces peeled, deveined shrimp, cut into ½-inch pieces
- 1 box (10 ounces) frozen chopped spinach, thawed and squeezed dry
- ½ cup drained petite diced tomatoes (from a 14.5-ounce can)
- 1 teaspoon dried oregano

Add shrimp, spinach, tomatoes, and oregano to simmering sauce.

527 calories per serving

Creamy Pasta with Scallops, Peas, and Saffron

SERVES 4 OR 5

- Creamy Light Pasta (page 206)
- 1⅓ cups frozen petite green peas
- 12 ounces bay scallops, preferably dry-packed and untreated (see page 31)
- ½ cup drained petite diced tomatoes (from a 14.5-ounce can)
- 1 large pinch saffron threads
- 1 teaspoon finely grated orange zest

Add peas, scallops, tomatoes, saffron, and orange zest to simmering sauce.

547 calories per serving

Creamy Pasta with Crab and Roasted Peppers

SERVES 4 OR 5

- Creamy Light Pasta (page 206)
- ⅓ cup diced drained jarred roasted red peppers
- 12 ounces pasteurized lump crabmeat, drained and picked over
- 4 scallions, sliced thin
- 2 teaspoons Old Bay Seasoning

Add peppers, crabmeat, scallions, and seasoning to simmering sauce.

536 calories per serving

Creamy Pasta with Clams, Italian Herbs, and Parsley

SERVES 4 OR 5

- Creamy Light Pasta (page 206)
- 3 cans (6 ounces each) chopped clams, drained; 1 cup juice reserved
- ½ teaspoon dried basil
- ¼ teaspoon dried oregano
- ¼ cup chopped fresh parsley leaves

Substitute clam juice for chicken broth. Add clams, basil, oregano, and parsley to simmering sauce.

506 calories per serving

Creamy Pasta with Spicy Chicken, Broccoli, and Basil

SERVES 4 OR 5

	Creamy Light Pasta (page 206)
3	cups broccoli florets
10–12	ounces shredded cooked chicken breast (about 2 cups)
½	cup drained petite diced tomatoes (from a 14.5-ounce can)
¼	cup chopped fresh basil leaves
½	teaspoon hot red pepper flakes

Add broccoli to boiling pasta during last 5 minutes of cooking. Add chicken, tomatoes, basil, and red pepper flakes to simmering sauce.

571 calories per serving

Mushroom-Flavored Creamy Pasta with Ham and Rosemary

SERVES 4 OR 5

	Creamy Light Pasta (page 206)
½	ounce dried wild mushrooms
1	cup (5 ounces) diced lean ham
½	cup drained petite diced tomatoes (from a 14.5-ounce can)
2	teaspoons minced fresh rosemary leaves
¼	cup chopped fresh parsley leaves (optional)

Add mushrooms to broth, milk, and garlic before microwaving. Using a slotted spoon, remove mushrooms from hot broth and coarsely chop. Add additional chicken broth or water to the milk-broth mixture, if necessary, to measure 2 cups before proceeding. Add mushrooms, ham, tomatoes, rosemary, and parsley, if using, to simmering sauce.

507 calories per serving

Create-Your-Own-Creamy-Pasta Combo

Firm vegetables (if using, add 3 cups of 1 of the following to boiling water with pasta):

Asparagus, trimmed and cut into bite-sized pieces
Broccoli florets
Winter squash, cut into bite-sized chunks

Frozen, jarred, or dried vegetables (add 1 or 2 of the following to sauce):

1 box (10 ounces) frozen chopped spinach, thawed and squeezed dry
1⅓ cups frozen petite green peas
1 box (9 ounces) frozen artichoke hearts, thawed and cut into bite-sized pieces
⅓ cup drained jarred roasted red peppers, cut into small dice
½ ounce dried mushrooms, microwaved first with evaporated milk mixture (see Mushroom-Flavored Creamy Pasta with Ham and Rosemary)

Chicken, seafood, or ham (add 12 ounces of 1 of the following to sauce unless otherwise specified):

Shredded cooked chicken breast strips or other cooked boneless, skinless chicken
Shrimp, peeled, deveined, and cut into ½-inch pieces
Smoked salmon, sliced thin (6 ounces)
Salmon fillet or tail end, cut into 2-inch chunks
Fully cooked lean chicken sausages, preferably Mediterranean-flavored, cut into bite-sized rounds
Pasteurized lump crabmeat, drained and picked over
3 cans (6 ounces each) chopped clams, drained (reserve 1 cup juice to use in place of chicken broth)
Ham, cut into small dice
Thin-sliced prosciutto

Herbs and/or flavorings (add to sauce):

½ cup drained petite diced tomatoes (from a 14.5-ounce can)
4 scallions, sliced thin
¼ cup chopped fresh herbs, such as dill, basil, parsley, chives
2 teaspoons minced fresh rosemary leaves (with ham and chicken)
1 teaspoon finely grated lemon or orange zest
½–1 teaspoon dried basil
¼–1 teaspoon dried oregano
½ teaspoon hot red pepper flakes
Pinch saffron threads (with chicken and seafood)

a red sauce pasta that welcomes additions

My light tomato sauce is the perfect vehicle for vegetables, meat, poultry, and seafood, making pasta more of a nutritionally complete meal. Firm vegetables, like asparagus and broccoli, and leafy green vegetables, like kale and spinach, cook with the pasta, while tender vegetables, such as peppers and mushrooms, are sautéed before adding the tomatoes. Shrimp, turkey sausage, or chicken simmers for a few minutes with the sauce as well.

My red sauce is the perfect vehicle for vegetables, meat, poultry, and seafood.

If you like a thicker, more pasta-hugging sauce, just heat a couple tablespoons of olive oil with a few minced garlic cloves. When the garlic starts to sizzle, add a can of crushed tomatoes (or Muir Glen ground peeled tomatoes; the fire-roasted variety is especially nice). When the sauce comes to a simmer, partially cover the pot and continue to simmer until thickened, about 10 minutes. You can add a little basil and/or oregano if you like.

Pasta with Just-Right Red Sauce

These tomato-based sauces complement the assertive taste of whole wheat pasta. My favorite most widely available brand is Ronzoni Healthy Harvest. Since whole wheat pasta contains more fiber than regular, you'll likely be satisfied with smaller portions.

SERVES 6

Salt

1 pound dried bite-sized pasta (whole wheat or white): farfalle (bow ties), fusilli (corkscrews), penne, ziti, rotelle (wagon wheels), elbow macaroni, or shells

1 pound firm or leafy green vegetables, or 1 pound tender vegetables (see recipes that follow or page 218)

1 tablespoon olive oil

Ground black pepper

2 thin slices (1 ounce) prosciutto (optional)

3 large garlic cloves, minced

Dried herbs and/or other flavorings (see recipes that follow or page 219)

1 can (14.5 ounces) petite diced tomatoes

1 can (8 ounces) tomato sauce

Chicken, seafood, or beans (see recipes that follow or page 219)

Fresh herbs and/or flavorings (see recipes that follow or page 219)

¼ cup grated Parmesan cheese, preferably Parmigiano-Reggiano, or crumbled feta cheese, plus extra for passing, if you like

Bring 2 quarts water and 1 tablespoon salt to a boil in a large soup kettle. Add pasta and, using the time given on the package as a guide, cook, partially covered and stirring frequently at first to prevent sticking, until just tender. If using a firm or leafy green vegetable, add during last 4 to

5 minutes of cooking. Drain pasta, reserving 1 cup pasta cooking liquid. Return pasta to pot.

Meanwhile, heat oil in a large skillet. If using tender vegetables, sauté, seasoning with salt and pepper to taste, until tender and golden, 5 to 7 minutes. Add prosciutto, if using, garlic, and dried herb or other flavoring. Continue to sauté until fragrant, 1 to 2 minutes longer. Add tomatoes and tomato sauce, bring to a simmer, reduce heat to low, and simmer to blend flavors, about 5 minutes. Add chicken, seafood, or beans and fresh herbs or flavorings. Simmer until seafood is just cooked or flavors have blended, 2 to 5 minutes longer.

Pour tomato sauce over pasta, add Parmesan or feta cheese and as much reserved cooking liquid as you like, and toss to coat. Serve, with extra Parmesan or feta cheese, if desired.

If there is any leftover pasta, pour it onto a baking sheet to cool quickly, then refrigerate. Save any remaining pasta cooking liquid to toss with pasta when reheating. (Leftover pasta can be refrigerated for up to 4 days. To reheat, microwave on high or warm over low heat, stirring in enough water or reserved pasta cooking liquid to make it moist again.)

About 322 calories per serving

#32

50 WAYS TO LOSE IT

Buy hardware and software for listening to music—you'll exercise longer.

Red Sauce with Shrimp, Spinach, and Lemon Zest

SERVES 6

- Pasta with Just-Right Red Sauce (page 213)
- 1 pound prewashed spinach
- 12 ounces peeled, deveined shrimp, cut into bite-sized pieces
- 1½ teaspoons finely grated lemon zest

Add spinach to boiling pasta during last 4 minutes of cooking. Add shrimp to simmering sauce. Add lemon zest with cheese.

383 calories per serving

Red Sauce with Crab, Mushrooms, and Basil

If you can afford a few extra calories, add a splash more oil to the pan before sautéing the mushrooms.

SERVES 6

- Pasta with Just-Right Red Sauce (page 213)
- 1 pound mushrooms, sliced
- 1 teaspoon dried basil
- 12 ounces pasteurized lump crabmeat, drained and picked over

Add mushrooms to skillet; add basil with garlic. Add crabmeat to simmering sauce.

402 calories per serving

Red Sauce with Scallops, Asparagus, and Orange Zest

SERVES 6

Pasta with Just-Right Red Sauce (page 213)
1 pound asparagus, tough ends snapped, cut into 1-inch pieces
¼ cup drained capers
12 ounces bay scallops, preferably dry-packed and untreated (see page 31)
1½ teaspoons finely grated orange zest

Add asparagus to boiling pasta during last 4 to 5 minutes of cooking. Add capers with garlic; add scallops to simmering sauce. Use Parmesan and add orange zest with cheese.

393 calories per serving

Red Sauce with Tuna, Onions, and Kalamata Olives

SERVES 6

Pasta with Just-Right Red Sauce (page 213)
1 large onion, halved and sliced thin
1 teaspoon dried oregano
¼ cup pitted, chopped kalamata olives
2 cans (6 ounces each) white albacore tuna packed in water (not drained)

Sauté onion in skillet; add oregano and olives with garlic. Add tuna to simmering sauce.

423 calories per serving

Red Sauce with White Beans, Kale, and Rosemary

SERVES 6

Pasta with Just-Right Red Sauce (page 213)
1 pound washed, trimmed kale (or escarole or curly endive), coarsely chopped
1 tablespoon minced fresh rosemary leaves
1 can (15.5 ounces) cannellini beans, drained

Add kale to boiling pasta during last 4 to 5 minutes of cooking. Add rosemary with garlic; add beans to simmering sauce.

417 calories per serving

Red Sauce with Chicken, Broccoli, and Sun-Dried Tomatoes

SERVES 6

- Pasta with Just-Right Red Sauce (page 213)
- 1 pound broccoli crowns, cut into florets
- 2 tablespoons finely chopped drained sun-dried tomatoes packed in oil
- 10–12 ounces cooked chicken breast, shredded (about 2 cups)

Add broccoli to boiling pasta during last 4 to 5 minutes of cooking. Add sun-dried tomatoes with garlic; add chicken to simmering sauce. Use Parmesan.

433 calories per serving

Red Sauce with Sausage, Broccoli Rabe, and Red Pepper

SERVES 6

- Pasta with Just-Right Red Sauce (page 213)
- 1 pound broccoli rabe, coarsely chopped
- ½ teaspoon hot red pepper flakes
- 12 ounces fully cooked lean chicken sausage, preferably Mediterranean-flavored

Add broccoli rabe to boiling pasta during last 4 to 5 minutes of cooking. Add red pepper flakes with garlic; add sausage to simmering sauce. Use Parmesan.

416 calories per serving

Create-Your-Own-Red-Sauce Combo

Firm or leafy green vegetables (use 1 pound of 1 vegetable or 8 ounces of 2 from this list or the one below):

Asparagus, trimmed and cut into bite-sized pieces

Broccoli florets, cut into bite-sized pieces, stems peeled and cut into ½-inch-thick coins

Broccoli rabe, stems peeled, if necessary, coarsely chopped

Butternut squash, peeled, halved, seeded, and cut into medium dice

Carrots, peeled and cut into bite-sized pieces

Cabbage, cored and shredded

Beet greens, collards, kale, mustard greens, Swiss chard, or turnip greens, stemmed and coarsely chopped

Spinach or arugula, stemmed (if mature)

Curly endive and escarole, trimmed and coarsely chopped

Tender vegetables (use 1 pound of 1 vegetable or 8 ounces of 2 from this list or the one above):

Bell peppers, stemmed, seeded, and cut into 1-by-¼-inch strips

Eggplant, trimmed and cut into ½-inch dice

Fennel, halved, cored, and sliced thin

Leeks, dark green tops discarded, quartered lengthwise up to but not through the root, rinsed thoroughly to remove grit, and sliced thin

Mushrooms, sliced (to save time, buy presliced)

Onions, halved root to stem end and sliced thin crosswise

Yellow squash, trimmed, quartered lengthwise, and cut into medium dice

Zucchini, trimmed, quartered, and cut into medium dice

Dried herbs and/or flavorings:

¼ cup drained capers

¼ cup coarsely chopped pitted black olives, such as kalamatas

2 tablespoons finely chopped drained sun-dried tomatoes packed in oil

1 tablespoon minced fresh rosemary leaves (treat this like a dried herb)

1 teaspoon dried basil

½ teaspoon hot red pepper flakes

Chicken, seafood, or beans (choose 12 ounces, unless otherwise specified, of 1 of the following):

Shredded cooked chicken (or chicken breast strips, available in most supermarkets with the other cooked meats)

Fully cooked lean chicken sausage, preferably Mediterranean-flavored, cut into bite-sized rounds

Fully cooked turkey meatballs (available in most supermarkets with the other cooked meats), quartered

Pasteurized lump crabmeat, drained and picked over

Peeled, deveined shrimp, cut into bite-sized pieces

Salmon fillet or tail end, or other boneless flaky fish, cut into 2-inch chunks

Canned clams (three 6-ounce cans), drained

Canned tuna (two 6-ounce cans), not drained

1 can (15.5 ounces) cannellini beans, drained

Fresh herbs and/or flavorings:

1½ teaspoons finely grated lemon or orange zest

¼ cup chopped fresh parsley or basil leaves

sear. pour. whisk. eat. 15-minute suppers

If you want to get dinner on the table in 15 minutes max and eat healthfully and well (as though you're at the finest restaurant in town), you need to know only two things: how to sear (a fancy word for brown) and how to use a measuring cup. That's it.

For chicken breasts or thighs, shrimp or scallops, pork tenderloin or chops, salmon or tuna, the method is the same. Searing demands high heat. Jump-start the process by warming the skillet over low heat.

Meanwhile, get out your measuring cup and make your choice from an incredibly diverse array of great pan sauces, most of them made with ordinary pantry ingredients.

Next coat the cuts (not the skillet, which would smoke excessively) with a little oil, which promotes browning and prevents sticking, and generously sprinkle with salt and pepper. Turn on the exhaust fan and turn up the heat: full blast on a gas stove or an aggressive medium-high on an electric range.

Depending on the thickness and density of your cut, cooking times will vary from 4 to 5 minutes for scallops and shrimp to 10 to 12 minutes for pork tenderloin and chicken thighs. Turn the meat only once to achieve a lovely seared surface, which makes for great flavor.

When the cuts are done, transfer to plates and carefully pour in the pan sauce ingredients. If the skillet is good and hot, the liquid should reduce by half in less than a minute. Instead of butter, whisk in a teensy bit of cornstarch mixed with water to give the sauce just enough body to cling to the meat. Continue to simmer the sauce until it is thick enough to coat the cut. If the sauce becomes too thick, simply add a little water. And when you don't have time to make a sauce, you can serve any of the cuts with just a wedge of lemon.

Get out your measuring cup and choose from an array of great pan sauces, made from ordinary ingredients.

Even if you're cooking for only one or two, double the recipe so that there's enough for another meal. Leftover seared poultry, pork, and seafood are especially nice for hearty main-course salads. (Save any extra pan sauce to toss with the salad as well.) The more you've got prepared, the easier it is to reach into the fridge and make the next meal.

Sear-and-Sauce Chicken Cutlets

Chicken breasts vary dramatically in size, the mass-produced variety being especially large. If there are dangling tenderloins, remove and cook them alongside the breasts, then reserve for another meal.

SERVES 4

Pan Sauce of your choice (pages 230–234)
4 medium (5–6 ounces each) or 2 large (8–12 ounces each) boneless, skinless chicken breasts, tenderloins removed (see headnote), patted dry
2 teaspoons olive, vegetable, or canola oil
Salt and ground black pepper

Heat a large (12-inch) nonstick skillet over low heat while preparing pan sauce ingredients and chicken. Lightly pound medium breasts with fist to a more or less even thickness or halve large breasts crosswise to make 4 cutlets. Place chicken cutlets and tenderloins in a medium bowl, drizzle with oil, season with salt and pepper to taste, and toss to coat evenly.

A couple of minutes before you are ready to sear chicken, turn on exhaust fan and increase heat under pan to a strong medium-high (electric range) or high (gas range). When skillet is very hot (a seasoned nonstick skillet will start to send up wisps of smoke), add chicken. Cook, turning only once, until chicken is well browned and just cooked through, 5 to 7 minutes for cutlets and about 4 minutes for tenderloins. (If chicken edge is still pink, prop cutlet against pan side and continue to cook, edge down, until it is no longer pink, 20 to 30 seconds.) Transfer chicken to plates.

Add pan sauce ingredients to skillet as instructed. Cook, pouring any accumulated chicken juices into the sauce, until reduced by half, usually less than a minute. Whisk in additional pan sauce ingredients as instructed, then cornstarch mixture, and cook until sauce is thick enough to coat chicken, which happens almost instantly. If sauce is too thick, add a little water to thin to proper consistency. Drizzle chicken with sauce and serve.

176 calories per serving (does not include pan sauce)

#33

50 WAYS TO LOSE IT

Thicken pan sauces with a little cornstarch and water rather than butter.

Sear-and-Sauce Chicken Thighs

Unlike a chicken breast, which is a single muscle, a chicken thigh cannot be pounded to an even thickness. Even though thighs must stay in the skillet long enough for the thickest muscles to cook, they contain bits of scattered fat that hold in juices and keep them moist.

SERVES 4

Pan Sauce of your choice (pages 230–234)
1¼–1½ pounds boneless, skinless chicken thighs, trimmed of excess fat and patted dry
2 teaspoons olive, vegetable, or canola oil
Salt and ground black pepper

Heat a large (12-inch) nonstick skillet over low heat while preparing pan sauce ingredients and chicken. Place chicken thighs in a medium bowl, drizzle with oil, season with salt and pepper to taste, and toss to coat evenly.

A couple of minutes before you are ready to sear chicken, turn on exhaust fan and increase heat under pan to a strong medium-high (electric range) or high (gas range). When skillet is very hot (a seasoned nonstick skillet will start to send up wisps of smoke), add chicken. Cook, turning only once, until thighs are well browned and just cooked through, 10 to 12 minutes. Transfer thighs to plates.

Add pan sauce ingredients to skillet as instructed. Cook, pouring any accumulated chicken juices into the sauce, until reduced by half, usually less than a minute. Whisk in additional pan sauce ingredients as instructed, then cornstarch mixture, and cook until sauce is thick enough to coat chicken, which happens almost instantly. If sauce is too thick, add a little water to thin to proper consistency. Drizzle chicken with sauce and serve.

189 calories for serving (does not include pan sauce)

Sear-and-Sauce Pork Tenderloin

You can cut the tenderloin crosswise into medallions, but it's more time-consuming cutting the pieces and turning them in the skillet. In this easier method, you just make a slit down the middle so that the tenderloin cooks evenly.

SERVES 4

- Pan Sauce of your choice (pages 230–234)
- 1 large pork tenderloin (1¼ pounds), patted dry
- 2 teaspoons olive, vegetable, or canola oil
- Salt and ground black pepper

Heat a large (12-inch) nonstick skillet over low heat while preparing pan sauce ingredients and pork. Split tenderloin lengthwise almost but not all the way through and pound lightly with your fist to a more or less even thickness. Place tenderloin in a medium bowl, drizzle with oil, season with salt and pepper to taste, and toss to coat evenly.

A couple of minutes before you are ready to sear tenderloin, turn on exhaust fan and increase heat under pan to a strong medium-high (electric range) or high (gas range). When skillet is very hot (a seasoned nonstick skillet will start to send up wisps of smoke), add tenderloin. Cook, turning only once, until tenderloin is well browned and just cooked through, about 10 minutes. Transfer tenderloin to a cutting board.

Add pan sauce ingredients to skillet as instructed. Cook, pouring any accumulated meat juices into the sauce, until reduced by half, usually less than a minute. Whisk in additional pan sauce ingredients as instructed, then cornstarch mixture, and cook until sauce is thick enough to coat pork, which happens almost instantly. If sauce is too thick, add a little water to thin to proper consistency. Cut tenderloin into thin slices, transfer a portion to each plate, drizzle with sauce, and serve.

185 calories per serving (does not include pan sauce)

Sear-and-Sauce Pork Loin Chops

Boneless pork chops are much easier to cook evenly than bone-in chops. You can also buy a pork loin and cut your own. If you like thick chops, simply cook one chop for every two people and split it. Remember to increase the cooking time accordingly.

SERVES 4

- Pan Sauce of your choice (pages 230–234)
- 4 pork loin chops (about 5 ounces each), patted dry
- 2 teaspoons olive, vegetable, or canola oil
- Salt and ground black pepper

Heat a large (12-inch) nonstick skillet over low heat while preparing pan sauce ingredients and chops. Place chops in a medium bowl, drizzle with oil, season with salt and pepper to taste, and toss to coat evenly.

A couple of minutes before you are ready to sear chops, turn on exhaust fan and increase heat under pan to a strong medium-high (electric range) or high (gas range). When skillet is very hot (a seasoned nonstick skillet will start to send up wisps of smoke), add chops. Cook, turning only once, until chops are well browned and just cooked through, 6 to 8 minutes. Transfer chops to plates.

Add pan sauce ingredients to skillet as instructed. Cook, pouring any accumulated meat juices into the sauce, until reduced by half, usually less than a minute. Whisk in additional pan sauce ingredients as instructed, then cornstarch mixture, and cook until sauce is thick enough to coat pork, which happens almost instantly. If sauce is too thick, add a little water to thin to proper consistency. Drizzle chops with sauce and serve.

220 calories per serving (does not include pan sauce)

Sear-and-Sauce Shrimp

SERVES 4

Pan Sauce of your choice (pages 230–234)
1¼ pounds peeled, deveined shrimp (16–20 count), patted dry
2 teaspoons olive, vegetable, or canola oil
Salt and ground black pepper

Heat a large (12-inch) nonstick skillet over low heat while preparing pan sauce ingredients and shrimp. Place shrimp in a medium bowl, drizzle with oil, season with salt and pepper to taste, and toss to coat evenly.

A couple of minutes before you are ready to sear shrimp, turn on exhaust fan and increase heat under pan to a strong medium-high (electric range) or high (gas range). When skillet is very hot (a seasoned nonstick skillet will start to send up wisps of smoke), add shrimp, tail end toward pan center. Cook until shrimp are well browned on one side, about 3 minutes. Starting with first shrimp added to pan, turn shrimp and continue to cook until cooked through, about 2 minutes longer. Transfer shrimp to plates.

Add pan sauce ingredients to skillet as instructed. Cook, pouring any accumulated shrimp juices into sauce, until reduced by half, usually less than a minute. Whisk in additional pan sauce ingredients as instructed, then cornstarch mixture, and cook until sauce is thick enough to coat shrimp, which happens almost instantly. If sauce is too thick, add a little water to thin to proper consistency. Drizzle shrimp with sauce and serve.

127 calories per serving (does not include pan sauce)

Sear-and-Sauce Sea Scallops

SERVES 4

Pan Sauce of your choice (pages 230–234)

12 large sea scallops (about 1¼ pounds), preferably dry-packed and untreated (see page 31), patted dry

2 teaspoons olive, vegetable, or canola oil

Salt and ground black pepper

Heat a large (12-inch) nonstick skillet over low heat while preparing pan sauce ingredients and scallops. Place scallops in a medium bowl, drizzle with oil, season with salt and pepper to taste, and toss to coat evenly.

A couple of minutes before you are ready to sear scallops, turn on exhaust fan and increase heat under pan to a strong medium-high (electric range) or high (gas range). When skillet is very hot (a seasoned nonstick skillet will start to send up wisps of smoke), add scallops. Cook, turning only once, until well browned and just cooked through, 4 to 5 minutes. Transfer scallops to plates.

Add pan sauce ingredients to skillet as instructed. Cook, pouring any accumulated scallop juices into the sauce, until reduced by half, usually less than a minute. Whisk in additional pan sauce ingredients as instructed, then cornstarch mixture, and cook until sauce is thick enough to coat scallops, which happens almost instantly. If sauce is too thick, add a little water to thin to proper consistency. Drizzle scallops with sauce and serve.

145 calories per serving (does not include pan sauce)

Sear-and-Sauce Salmon Fillets

This method also works for other steak fish, like swordfish and tuna. Try to avoid purchasing the salmon's thinner tail end. If you purchase a whole side, however, as I often do, cut off the tail end and reserve it for pasta sauces and soup.

SERVES 4

- **Pan Sauce of your choice (pages 230–234)**
- **4 center-cut skinned salmon fillets (1¼–1½ pounds total), patted dry**
- **2 teaspoons olive, vegetable, or canola oil**
- **Salt and ground black pepper**

Heat a large (12-inch) nonstick skillet over low heat while preparing pan sauce ingredients and salmon. Place salmon in a medium bowl, drizzle with oil, season with salt and pepper to taste, and toss to coat evenly.

A couple of minutes before you are ready to sear salmon, turn on exhaust fan and increase heat under pan to a strong medium-high (electric range) or high (gas range). When skillet is very hot (a seasoned nonstick skillet will start to send up wisps of smoke), add salmon. Cook, turning only once, until fillets develop a rich brown crust on both sides, about 6 minutes for medium-rare, 7 minutes for medium, and 8 minutes for medium-well. Transfer salmon to plates.

Add pan sauce ingredients to skillet as instructed. Cook, pouring any accumulated salmon juices into the sauce, until reduced by half, usually less than a minute. Whisk in additional pan sauce ingredients as instructed, then cornstarch mixture, and cook until sauce is thick enough to coat salmon, which happens almost instantly. If sauce is too thick, add a little water to thin to proper consistency. Drizzle salmon with sauce and serve.

200 calories per serving (does not include pan sauce)

Pan Sauces

EACH ONE SERVES 4

White Wine Cream Sauce with Chives

For chicken, pork, and seafood.

- ½ cup low-sodium chicken broth
- 2 tablespoons dry white wine or vermouth
- 1 tablespoon heavy cream
- 1 tablespoon snipped fresh chives
- ¼ teaspoon cornstarch, dissolved in 1 teaspoon cold water

Mix broth and wine or vermouth in a liquid measuring cup. Add to hot pan when instructed and reduce by half. Whisk in cream, then chives and cornstarch mixture.

21 calories per serving

Salsa Verde Cream Sauce with Cilantro

For chicken, pork, and seafood.

- ½ cup low-sodium chicken broth
- ½ cup store-bought salsa verde
- 1 tablespoon heavy cream
- 1 tablespoon chopped fresh cilantro leaves
- ¼ teaspoon cornstarch, dissolved in 1 teaspoon cold water

Mix broth and salsa verde in a liquid measuring cup. Add to hot pan when instructed and reduce by half. Whisk in cream, then cilantro and cornstarch mixture.

26 calories per serving

Mushroom-Thyme Cream Sauce

For chicken, pork, and seafood.

- ¾ cup low-sodium chicken broth
- ¼ cup finely chopped dried mushrooms
- Pinch dried thyme leaves
- 1 tablespoon heavy cream
- ¼ teaspoon cornstarch, dissolved in 1 teaspoon cold water

Heat broth, mushrooms, and thyme in a microwave-safe measuring cup until broth is very hot and mushrooms have softened, about 2 minutes. Add to hot pan when instructed and reduce by half. Whisk in cream, then cornstarch mixture.

49 calories per serving

Mustard Cream Sauce with Tarragon

For chicken, pork, and seafood.

- ⅔ cup low-sodium chicken broth
- 1 tablespoon Dijon mustard
- ⅛ teaspoon dried tarragon
- 1 tablespoon heavy cream
- ¼ teaspoon cornstarch, dissolved in 1 teaspoon cold water

Mix broth, mustard, and tarragon in a liquid measuring cup. Add to hot pan when instructed and reduce by half. Whisk in cream, then cornstarch mixture.

22 calories per serving

Light Tomato Sauce with Vinegar and Basil

For chicken, pork, fish, and seafood.

- ½ cup low-sodium chicken broth
- 2 tablespoons rice wine vinegar
- ¼ cup canned drained petite diced tomatoes, or 1 plum tomato, cut into small dice
- 2 tablespoons torn fresh basil leaves
- ¼ teaspoon cornstarch, dissolved in 1 teaspoon cold water

Mix broth, vinegar, tomatoes, and basil in a liquid measuring cup. Add to hot pan when instructed and reduce by half. Whisk in cornstarch mixture.

6 calories per serving

Orange-Dijon Pan Sauce

For chicken, pork, and seafood.

If serving with chicken or pork, you can add 1/4 cup dried cranberries and a tiny pinch of ground cloves to the orange juice mixture.

2/3 cup orange juice
1 teaspoon Dijon mustard
1/4 teaspoon cornstarch, dissolved in 1 teaspoon cold water

Mix juice and mustard in a liquid measuring cup. Add to hot pan when instructed and reduce by half. Whisk in cornstarch mixture.

21 calories per serving

Apricot Pan Sauce with Pistachios and Cumin

For chicken and pork.

1 can (5.5 ounces) apricot nectar
1 teaspoon Dijon mustard
1/8 teaspoon ground cumin
1 tablespoon chopped dried apricots
1/4 teaspoon cornstarch, dissolved in 1 teaspoon cold water
1 tablespoon chopped roasted pistachios

Mix nectar, mustard, cumin, and apricots in a liquid measuring cup. Add to hot pan when instructed and reduce by half. Whisk in cornstarch mixture. Sprinkle pistachios over meat before serving.

42 calories per serving

Prune Pan Sauce with Warm Spices

For chicken and pork.

- 1 can (5.5 ounces) prune juice
- 1 teaspoon Dijon mustard
- 1 tablespoon finely chopped prunes
- Tiny pinch each ground cloves and ground cinnamon
- ¼ teaspoon cornstarch, dissolved in 1 teaspoon cold water

Mix juice, mustard, prunes, cloves, and cinnamon in a liquid measuring cup. Add to hot pan when instructed and reduce by half. Whisk in cornstarch mixture.

36 calories per serving

Marsala Pan Sauce with Raisins or Prunes

For chicken and pork.

This sauce can also be made with port or sweet vermouth, with or without the raisins.

- ⅔ cup Marsala
- ¼ cup raisins or chopped prunes
- ¼ teaspoon cornstarch, dissolved in 1 teaspoon cold water

Mix Marsala and raisins or prunes in a liquid measuring cup. Add to hot pan when instructed and reduce by half. Whisk in cornstarch mixture.

63 calories per serving

Cherry-Balsamic Pan Sauce with Toasted Almonds

For chicken and pork.

- ½ cup low-sodium chicken broth
- 2 tablespoons balsamic vinegar
- 2 tablespoons cherry preserves or fruit spread
- ¼ teaspoon cornstarch, dissolved in 1 teaspoon cold water
- 1 tablespoon coarsely chopped toasted almonds

Mix broth, vinegar, and preserves or fruit spread in a liquid measuring cup. Add to hot pan when instructed and reduce by half. Whisk in cornstarch mixture. Sprinkle almonds over meat before serving.

43 calories per serving

Red Wine Pan Sauce with Garlic, Olives, and Oregano

For chicken, pork, and salmon.

- 1/3 cup dry red wine
- 1/3 cup low-sodium chicken broth
- 2 teaspoons Dijon mustard
- 1/4 cup pitted, coarsely chopped kalamata olives
- 2 medium garlic cloves, minced
- 1/2 teaspoon dried oregano
- 1/4 teaspoon cornstarch, dissolved in 1 teaspoon cold water

Mix wine, broth, mustard, olives, garlic, and oregano in a liquid measuring cup. Add to hot pan when instructed and reduce by half. Whisk in cornstarch mixture.

38 calories per serving

Apple-Ginger Pan Sauce

For chicken and pork.

- 1 can (5.5 ounces) apple juice
- 2 teaspoons low-sodium soy sauce
- 1/2 teaspoon ground ginger
- 1/4 teaspoon cornstarch, dissolved in 1 teaspoon cold water

Mix juice, soy sauce, and ginger in a liquid measuring cup. Add to hot pan when instructed and reduce by half. Whisk in cornstarch mixture.

21 calories per serving

perfect fish every time—no turning required

My method of baking fish solves several problems encountered in sautéing and uses a lot less oil. When you're serving four, either you have to cook the fillets in batches or you need two skillets. And since the fillets are delicate, they often fall apart when turned.

By arranging the fish fillets and vegetables on a baking sheet and turning on the oven after the fish is in, you get succulent, perfectly cooked fish (no turning required) and golden, tender-crisp vegetables effortlessly.

Just shove the pan in the oven and turn it on.

Arrange the fillets in a single layer, then lightly oil (or butter) and season them. Don't spread the fat with a brush—you'll lose half of it in the bristles. Instead use a spreader or butter knife. Toss the vegetables with a little oil and seasoning as well. Then just shove the pan in the oven and turn it on. While the fish and vegetables cook, chop some fresh herbs for sprinkling, make a quick relish, or sit down and enjoy a first-course salad. In just 15 minutes, dinner is ready.

This technique works well with fish fillets, and you can also cook salmon, swordfish, and tuna in the same way. Simply increase the roasting time by a few minutes.

I have specified vegetables for each of the following recipes, but they are interchangeable.

Baked Fish with Asparagus, Lemon, and Fresh Herbs

Tarragon is stronger than the other herbs, so if you use it, don't add more than a teaspoon to the mix.

SERVES 4

- 1½ pounds fish fillets (trout, sole, catfish, tilapia, red snapper, cod, turbot)
- 1 tablespoon extra-virgin olive oil
- Salt and ground white pepper
- 20 medium asparagus spears, tough ends snapped
- ¼ cup chopped mixed fresh herbs (basil, parsley, cilantro, dill, tarragon; see headnote)
- ½ teaspoon finely grated lemon zest
- 1 lemon, quartered

Spray a large (18-by-12-inch) rimmed baking sheet with vegetable cooking spray. Arrange fish in a single layer on baking sheet, leaving room for asparagus. Spread 2 teaspoons of the oil over fish and sprinkle with salt and pepper. Toss asparagus with remaining 1 teaspoon oil and sprinkle with salt and pepper. Arrange asparagus in a single layer on baking sheet with fish.

Place on bottom rack of oven and turn oven to 400 degrees. Bake until fish is opaque and asparagus is tender-crisp, 15 to 17 minutes. Combine herbs and lemon zest and sprinkle evenly over fish. Serve immediately with lemon wedges.

About 253 calories per serving

Baked Fish with Oven-Sautéed Tomatoes, Basil, and Garlic

SERVES 4

1½ pounds fish fillets (trout, sole, catfish, tilapia, red snapper, cod, turbot)
4 teaspoons extra-virgin olive oil
Salt and ground black pepper
1 teaspoon dried basil
1 teaspoon garlic powder
1 pound (heaping 2½ cups) cherry tomatoes
¼ cup chopped fresh parsley leaves
1 lemon, quartered

Spray a large (18-by-12-inch) rimmed baking sheet with vegetable cooking spray. Arrange fish in a single layer on baking sheet, leaving room for tomatoes. Spread 2 teaspoons of the oil over fish and sprinkle with salt, pepper, and ½ teaspoon each basil and garlic powder. Sprinkle tomatoes with salt, pepper, remaining 2 teaspoons oil, and remaining ½ teaspoon each basil and garlic powder. Spread in a single layer on baking sheet with fish.

Place on bottom rack of oven and turn oven to 400 degrees. Bake until fish is opaque and cherry tomatoes have collapsed, 15 to 17 minutes. Remove from oven. Sprinkle fish with parsley and serve immediately with lemon wedges.

About 271 calories per serving

Baked Fish with Green Beans and Capers

SERVES 4

- 1½ pounds fish fillets (trout, sole, catfish, tilapia, red snapper, cod, turbot)
- 3 tablespoons extra-virgin olive oil
- Salt and ground black pepper
- 1 pound trimmed green beans
- 2 shallots, minced
- ¼ cup drained capers
- 2 tablespoons fresh lemon juice

Spray a large (18-by-12-inch) rimmed baking sheet with vegetable cooking spray. Arrange fish in a single layer on baking sheet, leaving room for green beans. Spread 2 teaspoons of the oil over fish and sprinkle with salt and pepper. Toss green beans with 1 teaspoon oil and sprinkle with salt and pepper. Arrange green beans in a more or less single layer on baking sheet with fish.

Place on bottom rack of oven and turn oven to 400 degrees. Bake until fish is opaque and beans are tender-crisp, about 15 minutes.

Meanwhile, in a small bowl, mix remaining 2 tablespoons oil with shallots, capers, and lemon juice. Spoon caper sauce over fish and serve.

About 336 calories per serving

#34

50 WAYS TO LOSE IT

Serve a vegetable and salad (but skip the starch) with your main course.

Baked Fish with Mushrooms and Thyme

SERVES 4

- 1½ pounds fish fillets (trout, sole, catfish, tilapia, red snapper, cod, turbot)
- 4 teaspoons extra-virgin olive oil
- Salt and ground black pepper
- 1 teaspoon dried thyme leaves
- 1 pound trimmed white or baby bella mushrooms
- Juice of ½ lemon

Spray a large (18-by-12-inch) rimmed baking sheet with vegetable cooking spray. Arrange fish in a single layer on baking sheet, leaving room for mushrooms. Spread 2 teaspoons of the oil over fish and sprinkle with salt, pepper, and ½ teaspoon thyme. Toss mushrooms with remaining 2 teaspoons oil and sprinkle with salt, pepper, and remaining ½ teaspoon thyme. Arrange mushrooms in a more or less single layer on baking sheet with fish.

Place on bottom rack of oven and turn oven to 400 degrees. Bake until fish is opaque, 15 to 17 minutes. Remove fish; spread mushrooms over baking sheet and continue to roast until golden brown, 3 to 5 minutes longer. Remove from oven. Sprinkle mushrooms with lemon juice, using a metal spatula to loosen browned bits. Serve fish with mushrooms alongside.

About 270 calories per serving

Baked Fish with Spinach and Asian Drizzle

SERVES 4

- 1 pound prewashed spinach
- 4 teaspoons vegetable or canola oil
- 1 teaspoon garlic powder
- 1½ pounds fish fillets (trout, sole, catfish, tilapia, red snapper, cod, turbot)
- Salt
- Lime-Ginger or Soy-Sesame Drizzle (recipes follow)

Spray a large (18-by-12-inch) rimmed baking sheet with vegetable cooking spray. On baking sheet, toss spinach with 2 teaspoons of the oil and ½ teaspoon garlic powder. Arrange fish over spinach, spread with remaining 2 teaspoons oil, and sprinkle lightly with salt and remaining ½ teaspoon garlic powder.

Place on bottom rack of oven and turn oven to 400 degrees. Bake until fish is opaque and spinach has wilted, 15 to 17 minutes. Meanwhile, prepare sauce.

Drizzle sauce over fish and spinach and serve.

About 286 calories per serving with lime drizzle; 295 calories with soy sauce drizzle

Lime-Ginger Drizzle

- 2 tablespoons fresh lime juice
- 2 tablespoons Asian fish sauce
- ½ teaspoon ground ginger
- ½ teaspoon hot red pepper flakes
- 2 teaspoons sugar

Whisk all ingredients in a small bowl.

14 calories per serving

Soy-Sesame Drizzle

- 2 tablespoons soy sauce
- 2 tablespoons rice wine vinegar
- 1 teaspoon toasted sesame oil
- ½ teaspoon hot red pepper flakes
- 2 teaspoons sugar

Whisk all ingredients in a small bowl.

23 calories per serving

#35

50 WAYS TO LOSE IT

For brown rice that's quick, try Success brand precooked brown rice in 1-cup containers.

wrap it up!

For a meal that's flexible, quick, and complete, foil packs are it. With a choice of chicken, pork, or seafood, six flavoring options, and ten vegetables, you can create a packet based on whatever meat or seafood, flavorings, and vegetables you've got on hand or feel like enjoying.

While the oven preheats, simply toss and wrap the meat or seafood, flavoring, and vegetables in foil. Then put the packets in the oven, and 15 minutes later, you've got a colorful dinner. While the packets cook, you can relax with a glass of wine. How civil is that!

For a meal that's flexible, quick, and complete, foil packs are it.

To ensure that the meat and vegetables cook evenly, place the oven rack in the lowest position (or make sure the grill is good and hot) and arrange the meat or seafood in a single layer over the vegetables. Before opening the packs, let them rest for a few minutes to allow the residual heat to gently finish the cooking. If you want to take advantage of all the flavorful juices, accompany these dishes with a small amount of rice.

Mix-and-Match Foil Packets

The beauty here is that regardless of which meat or seafood or vegetable you choose, the baking time is the same.

SERVES 4

Pick 1 (1¼–1½ pounds):

Boneless, skinless chicken breasts, sliced into ½-inch-thick strips
Pork tenderloin, sliced crosswise into ½-inch-thick rounds
Extra-large peeled, deveined shrimp (21–25 count)
Sea scallops, preferably dry-packed and untreated (see page 31)
Center-cut skinned salmon fillets

Pick a Flavoring:

LEMON DILL

- ¼ cup extra-virgin olive oil
- 4 large garlic cloves, minced
- 4 large scallions, sliced thin
- ¼ cup chopped fresh dill
- 1 teaspoon each salt and ground black pepper
- 1 teaspoon finely grated lemon zest

About 315 calories per serving

BARBECUE

- ¼ cup olive oil
- 4 large garlic cloves, minced
- 4 large scallions, sliced thin
- ½ cup barbecue sauce
- 1 teaspoon each salt and ground black pepper

About 375 calories per serving

TARRAGON MUSTARD CREAM

- ¼ cup heavy cream
- 4 large garlic cloves, minced
- 4 large scallions, sliced thin
- ½ cup Dijon mustard
- 1 teaspoon each salt and ground black pepper
- 2 teaspoons dried tarragon

About 290 calories per serving

SOY SESAME

- 3 tablespoons vegetable oil
- 4 large garlic cloves, minced
- ¼ cup soy sauce
- 2 teaspoons rice wine vinegar
- 2 teaspoons toasted sesame oil
- 1 teaspoon hot red pepper flakes
- 1 teaspoon sugar

About 310 calories per serving

TOMATO, ITALIAN HERBS, AND CAPERS

- ¼ cup extra-virgin olive oil
- 4 large garlic cloves, minced
- 1 cup canned crushed tomatoes
- 2 teaspoons dried Italian seasoning
- ¼ cup drained capers
- 1 teaspoon each salt and ground black pepper

About 327 calories per serving

TOMATO, ORANGE, AND SAFFRON

- ¼ cup extra-virgin olive oil
- 1 cup canned crushed tomatoes
- ¼ cup pitted, chopped oil-cured olives
- 4 large garlic cloves, minced
- 4 large scallions, sliced thin

1 teaspoon each salt and ground black pepper

1 teaspoon finely grated orange zest

¼ teaspoon saffron threads

About 355 calories per serving

Pick a Vegetable (1 pound of 1 of the following):

Trimmed asparagus spears, cut into 1-inch lengths

Bell peppers (1 each red and yellow), stemmed, seeded, and cut into ¼-inch-wide strips

Sliced mushrooms

Bok choy, halved and sliced thin

Zucchini or yellow squash, trimmed and sliced thin (halve lengthwise if large)

Eggplant, trimmed and sliced thin (halve lengthwise if large)

Bean sprouts

Sugar snap or snow peas

Cherry or grape tomatoes

Fennel, trimmed, halved, cored, and sliced thin

Adjust oven rack to lowest position and heat oven to 500 degrees. Or heat gas grill, igniting all burners on high, for at least 10 minutes.

Gently toss chicken, pork, or seafood with flavoring and vegetable in a large bowl. Divide mixture among 4 approximately 18-by-12-inch sheets of heavy-duty aluminum foil, arranging meat or seafood atop the vegetables, each in a more or less single layer. Bring long sides of foil together, fold over about ½ inch, and crimp to seal. Repeat folding and crimping twice more. Fold ends in twice to seal completely.

If baking, set foil packets on a large baking sheet and bake for 15 minutes. Remove from oven, let stand for 3 minutes, and serve.

If grilling, set foil packets on hot rack, cover, and grill for 8 minutes. Remove from grill, let stand for 3 minutes, and serve.

weeknight grilled dinners with sex appeal

Grilled pork tenderloin, boneless pork chops, chicken breasts and thighs, turkey cutlets, salmon fillets, and shrimp are perfect for a weeknight diet. They cook quickly, and they're relatively lean. Without help, though, they tend to overcook before they develop the sexy grill marks.

Add a little sugar to a spice rub—or lightly sprinkle it right onto the meat—and you get gorgeous sear marks in half the time. And those sear marks aren't just for show: they dramatically increase flavor, and the reduced grill time ensures juicy, tender results.

Simple enough for ordinary nights, these dinners impress guests.

Serving the cuts with a wedge of lemon or lime is enough, but there's nothing like a fresh salsa to give your dinner pizzazz. Make it first to allow time for the flavors to meld and develop. Next preheat the grill. A hot grill is important. For this reason, preheat it—all burners on high, grill lid closed—for 10 to 15 minutes. Meanwhile, prepare the rub or paste. Lightly toss the cuts with oil to help the seasonings adhere and give them an attractive sheen, then cover the cuts with the rub or paste. By the time the cuts are coated, the grill should be good and hot.

Clean the hot grill rack with a wire brush, then, using spring-action tongs, rub the rack with a vegetable-oil-soaked rag to keep the cuts from sticking.

Place the cuts on the grill, close the grill lid, and set the timer. Unless you see excessive smoke pouring from the grill, resist the temptation to open the lid. The cuts don't need to be turned more than once. So don't peek and poke. I wash up some dishes or set the table while they're cooking. Simple enough for ordinary nights, these dinners impress guests. And since there are almost always leftovers, you'll have the makings for tomorrow's hearty main-course salad.

Spiced-Up Grilled Boneless Pork, Poultry, or Salmon

If you don't have time to make a spice rub or paste, simply toss the cuts with oil, salt, pepper, and 2 teaspoons brown sugar.

SERVES 6

Salsa of choice (optional; pages 256–258)
Spice rub or paste of choice (pages 251–253)

CHOOSE 1 OF THE FOLLOWING:

2 pork tenderloins (about 1 pound each), split lengthwise almost but not all the way through

6 boneless pork loin chops, about ¾ inch thick

6 boneless, skinless chicken breasts, tenderloins removed, thick end of each breast pounded lightly with fists to about ¾ inch thick

8 large boneless, skinless chicken thighs (10–12 medium), trimmed of excess fat

8 turkey cutlets

6 center-cut salmon fillets

1 tablespoon vegetable oil

If serving a salsa, prepare it now.

Heat gas grill, igniting all burners on high, grill lid closed, for at least 10 minutes.

Meanwhile, prepare spice rub or paste. Place selected meat, poultry, or salmon in a medium bowl. If using spice rub, drizzle with oil, then sprinkle with spice rub. If using paste, stir oil into paste, then add to bowl with meat, poultry, or salmon. Toss, spreading with fingertips if necessary, to coat evenly. Clean hot grill rack with a wire brush, then, using spring-action tongs, rub rack with a vegetable-oil-soaked rag.

Place prepared cuts on hot grill rack, being careful not to crowd. Close grill lid and cook, turning only once about halfway through, until cuts have impressive grill marks on both sides, are firm to the touch, and are just opaque throughout.

Total cooking times:

4 to 5 minutes for salmon and turkey cutlets

6 to 8 minutes for pork chops and chicken breasts, depending on thickness

8 to 10 minutes for pork tenderloin

10 to 12 minutes for chicken thighs, depending on thickness

Transfer to a serving platter and let rest for 5 minutes. Spoon salsa alongside, if using, and serve.

About 208 calories per serving (for pork tenderloin; does not include salsa)

#36

50 WAYS TO LOSE IT

Take your eating and exercise rituals wherever you go.

Spicy Grilled Shrimp

Domestic wild-caught shrimp taste better than farm-raised shrimp from Asia. Large shrimp stay juicy when grilled. If you don't have time to make a spice rub or paste, simply toss the shrimp with oil, salt, pepper, and 2 teaspoons brown sugar.

SERVES 6

Salsa of choice (optional; pages 256–258)
Spice rub or paste of choice (pages 251–253)
2 pounds peeled, deveined shrimp (15–20 count), wild-caught if possible
1 tablespoon vegetable oil

If serving a salsa, prepare it now.

Heat gas grill, igniting all burners on high, grill lid closed, for at least 10 minutes.

Meanwhile, prepare spice rub or paste. Place shrimp in a medium bowl, drizzle with oil, and add spice rub. If using a paste, stir oil into paste, then add to bowl with shrimp. Toss, spreading with fingertips if necessary, to coat evenly. Thread shrimp onto 6 metal or bamboo skewers. (If using bamboo skewers, leave as little exposed wood as possible at both ends to keep them from charring.) Clean hot grill rack with a wire brush, then, using spring-action tongs, rub rack with a vegetable-oil-soaked rag.

Place skewered shrimp on hot grill rack, being careful not to crowd. Close grill lid and cook, turning only once about halfway through, until shrimp turn pink, have grill marks on both sides, and are just opaque throughout, about 4 minutes total. Let rest for a couple of minutes. Spoon salsa alongside, if using, and serve.

About 147 calories per serving (does not include salsa)

Simple Spice Rubs and Pastes

Each of the following rubs and pastes is enough to flavor 2 pork tenderloins, 6 boneless pork loin chops, 6 boneless, skinless chicken breasts, 8 to 10 boneless, skinless chicken thighs, 8 turkey cutlets, 6 salmon fillets, or 2 pounds shrimp.

Mix all ingredients in a small bowl.

Basic Paprika Garlic Spice Rub

- 2 teaspoons dark brown sugar
- 1 tablespoon paprika
- 1½ teaspoons ground black pepper
- 1½ teaspoons garlic powder
- 1 teaspoon salt

12 calories per serving

Fennel Garlic Spice Rub

- 2 teaspoons dark brown sugar
- 2 teaspoons chopped fennel seeds
- 1½ teaspoons paprika
- 1½ teaspoons garlic powder
- 1 teaspoon salt

12 calories per serving

Cumin and Coriander Spice Rub

- 2 teaspoons dark brown sugar
- 1½ teaspoons garlic powder
- 1½ teaspoons ground coriander
- 1½ teaspoons ground cumin
- ½ teaspoon ground ginger
- ½ teaspoon turmeric
- 1 teaspoon salt

12 calories per serving

Warm Spice Rub

2 teaspoons dark brown sugar
2 teaspoons paprika
1½ teaspoons garlic powder
1½ teaspoons ground ginger
1 teaspoon salt
½ teaspoon ground cinnamon
⅛ teaspoon ground cloves

12 calories per serving

Spicy Rosemary Rub

1 tablespoon minced fresh rosemary leaves
2 teaspoons dark brown sugar
1 teaspoon salt
1 teaspoon ground black pepper
1 teaspoon hot red pepper flakes

8 calories per serving

Garlicky Chinese Five-Spice Rub

Drizzle the cuts with a little soy sauce as they come off the grill.

2 tablespoons Chinese five-spice powder
2 teaspoons dark brown sugar
1 teaspoon garlic powder
½ teaspoon salt

16 calories per serving

#37
50 WAYS TO LOSE IT

Sit down and savor each meal—no eating at the counter.

Caribbean Spice Paste

Rather than tossing the cuts with the 1 tablespoon oil, stir the oil into this paste instead.

- 1/4 cup classic yellow mustard
- 2 teaspoons hot red pepper sauce (Tabasco brand is hotter)
- 2 teaspoons dark brown sugar
- 1 tablespoon dried thyme leaves
- 1 teaspoon salt
- 1 1/2 teaspoons ground allspice
- 1 teaspoon garlic powder
- 1 teaspoon ground black pepper
- 1/2 teaspoon ground cinnamon

19 calories per serving

Tandoori Paste

Rather than tossing the cuts with the 1 tablespoon oil, stir the oil into this paste instead.

- 1 1/2 tablespoons ground cumin
- 1 1/2 teaspoons curry powder
- 1 teaspoon garlic powder
- 1 teaspoon salt
- 1/2 teaspoon ground ginger
- 1/4 teaspoon cayenne pepper
- 3 tablespoons red wine vinegar
- 1/2 cup low-fat plain yogurt

19 calories per serving

Grilled Swordfish or Tuna Steaks

Tomatoes and cucumbers are especially nice for the salsa (see page 256).

As with any of the grilled cuts, if there's no time to make a salsa, simply serve the fish with lemon or lime wedges.

To give the fish a subtle sweet-and-sour feel, add 2 teaspoons each dark brown sugar and vinegar to the marinade.

If there's time, place the fish and soy mixture in a zipper-lock bag and refrigerate overnight.

SERVES 6

- Salsa or relish of choice (optional; pages 256–258)
- 1 tablespoon vegetable oil
- ¼ cup soy sauce
- ½ teaspoon ground ginger
- ½ teaspoon garlic powder
- ½ teaspoon hot red pepper flakes
- 2 pounds swordfish or tuna steaks, about 1 inch thick, cut into 6 portions

If serving a salsa, prepare it now.

Heat gas grill, igniting all burners on high, grill lid closed, for at least 10 minutes.

Meanwhile, mix oil, soy sauce, ginger, garlic powder, and red pepper flakes in a medium bowl; add fish and toss to coat. Clean hot grill rack with a wire brush, then, using spring-action tongs, rub rack with a vegetable-oil-soaked rag.

Place fish on hot grill rack, being careful not to crowd. Close grill lid and cook, turning only once about halfway through, until fish steaks have grill marks on both sides, about 6 minutes for medium and 7 to 8 minutes for medium-well. Let rest for a couple of minutes. Spoon salsa or relish alongside, if using, and serve.

192 calories per serving (does not include salsa or relish)

Seared Steak with Rosemary and Garlic

For my weeknight beef fix, I love full-flavored, yet lean, sirloin steak. Since leftovers are great warmed up and tossed into the next day's lunch salad, grill more than you need.

SERVES 6

1 tablespoon olive oil
2 tablespoons steak sauce, such as A.1.
2 tablespoons soy sauce
1 tablespoon minced fresh rosemary leaves
1 teaspoon garlic powder
2 teaspoons ground black pepper
1 teaspoon paprika
2 pounds boneless sirloin steak, about 1 inch thick
Salt

Mix oil, steak sauce, soy sauce, rosemary, garlic powder, pepper, and paprika in a small bowl. Place steak on a plate; prick all over on both sides with a fork. Pour half the marinade on one side; spread until absorbed. Turn steak over and repeat procedure on remaining side; let stand while grill heats.

Heat gas grill, igniting all burners on high, grill lid closed, for at least 10 minutes. Clean hot grill rack with a wire brush, then, using spring-action tongs, rub rack with a vegetable-oil-soaked rag.

Place steak on hot grill rack, close grill lid, and cook, turning only once about halfway through, until steak has grill marks on each side, about 6 minutes total for medium-rare, 7 to 8 minutes total for medium. Remove from grill and let rest for 5 minutes. Slice or cut into portions, sprinkle lightly with salt, and serve.

224 calories per serving

Create-Your-Own Fruit Salsa

Use whatever seasonal fruit you've got: mangoes, peaches, nectarines, apricots, plums, oranges, grapefruit, grapes, melons (including watermelon, honeydew, and cantaloupe), strawberries, blueberries, apples, or pears. Or use a mix of fruit—apples and grapes, for example, or oranges and grapefruit.

Choose bell pepper color to contrast with the fruit—red bell pepper with pineapple or yellow bell pepper with watermelon, for instance.

You can also make this salsa with 2 cups finely diced tomatoes and/or cucumbers instead of fruit, which is great with Grilled Swordfish or Tuna Steaks (page 254).

MAKES A HEAPING 2 CUPS, SERVING 6

- 2 cups finely diced fresh fruit (see headnote)
- ½ medium yellow, red, or green bell pepper, cut into small dice (see headnote)
- 3 medium scallions, sliced thin, or ½ small red onion, cut into small dice
- 1 small jalapeño pepper, stemmed, seeded, and minced
- 2–3 tablespoons fresh lime juice or rice wine vinegar
- 2–3 tablespoons chopped fresh cilantro, basil, parsley, or mint leaves
- Salt and ground black pepper

Mix all ingredients in a medium bowl, using the smaller quantity of lime juice or vinegar and fresh herbs, and a sprinkling of salt and pepper. Let stand for 10 to 30 minutes. Before serving, taste and adjust seasonings, including additional lime juice or vinegar, herbs, and salt and pepper.

About 35 calories per serving

Variations on a Salsa Theme

Mix all ingredients in a medium bowl and let stand for 10 to 30 minutes. Before serving, taste and adjust seasonings, including additional lime juice or vinegar, fresh herbs, and salt and pepper.

EACH OF THESE RECIPES MAKES A HEAPING 2 CUPS, SERVING 6

Pineapple Salsa with Radishes, Peppers, and Cilantro

- ½ medium pineapple, peeled, quartered, cored, and cut into small dice (about 2 cups)
- ½ medium yellow or red bell pepper, cut into small dice
- 4 large radishes, trimmed and cut into small dice
- 2 tablespoons chopped fresh cilantro leaves
- 2 tablespoons rice wine vinegar
- Salt and ground black pepper

22 calories per serving

Green Grape Salsa with Scallions and Mint

- 2 cups quartered seedless green grapes
- ½ medium green bell pepper, cut into small dice
- 3 medium scallions, sliced thin
- 1 small jalapeño pepper, stemmed, seeded, and minced
- 3 tablespoons chopped fresh mint leaves
- 2 tablespoons fresh lime juice
- Salt and ground black pepper

47 calories per serving

Mango Peanut Salsa

- 1 medium mango, peeled, pitted, and cut into small dice (about 2 cups)
- ¼ cup coarsely chopped roasted peanuts
- ½ medium red bell pepper, cut into small dice
- 3 medium scallions, sliced thin
- 1 small jalapeño pepper, stemmed, seeded, and minced
- 3 tablespoons chopped fresh cilantro leaves
- 3 tablespoons fresh lime juice

65 calories per serving

Cherry Tomato Relish with Capers and Green Olives

- 2 cups quartered grape or cherry tomatoes
- ½ small red onion, cut into small dice
- 1 large garlic clove, minced
- 2 tablespoons drained capers
- ¼ cup chopped pimiento-stuffed green olives
- 2 tablespoons torn fresh basil leaves
- 1 tablespoon extra-virgin olive oil
- ½ teaspoon finely grated lemon zest
- 2 teaspoons fresh lemon juice
- ¼ teaspoon each salt and ground black pepper

48 calories per serving

#38
50 WAYS TO LOSE IT

Grill fruit—apples, pears, peaches, and plums—and serve as a first course, side dish, or dessert.

big-flavored vegetables: no thinking required

When you make a weeknight main course, there's not much time to spend on vegetables. In fact, you don't have to. I rely primarily on three techniques, all of which cook the vegetables as quickly as possible, leaving them tender but not overdone. And all three methods ensure that flavor is preserved.

Roasting allows you to cook a large quantity of mixed vegetables with very little effort. Preparation is minimal. Onions, new potatoes, carrots, and small zucchini, for example, are simply halved. After that, just toss them with olive oil, salt, pepper, and an herb, if you like, and arrange them cut side down on a rimmed baking sheet. Pop them in the oven and set the temperature to 425 degrees, and in 20 to 25 minutes, you've got fantastic caramel-brown vegetables for dinner, with enough left over for another meal.

These three methods cook vegetables as quickly as possible, ensuring that not one ounce of flavor is lost.

In principle, gas grilling is identical to roasting. Both produce two kinds of heat—the direct kind from the gas or electric burner and the indirect kind from heat buildup in the enclosed space. To get the full effect of both direct and enveloping heat, cook the vegetables on a fully preheated grill. Because of the super-hot direct and indirect heat, they cook more quickly than in the oven.

I don't bother with grill baskets or screens. I simply stick with vegetables that can't fall through the grate, which disqualifies only a few: cherry tomatoes, green beans, brussels sprouts, pearl onions, and certain baby vegetables. All the others—if they are left in large enough pieces or, as with asparagus, are turned perpendicular to the grate—cook to perfection.

Steam-sautéing is another super-quick method for cooking fresh vegetables. In one seamless process, they steam in a very small amount of salted, oiled water, and by the time they're cooked, the water has evaporated, the oil kicks in, and they start to sauté.

Grilled Vegetables

SERVES 8

Generous 8 cups of any of the vegetables on page 262
3 tablespoons olive oil
1 teaspoon dried basil, tarragon, or thyme leaves
Salt and ground black pepper

Heat gas grill, igniting all burners on high, with grill lid closed, for at least 10 minutes. While grill heats, toss vegetables with oil, basil, and salt and pepper to taste. Clean hot grill rack with a wire brush, then, using spring-action tongs, rub rack with a vegetable-oil-soaked rag.

With the exception of asparagus spears, which are added at halfway point, arrange vegetables on hot grill rack, being careful not to crowd. Cover and cook, turning only once about halfway through, until vegetables have grill marks on both sides and are tender-crisp, about 10 minutes. Serve.

About 100 calories per serving

#39

50 WAYS TO LOSE IT

Walk a minute, run a minute.

A Grill Full of Vegetables

Slice the vegetables thinner than you would if you were roasting them. The thinner the vegetable, the more quickly it cooks. And the larger the surface exposed to the fire, the more area that browns and the more caramelized flavor you'll get. Leave the onions and shallots unpeeled. They're prettier and the prep is simpler.

Grilled Vegetable Possibilities:

Medium carrots and parsnips, peeled and halved lengthwise (if they're long, halve them crosswise as well)

Medium sweet potatoes, peeled and quartered lengthwise

Small onions, unpeeled, halved lengthwise or crosswise (don't use large onions, which require lower, slower heat)

Large shallots, unpeeled, halved lengthwise

Medium turnips, peeled and sliced into 4 rounds

Rutabagas, peeled and cut into thick slices (if large, halve lengthwise and cut into thick half slices)

Medium beets, peeled and sliced into 4 rounds (if small, halve lengthwise)

Winter squash, peeled, seeded, and cut into 2-inch chunks (most produce departments carry peeled, cut winter squash)

Asparagus, tough ends snapped

New or small red potatoes, halved

Leeks, trimmed of dark green part, halved lengthwise, and washed to remove grit

Fennel, fronds trimmed and bulb quartered if small or cut into sixths if large

Small zucchini, halved lengthwise (if large, slice lengthwise into 3–4 pieces)

Small yellow squash, halved lengthwise (if large, slice lengthwise into 3–4 pieces)

Small eggplant, halved lengthwise (if large, quarter lengthwise)

Small portobello mushrooms, stemmed (not baby bellas)

Grilled Fruit

If you're grilling the main course and the vegetables, why not toss a little fruit on as well? Fill the core of a grilled pear, peach, or apple half with a tablespoon of your favorite goat cheese or blue cheese. Lay the fruit on a paper-thin slice of prosciutto, and you've got a first-class first course, or perch them on a bed of lightly dressed mixed greens.

Serve a plank of grilled pineapple alongside skewered grilled shrimp. What about a grilled peach or pear half with grilled pork chops or a sliced tenderloin?

Topped with a little yogurt, perhaps a sprinkling of chopped nuts, a grilled peach, pear, or apple half is a perfect way to end the meal.

SERVES 6

CHOOSE 1 OF THE FOLLOWING:

3 firm but ripe pears, halved and cored
3 firm but ripe peaches or nectarines, halved and pitted
3 crisp apples, such as Granny Smith, halved and cored
1 pineapple, peeled, halved, cored, and cut into 6 wedges

1 tablespoon olive oil

Heat gas grill, igniting all burners on high, with grill lid closed, for at least 10 minutes. While grill heats, toss fruit with oil. Clean hot grill rack with a wire brush, then, using spring-action tongs, rub rack with a vegetable-oil-soaked rag.

Arrange fruit on hot grill rack. Cover and cook, turning only once about halfway through, until fruit has grill marks on both sides and is just cooked through, about 10 minutes. Serve.

About 54 calories per serving

a big pan of roasted vegetables

Since it's so simple, I like to roast a lot of vegetables at once. Depending on the number of diners, there are usually enough leftover roasted vegetables for another meal. You can toss them in soups, drizzle them with vinaigrette for a first-course salad, or add them to a hearty main-course salad a day or two later.

Unlike most roasted-vegetable techniques, this one starts with a cold oven. That means the heating element is in preheat mode and fully on for the entire time the vegetables are roasting. Not only do they cook quickly, they also (more important) brown quickly. The usual 45-minute cooking time is reduced to a mere 20 to 25 minutes.

The usual 45-minute cooking time is reduced to a mere 20 to 25 minutes.

Every oven and every roasting pan are different, so cooking times may vary. Understand the principle: you're using the oven element like a big stovetop burner to cook and brown the vegetables as quickly as possible. If you have an especially thin pan, your vegetables may brown faster. If so, turn them sooner than the suggested 20 minutes.

When you turn them at the 20-minute point, certain vegetables—eggplant and sweet potatoes, for example—may stick a little. (Using vegetable cooking spray helps.) If so, just continue turning the other vegetables. By the time you've finished, the steam will have loosened them, and they'll be ready to turn.

I find that a generously filled 2-quart (8-cup) Pyrex measuring cup works best to measure the vegetables, which I like to leave in their natural shape whenever possible. If you don't have one, just make sure there are enough vegetables to fit in a single layer on the baking sheet.

Roasted Fall/Winter Vegetables

SERVES 8

USE A GENEROUS 8 CUPS OF ANY COMBINATION OF THE FOLLOWING:

- Medium carrots, peeled and halved lengthwise
- Medium sweet potatoes, peeled, halved lengthwise, and cut into 2-inch chunks
- Small onions, unpeeled, halved lengthwise or crosswise
- Large shallots, unpeeled, halved lengthwise
- Medium turnips, peeled and halved
- Rutabagas, peeled and cut into 2-inch chunks
- Medium beets, peeled and halved
- Winter squash, peeled, seeded, and cut into 2-inch chunks (most produce departments carry peeled, cut winter squash)
- Parsnips, peeled and halved lengthwise

3 tablespoons olive oil
1 teaspoon dried thyme leaves
Salt and ground black pepper

Coat a large (18-by-12-inch) rimmed baking sheet with vegetable cooking spray. Toss vegetables with oil, thyme, and salt and pepper to taste. Arrange vegetables on baking sheet, cut side down. Place pan on lowest rack in a cold oven. Set oven to 425 degrees and roast until cut sides are caramel-brown in color, about 20 minutes. Turn vegetables over and continue to cook until just tender, about 5 minutes longer. Serve. (Each person can slip the onions and shallots from their skins at the table.)

About 118 calories per serving

Roasted Spring Vegetables

SERVES 8

USE A GENEROUS 8 CUPS OF ANY COMBINATION OF THE FOLLOWING:

- Carrots, peeled and halved lengthwise
- Asparagus, tough ends snapped
- New or small red potatoes, halved
- Leeks, trimmed of dark green part, halved lengthwise, and washed to remove grit, or frozen pearl onions, not thawed
- Fennel, fronds trimmed and bulb quartered if small or cut into sixths if large

3 tablespoons olive oil
1 teaspoon dried tarragon
Salt and ground black pepper

Coat a large (18-by-12-inch) rimmed baking sheet with vegetable cooking spray. Toss vegetables with oil, tarragon, and salt and pepper to taste. If using asparagus, set spears aside. Arrange vegetables on baking sheet, cut side down. Place pan on lowest rack in a cold oven. Set oven to 425 degrees and roast until cut sides are caramel-brown in color, about 20 minutes. Turn vegetables over, add asparagus, and continue to cook until asparagus is bright green and tender, about 5 minutes longer (or perhaps a little more if asparagus is especially thick). Serve.

About 112 calories per serving

Roasted Summer Vegetables

SERVES 8

USE A GENEROUS 8 CUPS OF ANY COMBINATION OF THE FOLLOWING:

- Small zucchini, halved lengthwise (if large, halve again crosswise)
- Small yellow squash, halved lengthwise (if large, halve again crosswise)
- Small eggplant, halved lengthwise (if large, quartered lengthwise and cut into large chunks)
- Cauliflower, cored, broken into large florets, florets halved
- Cherry tomatoes

3 tablespoons olive oil
1 teaspoon dried basil
Salt and ground black pepper

Coat a large (18-by-12-inch) rimmed baking sheet with vegetable cooking spray. Toss vegetables (except cherry tomatoes, if using) with oil, basil, and salt and pepper to taste. Arrange vegetables on baking sheet, cut side down. If using cherry tomatoes, add to bowl, toss to coat with residual oil, season with salt and pepper to taste, and set aside. Place pan on lowest rack in a cold oven. Set oven to 425 degrees and roast until cut sides are caramel-brown in color, about 20 minutes. Turn vegetables over, add cherry tomatoes, if using, and continue to cook until vegetables are just tender and tomatoes have softened, about 5 minutes longer. Serve.

About 69 calories per serving

Roasted Green Beans with Cherry Tomatoes and Oregano

SERVES 6

1 pound thin green beans, trimmed
1 pint cherry tomatoes
2 tablespoons olive oil
1 teaspoon dried oregano
Salt and ground black pepper

Toss beans and tomatoes with olive oil, oregano, and salt and pepper to taste in a medium bowl. Arrange on a large (18-by-12-inch) rimmed baking sheet. Place pan on lowest rack in a cold oven. Set oven to 425 degrees and roast, giving pan an occasional shake after 15 minutes, until tomatoes collapse and beans are tender and golden, about 20 minutes total. Serve.

80 calories per serving

#40

50 WAYS TO LOSE IT

Decide realistically how much you can exercise, then be faithful.

Roasted Buttered Brussels Sprouts with Dijon and Lemon

SERVES 8

- 3 boxes (10 ounces each) frozen brussels sprouts, separated as much as possible
- 2 tablespoons olive oil
- Salt and ground black pepper
- 1 tablespoon butter, melted
- 2 tablespoons Dijon mustard
- 1 teaspoon finely grated lemon zest
- 1 teaspoon fresh lemon juice

Toss frozen brussels sprouts with olive oil and salt and pepper to taste in a medium bowl. Arrange on a large (18-by-12-inch) rimmed baking sheet. Place pan on lowest rack in a cold oven. Set oven to 425 degrees and roast, giving pan a shake after 15 minutes, until all the moisture has evaporated and brussels sprouts have turned golden brown, about 20 minutes total. Return brussels sprouts to bowl and stir in butter, mustard, lemon zest, and juice. Serve.

91 calories per serving

Roasted Mushrooms with Garlic and Thyme

SERVES 8

- 2 packages (10 ounces each) baby bella or domestic white mushrooms, trimmed and, if large, halved
- 3 tablespoons olive oil
- ½ teaspoon dried thyme leaves
- Salt and ground black pepper
- 2 large garlic cloves, minced

Toss mushrooms with olive oil, thyme, and salt and pepper to taste in a medium bowl. Arrange on a large (18-by-12-inch) rimmed baking sheet. Place pan on lowest rack in a cold oven. Set oven to 425 degrees and roast until all the moisture has evaporated and mushrooms are golden brown, about 20 minutes. Remove from oven, stir in garlic, let stand for a couple of minutes, and serve.

50 calories per serving

#41

50 WAYS TO LOSE IT

Stocking your pantry with mix-and-match ingredients that can be used in soups, salads, and main dishes makes eating healthy easier.

quicker than quick: steam-sautéing

When I serve a pan-seared main course, chances are there's a steam-sautéed vegetable on the plate as well. Just as searing is one of the quickest methods for cooking meat, poultry, and fish, steam-sautéing is the quickest vegetable-cooking method.

Simply place a pound of vegetables in a Dutch oven or medium skillet (a saucepan's surface area is too small), along with a smidgen of water and a little fat and salt. Cover and turn the burner on high. Because there's such a tiny amount of water, it heats almost instantly. The quickly generated steam cooks the vegetable so fast that by the time the water has evaporated, the vegetable has cooked. The fat's there for flavor and to keep the vegetables from scorching.

You can double the vegetables to 2 pounds; just be sure to use a deep 11- to 12-inch skillet. The larger surface allows the water to heat more quickly and the vegetables to cook more evenly. And if you're having a dinner party and need to cook even more vegetables, you can use a roasting pan covered with heavy-duty foil and set over two burners on high.

Steam-Sautéed Vegetables

SERVES 4

Choose 1 pound of 1 vegetable or a combination of vegetables:

Carrots, peeled and sliced thin (or buy baby carrots)

Asparagus, tough ends snapped

Snow peas or sugar snap peas, strings removed (or buy peas that are already strung)

Green beans or yellow wax beans, trimmed (or buy beans that are already trimmed)

Broccoli, crowns cut into medium florets, stems peeled and cut into thick coins (or 1 large crown per person split lengthwise)

Cauliflower, trimmed and cut into medium florets (or buy florets)

Winter squash, peeled, seeded, and cut into medium dice (or buy peeled, seeded squash)

Frozen brussels sprouts (one and a half 10-ounce boxes)

Turnips or rutabagas, peeled and cut into medium dice

Parsnips, peeled and cut into thick coins

Cabbage, cored and coarsely shredded (or buy coleslaw mix)

⅓ cup water

2 teaspoons olive oil

Scant ½ teaspoon salt

Dried herbs and spices (optional):

- ¼ teaspoon potent or fiery spices (nutmeg, cloves, or hot red pepper flakes)
- ½ teaspoon less potent spice (ground cumin, ground coriander, ground ginger, or caraway seeds) or potent dried herb (thyme, tarragon, herbes de Provence, oregano, or *fresh* rosemary—treat rosemary like a dried herb)
- 1 teaspoon spice blend (curry or chili powder) or milder dried herb (basil)

Fresh herbs and aromatics (optional):

- 2 medium garlic cloves, minced
- 1 tablespoon minced fresh ginger
- ½ teaspoon finely grated orange or lemon zest (you may want a little squeeze of lemon juice as well)
- 1½ teaspoons chopped fresh herb (tarragon, dill, or thyme)
- 1 tablespoon chopped mild soft fresh herb (parsley, cilantro, mint, or basil)

Place vegetables, water, oil, salt, and dried herb or spice, if using, in a medium (5½-quart) Dutch oven or skillet. Cover, turn burner on high, and cook until water has mostly evaporated and vegetables are bright and just tender, 5 to 7 minutes. Remove lid and continue to cook until liquid thickens to a sauce or completely evaporates and vegetables start to sauté. Stir in fresh herb or aromatic, if using, and serve.

About 35 calories per serving

#42
50 WAYS TO LOSE IT

To control calories, use measuring cups and spoons for cooking and serving.

Quick Tomato-Stewed Zucchini with Basil and Garlic

Tomatoes, not water, steam and flavor ordinarily bland zucchini. This method also works with green beans and yellow squash.

SERVES 4

- 1 tablespoon olive oil
- 2 large garlic cloves, minced
- 1 can (14.5 ounces) petite diced tomatoes
- 1 pound zucchini, trimmed and sliced thin
- ½ teaspoon dried basil
- Scant ½ teaspoon salt
- Ground black pepper

Place oil and garlic in a medium skillet or small Dutch oven over high heat. When garlic starts to sizzle and turn golden, stir in tomatoes, zucchini, basil, and salt and pepper to taste. Cover and steam until tomato liquid has evaporated and zucchini is tender, 8 to 10 minutes. Serve.

71 calories per serving

#43

50 WAYS TO LOSE IT

Let your clothes be your scale. Weigh yourself only once a month.

Rich and Creamy Cauliflower Puree

Steaming cauliflower in chicken broth steps up the flavor, and pureeing it with evaporated milk gives it an intensely rich, luxurious taste and texture without the added calories of heavy cream. Although similar in look and flavor to mashed potatoes, this dish is significantly less caloric.

SERVES 6 TO 8

- 1 large head cauliflower, cored and cut into medium florets
- ⅔ cup chicken broth
- ½ teaspoon salt
- ¼ teaspoon ground black or white pepper
- 1 small can (5 ounces) evaporated milk

Place cauliflower and broth in a medium (5½-quart) Dutch oven over high heat. Cover and steam until cauliflower is tender and broth has almost evaporated, about 10 minutes.

Transfer cauliflower to a blender and add salt and pepper. Remove pop-out center and, with motor running, pour in evaporated milk and blend, stopping blender once or twice to stir in unprocessed cauliflower, until puree is silky smooth. Taste and add more salt and pepper, if needed. Serve. (Cauliflower can be covered and refrigerated for up to 3 days.)

67 calories per serving

#44

50 WAYS TO LOSE IT

Give yourself an occasional nonfood treat (a movie, a massage, a manicure) for a job well done.

dessert too

One thing I know: you cannot forswear sugary things to lose weight. You have to determine what you legitimately need to be happy and then stick with it.

Several years ago, my brother-in-law lost nearly two hundred pounds. To keep motivated to maintain that incredible weight loss, he allows himself a couple of low-fat cookies every day and one decadent dessert a week. This strategy has worked for him. If you forgo having nuts and a glass of wine before dinner and you're committed to regular exercise, it's very possible to enjoy a light daily dessert. You're not going to get away with a large hunk of chocolate cake, an oversize bowl of premium ice cream, or a big wedge of pie on a regular basis. You can, however, savor a small dish of vanilla or chocolate pudding, a goblet of light strawberry mousse, or a ramekin of creamy caramel custard or orange panna cotta. Most of these desserts, especially the pudding, require minimal preparation, so make a batch of six or eight on the weekend to have during the week.

One thing I know: you cannot forswear sugary things to lose weight.

Made with light cream cheese and a crumb coating instead of a full crust, cheesecake is another dessert you can enjoy regularly. If you invest in mini springform pans, you can make several small cheesecakes at one time and freeze them. Stored in the freezer, they stay fresh, they're less of a temptation, and you can pull them out as needed. To keep it interesting, you can divide the batter and flavor each portion differently.

Breakfast Fruit Parfait with Yogurt and Drizzled Honey (page 49) also makes a perfect end to a meal. For you, however, the perfect end may be a crisp fragrant cookie or two. If so, there are several with very reasonable calorie counts in the Time for Tea chapter (page 139).

If chocolate is your passion, weigh out an ounce of good-quality bittersweet (it's surprisingly not that caloric) and pair it with seasonal fruit—apples in the fall and winter, strawberries in the spring, and raspberries and cherries in the summer.

Tart shells made from egg roll wraps are perfect for those who need a daily sweet fix. First, they're simple to make. Brushed lightly with butter and sprinkled with a little graham cracker–sugar topping, they're baked in mini muffin pans. The dough is thin, and other than the tiny bit of surface butter, they're quite low in calories. They're versatile too. Fill them with chocolate pudding and banana slices, lemon curd and raspberries, vanilla pudding and toasted flaked coconut, or a tablespoon of your favorite ice cream or sorbet.

Remember: your sweet tooth is not in charge. You are. So sit down and have a friendly conversation. Find out what it really needs. As you listen and decide, be generous. You can always cut back.

You'll eventually see that it is possible to live a healthy, happy life that includes dessert. In other words, you *can* have your cake and eat it too.

#45
50 WAYS TO LOSE IT

Give away the "old you" clothes as you shrink.

RECIPES

FRUIT DESSERTS

Chocolate 'n' Cherries 282
Perfect Berry Sauce with Sour Cream Mounds or Angel Food Cake 283
Peach Melba 284
Mango Fruit Salad with Mint and Honey-Lime Dressing 285

MOUSSES, PUDDINGS, AND CREAM TARTLETS

Strawberry Mousse 286
Light Orange Panna Cotta with Fresh Raspberries 287
Caramel Crème 288
Double Chocolate Pudding 289
Vanilla Pudding 290
Crisp Mini Tart Shells 291
Chocolate Tartlets 292
  Banana Cream Tartlets 292
  Coconut Cream Tartlets 293
  Lemon Curd Tartlets 293

CHEESECAKES

Creamy Cheesecake 294
  Lemon 295
  Lime 295
  Tiramisu 295
  Chocolate Orange 296

Chocolate 'n' Cherries

If cherries aren't in season, I serve the dark chocolate with 2 crisp apples, cored and quartered, a pint of strawberries, or a half pint of raspberries.

SERVES 4

1 4-ounce bar good-quality bittersweet chocolate, broken into 4 pieces
2 cups Bing cherries

Arrange chocolate and cherries on four dessert plates. Serve.

187 calories per serving

#46
50 WAYS TO LOSE IT

Keep desserts satisfying but small.

Perfect Berry Sauce with Sour Cream Mounds or Angel Food Cake

Brightly flavored and refreshingly intense, this sauce is made from pureed frozen berries, which, along with the jam, give it great body and taste. Seasonal fresh berries contribute to the supple texture.

MAKES 2 CUPS SAUCE, SERVING 8

Perfect Berry Sauce

- 1 package (12 ounces) frozen raspberries, blackberries, or strawberries, partially thawed (1½–2 minutes on high power in microwave)
- ½ cup seedless raspberry, blackberry, or strawberry jam
- ½ teaspoon finely grated orange zest
- 1½ cups fresh raspberries, blackberries, or small strawberries, hulled and quartered

- 2 cups light sour cream, or 1 store-bought angel food cake

Puree partially thawed fruit, jam, and zest in a food processor. Put through a strainer and discard seeds. Stir fresh berries into sauce and refrigerate until ready to serve. (Sauce can be covered and refrigerated for up to 5 days.)

Spoon ¼ cup sour cream onto each of eight dessert plates (or into each of eight goblets) or place a portion of angel food cake on a plate. Spoon ¼ cup sauce around each mound of sour cream or piece of cake. Serve.

About 170 calories per serving

Peach Melba

SERVES 8

- ¼ cup peach schnapps
- 4 large peaches, unpeeled, halved and pitted
- Perfect Berry Sauce (page 283) made with raspberries
- ½ cup toasted slivered almonds

Pour peach schnapps in a microwave-safe pan large enough to hold peaches in a single layer. Place peaches cut side down in pan. Microwave on high power for 3 minutes. Turn peaches over and continue to microwave until they are soft but still hold their shape, about 2 minutes longer. Let stand until cool enough to handle, then peel. Refrigerate until ready to serve.

To serve, place a peach half in each of eight small bowls. Pour ¼ cup berry sauce around each peach, sprinkle each dessert with 1 tablespoon almonds, and serve immediately.

186 calories per serving

#47

50 WAYS TO LOSE IT

Work on relationships in which you might be giving too much. (Consider a therapist for help.)

Mango Fruit Salad with Mint and Honey-Lime Dressing

This fruit salad keeps for up to 3 days in the refrigerator, so even if you're not serving 8 people, go ahead and make the full recipe. It's also a great first course served atop a bed of mixed baby field greens lightly dressed with olive oil, salt, pepper, and a few drops of lime juice.

SERVES 8

- 2 tablespoons minced fresh ginger
- 1 teaspoon finely grated lime zest
- 2 tablespoons fresh lime juice
- ¼ cup honey
- 2 medium mangoes, peeled, pitted, and cut into bite-sized chunks
- 3 cups seedless green grapes
- 1½ cups fresh blueberries
- ¼ cup chopped fresh mint, plus extra sprigs for garnish

Whisk ginger, lime zest, juice, and honey in a small bowl; set aside. Mix mangoes, grapes, blueberries, and mint in a large bowl. Add dressing and toss to coat. (Salad can be covered and refrigerated for up to 3 days.) To serve, spoon into eight bowls or goblets and garnish with mint sprigs.

127 calories per serving

Strawberry Mousse

Made with frozen strawberries, this excellent dessert sets up quite quickly.

SERVES 8

- 1 container (24 ounces) frozen sweetened strawberries
- 1 cup ricotta cheese
- 2 packages (4½ teaspoons) unflavored gelatin
- 2 tablespoons fresh lemon juice
- 4 large egg whites
- ¼ cup sugar
- 1 pint strawberries, hulled and sliced

Microwave frozen strawberries on high power until they are partially thawed and mixture breaks up easily with a fork, 1½ to 2 minutes. Reserve 2 tablespoons of the juice. Transfer strawberries to a food processor, add ricotta, and process until smooth.

Meanwhile, mix gelatin with lemon juice and reserved strawberry juice in a small microwave-safe bowl until gelatin softens, about 1 minute. Microwave on high power until gelatin has fully dissolved and liquid is clear, about 45 seconds. Pour gelatin mixture into food processor with ricotta mixture and process until fully incorporated. Transfer to a large bowl and refrigerate.

Beat egg whites with an electric mixer on medium-high speed until foamy and starting to peak. Gradually beat in sugar until glossy stiff peaks form. Fold whipped whites into strawberry mixture until thoroughly blended. Cover and refrigerate for at least 1 hour. (Mousse can be refrigerated overnight.)

Spoon into eight stemmed glasses, garnish with sliced strawberries, and serve.

173 calories per serving

Light Orange Panna Cotta with Fresh Raspberries

SERVES 4

- 1 can (12 ounces) evaporated milk
- ¼ cup sugar
- 1 teaspoon finely grated orange zest
- 1¼ teaspoons unflavored gelatin
- 1 tablespoon orange-flavored liqueur, such as Cointreau or Grand Marnier
- ½ pint raspberries

Whisk milk, sugar, orange zest, and gelatin in a small saucepan until gelatin softens and sugar dissolves. Bring milk mixture to a simmer. Remove from heat and stir in liqueur. Pour a scant ½ cup into each of four 6-ounce custard cups. Refrigerate until set, about 2 hours. (Panna cotta can be covered with plastic wrap and refrigerated for up to 5 days.)

To serve, run a thin-bladed knife around inside edge of custard cup. Turn out each panna cotta onto a small dessert plate, garnish with raspberries, and serve.

189 calories per serving

#48
50 WAYS TO LOSE IT

Substitute evaporated milk (either 2% or regular) for heavy cream: 12.5 or 20 calories per tablespoon vs. 60 calories per tablespoon.

Caramel Crème

If you're looking for crème brûlée without all the calories, here's your answer. For a dessert that tastes every bit as good as the one made with heavy cream, use regular evaporated milk. For a very good but lighter dessert, use 2% evaporated milk.

And if you want a crisp sugar top, adjust oven rack to highest setting and turn broiler on high. Place the chilled custard cups in a 13-by-9-inch baking dish and fill with ice water to come halfway up the sides of the cups. Sprinkle each dessert with ½ teaspoon sugar. Broil until sugar bubbles and edges turn golden brown, 1 to 2 minutes.

SERVES 6

- 1 can (12 ounces) evaporated milk
- 6 tablespoons dark brown sugar
- 1 large egg plus 1 egg yolk
- 1 teaspoon vanilla extract

Adjust oven rack to lower-middle position and heat oven to 325 degrees. Set six custard cups in a 13-by-9-inch baking dish. Bring 1 quart water to a boil in a medium saucepan.

Bring the milk and sugar to a simmer in a small saucepan, stirring, until sugar dissolves. Meanwhile, whisk egg, yolk, and vanilla in a 1-quart Pyrex measuring cup. Gradually whisk milk mixture into eggs, then pour into custard cups. Set pan in oven; carefully pour hot water into pan halfway up sides of cups. Bake until custards are set, 20 to 25 minutes. Remove custards from baking dish and cool slightly. Cover with plastic wrap and refrigerate until chilled, about 2 hours. Serve. (Custards can be refrigerated for up to 5 days.)

147 calories per serving

Double Chocolate Pudding

I like whole milk's richness in this pudding. If you prefer to use reduced- or low-fat milk, you could have a larger portion.

SERVES 6 OR MAKES UP TO 3 DOZEN TARTLETS (SEE PAGE 291)

- 2 cups whole milk
- ½ cup sugar
- ¼ cup unsweetened cocoa powder
- 2 tablespoons cornstarch
- 1 teaspoon instant coffee or espresso powder
- ⅛ teaspoon salt
- 2 ounces bittersweet chocolate, coarsely chopped
- 2 teaspoons vanilla extract

Microwave milk in a 1-quart Pyrex measuring cup until steamy hot, 3 to 4 minutes. Meanwhile, whisk sugar, cocoa powder, cornstarch, instant coffee or espresso powder, and salt in a medium saucepan. Over medium heat, vigorously whisk in milk. Continue to whisk until mixture thickens to pudding consistency, just a couple of minutes. Remove from heat and whisk in chocolate and vanilla until chocolate melts.

Pour into six custard cups or into an airtight container. Serve warm or cover surface with a sheet of plastic to keep a skin from forming, chill, and serve cold. (Pudding can be refrigerated for up to 5 days.)

190 calories per serving

Vanilla Pudding

Whole milk is key to the pudding's rich flavor and texture.

SERVES 6 OR MAKES UP TO 3 DOZEN TARTLETS (SEE PAGES 292–293)

- 2 cups whole milk
- ½ cup sugar
- 2 tablespoons cornstarch
- ⅛ teaspoon salt
- 2 large egg yolks
- 2 teaspoons vanilla extract

Microwave milk in a 1-quart Pyrex measuring cup until steamy hot, 3 to 4 minutes. Meanwhile, whisk sugar, cornstarch, and salt in a medium saucepan. Whisk in egg yolks, then turn heat to medium and vigorously whisk in milk. Continue to whisk until mixture thickens to pudding consistency, just a couple of minutes. Remove from heat and stir in vanilla.

Pour into six custard cups or into an airtight container. Serve warm or cover surface with a sheet of plastic to keep skin from forming, refrigerate, and serve cold. (Pudding can be refrigerated for up to 5 days.)

145 calories per serving

Crisp Mini Tart Shells

Make a batch of these and store them in a tin—they'll stay fresh for 2 to 3 weeks.

Round wonton wrappers can be substituted for the egg roll wraps. If you have just one or two mini muffin tins, bake the tart shells in batches or simply halve the recipe. When sealed tightly, the egg roll wraps can be refrigerated for a week or two or frozen for a couple of months.

MAKES 4 DOZEN

- ½ cup sugar
- ½ cup graham cracker crumbs
- 12 egg roll wraps, stacked and cut into 48 squares
- ¾ stick (6 tablespoons) unsalted butter, melted

Adjust oven racks to lowest and lower-middle positions and heat oven to 325 degrees. Spray forty-eight mini muffin cups with vegetable cooking spray.

Mix sugar and graham cracker crumbs in a small bowl.

Working in 4 batches and keeping the rest covered, place 12 wrappers on work surface. Brush top with melted butter and, holding wrapper over graham cracker mixture, sprinkle to adhere. Turn wrappers crumb side down, brush other side with butter, and sprinkle with crumb mixture. Fit wrappers into muffin cups.

Place two muffin tins each on upper and lower oven racks and bake, switching tins from side to side and from upper to lower positions after 10 minutes, until golden brown and crisp, 15 to 18 minutes. Immediately turn shells out onto a wire rack to cool before filling (see pages 292–293). (Tartlet shells can be stored in an airtight tin for up to 3 weeks.)

38 calories per tart shell

Chocolate Tartlets

Since the chocolate pudding is so easy, I highly recommend making it from scratch. If, however, you need a quick sweet fix, use store-bought chocolate pudding and doctor it as suggested below.

MAKES UP TO 3 DOZEN

- Double Chocolate Pudding (page 289), or six 4-ounce dark chocolate pudding cups, preferably Swiss Miss
- 1½ teaspoons instant coffee or espresso powder, for store-bought pudding
- 3 dozen Crisp Mini Tart Shells (page 291)
- Banana slices, fresh raspberries, toasted sliced almonds, or chopped roasted pistachios, for garnish

If using store-bought chocolate pudding cups, spoon pudding into a medium bowl and whisk in instant coffee or espresso powder.

Fill each tartlet with 1 tablespoon pudding, top with 2 banana slices or other garnishes, and serve.

About 78 calories per tartlet

Banana Cream Tartlets

There's no disguising the artificial flavor in vanilla pudding cups—you need homemade here.

Fill each tartlet with 1 tablespoon Vanilla Pudding (page 290). Top with 2 banana slices and serve.

71 calories per tartlet

Coconut Cream Tartlets

Scatter ½ cup flaked sweetened or unsweetened coconut in an 8-inch square baking pan. Toast on lower-middle rack of a 325-degree oven, stirring every 5 minutes, until evenly golden brown, about 15 minutes.

Fill each tartlet with 1 tablespoon Vanilla Pudding (page 290). Lightly sprinkle with toasted coconut and serve.

67 calories per tartlet

Lemon Curd Tartlets

Fill each tartlet with 1 tablespoon store-bought lemon curd. Top with a fresh raspberry, if you like, and serve.

71 calories per tartlet

#49

50 WAYS TO LOSE IT

Remember, losing weight is not a race to complete but a new way of life.

Creamy Cheesecake

For a creamy, silky texture, bake the cheesecake in a water bath. To ensure that the springform pan doesn't leak in the water, double-wrap the bottom and sides with heavy-duty foil. You can make one big cheesecake or five small ones, but unless you have an extra-large roasting pan, there may be room for only four of the small pans. If so, set the fifth cheesecake in an 8- or 9-inch baking pan filled with boiling water. Or refrigerate the batter and bake it at a later time.

SERVES 16 TO 20

- 1 tablespoon butter, softened
- 3 tablespoons crumbs from Famous Chocolate Wafers or graham crackers, or 24 soft ladyfingers (one 3-ounce package)
- 3 8-ounce packages light Neufchatel cream cheese
- 1 cup sugar
- 3 large eggs
- 2 teaspoons vanilla extract
- ¼ cup heavy cream
- ¼ cup light sour cream

Adjust oven rack to middle position and heat oven to 325 degrees. Bring 2 quarts water to a boil. Brush one 9-inch or five 4½-inch springform pans with butter. Add crumbs, tilting pan(s) in all directions to coat evenly, or line pan sides with ladyfingers. (If using 4½-inch pans, halve ladyfingers crosswise to fit.) Cover exterior of pan(s) with two sheets of heavy-duty foil to prevent water from seeping in; set in a roasting pan.

Beat cream cheese with an electric mixer until smooth. Gradually add sugar and beat on medium speed until fully incorporated. Scrape down bowl sides and beat again until smooth. Beat in eggs, one at a time, scraping down bowl after each addition to ensure a creamy texture. Slowly beat in vanilla, then cream and sour cream.

Pour batter into prepared pan(s). Set roasting pan on oven rack and pour in enough boiling water to come about halfway up sides of springform pan(s). Bake until cake edges are set but center still jiggles, 30 to 35 minutes for small cakes and 40 to 45 minutes for large cake. Turn off heat, leave oven door ajar, and let cheesecake(s) sit in oven so that cake continues to cook in the residual heat, 15 to 20 minutes. Remove pan(s) from water bath and set on a wire rack. Let cool to room temperature. Cover and refrigerate until well chilled, about 3 hours. (Cheesecake(s) can be refrigerated for up to 5 days.) Loosen sides of pan(s), slice, and serve.

About 199 calories per serving

Lemon Cheesecake

Use ladyfingers or graham crackers for crust. Stir 4 teaspoons finely grated lemon zest into batter.

About 214 calories per serving

Lime Cheesecake

Use ladyfingers or graham crackers for crust. Stir 4 teaspoons finely grated lime zest into batter.

About 214 calories per serving

Tiramisu Cheesecake

Brush soft ladyfingers (one 3-ounce package) with a mixture of 6 tablespoons strong coffee and 2 tablespoons rum. Line pan sides with ladyfingers. Stir 3 tablespoons espresso powder into batter. When ready to serve, shave a 4-ounce bar of semisweet or bittersweet chocolate with a vegetable peeler onto cheesecake(s).

About 254 calories per serving

Chocolate Orange Cheesecake

Use Famous Chocolate Wafers for crust. Stir 4 teaspoons finely grated orange zest and ½ cup orange marmalade into batter. When ready to serve, shave a 4-ounce bar of bittersweet chocolate with a vegetable peeler onto cheesecake(s).

About 260 calories per serving

#50

50 WAYS TO LOSE IT

Don't let anyone or anything get in the way of your achieving your goal.

INDEX

almond(s)
  and cherries granola, 53
  cherry cookies, 153
  crunchy granola, 53
  and currants, rosemary cookies with, 153
  miniature apricot-cherry bars with oatmeal crumble topping, 156–57
  multigrain pancakes, 67
  peach melba, 284
  strawberry bars, 161
  toasted, and watermelon-blueberry parfait, 49
anise cookies with pine nuts, 154
appetizers
  bar nuts à la Union Square Cafe, 173
  classic Texas caviar, 178
  deviled eggs for two, 179
  I can't believe they're not fried tortilla chips, 173
  pita crisps; variations, 174–75
  roasted pumpkin seeds with chili and lime, 171
  roasted pumpkin seeds with curry and cayenne, 171
  seasoned roasted peanuts, 170
  smoked salmon tartare, 177
  wine biscuits with cracked black pepper, 176
apple(s)
  -ginger pan sauce, 234
  -grape and toasted walnut parfait, 50
  grilled fruit, 263
  sausage, and sage, quiche with, 80
  whole wheat muffins, mini, with cinnamon glaze, 146
apricot
  -cherry bars, miniature, with oatmeal crumble topping, 156–57
  pan sauce with pistachios and cumin, 232
  pistachio bars, 161
artichoke heart, seared tuna, mushroom, and shaved Parmesan salad, 104
arugula
  BLT omelet, 75
  and prosciutto, fresh tomato flatbread with, 193
  and tomatoes, ham and lentil soup with, 133
asparagus
  ham, and Swiss cheese, quiche with, 80
  lemon, and fresh herbs, baked fish with, 236
  salmon, and dill, creamy pasta with, 208
  scallop and rice soup with tomato, 118
  scallops, and orange zest, red sauce with, 216
  soup, cream of, 126

bacon. *See also* Canadian bacon
  BLT omelet, 75
  leeks, and goat cheese, quiche with, 78–79
  watercress, and blue cheese omelet, 75
balsamic vinaigrette, low-fat, 96
banana(s), 28
  chocolate fruit smoothies; variations, 45
  cream tartlets, 292
  -nutmeg multigrain pancakes, 67
  peanut cookies, 152
  -pineapple and roasted cashew parfait, 50
  pizza with peanut butter and chocolate, 63
  tropical granola, 53
  vanilla fruit smoothies; variations, 46–47
  whole wheat muffins, mini, with nutmeg glaze, 147
barbecue chicken flatbread, 202

barbecue foil packet flavoring, 243
bars
  apricot-cherry, miniature, with oatmeal crumble topping, 156–57
  apricot pistachio, 161
  fruit, simplest, 160–61
  lemon coconut, 161
  peach pecan, 161
  strawberry almond, 161
bean(s), 25
  black, and chicken, creamy chili-corn soup with, 136
  black, and chicken soup, Mexican, 113
  black, and ham soup, Brazilian, 112–13
  black, chicken, tomato, and corn salad, 97
  black, seared scallop, orange, and avocado salad, 100
  black, soup, creamy, with cumin and salsa verde, 129
  chicken, apricot, chickpea, and red onion salad, 97
  classic Texas caviar, 178
  creamy chickpea soup with garam masala and cilantro, 130
  create-your-own-red-sauce combo, 218–19
  green, and capers, baked fish with, 238
  green, roasted, with cherry tomatoes and oregano, 268
  ham and lentil soup with tomatoes and arugula, 133
  lima, and corn, chicken soup with, 112
  meal-in-a-bowl salad; variations, 92–104
  Moroccan lentil soup, 134
  pasta with just-right red sauce; variations, 213–17
  pork and Hoppin' John soup with collards and peppers, 117
  refried, and pepper Jack, slaw-topped Mexican flatbread with, 200
  white, and ham soup with cabbage, carrots, and caraway, 116
  white, and sausage soup, spicy, with winter squash and broccoli rabe, 114–15
  white, kale, and rosemary, red sauce with, 216–17
  white, salsa verde, and corn, chicken flatbread with, 197
  white, soup, creamy, with rosemary and basil, 131–32
  white, tuna, olive, and tomato salad, 99
beef
  seared steak with rosemary and garlic, 255
  berry(ies). *See also* blueberry(ies); cranberry(ies); raspberry(ies)
  cantaloupe-strawberry and Grape-Nut parfaits, 50
  honeydew-blackberry and granola parfait, 50
  sauce, perfect, with sour cream mounds or angel food cake, 283
  strawberry almond bars, 161
  strawberry mousse, 286
biscotti
  cherry almond, 163
  cranberry orange (or lemon), 163
  my favorite, 162–63
  orange (or lemon) pistachio, 163
  raisin, spiced, 163
biscuits, wine, with cracked black pepper, 176
blackberry-honeydew and granola parfait, 50
black-eyed peas
  classic Texas caviar, 178
  pork and Hoppin' John soup with collards and peppers, 117
black forest smoothie, 45
blueberry(ies)
  -lemon multigrain pancakes, 67
  -lemon smoothie, 47
  mango fruit salad with mint and honey-lime dressing, 285
  orange-berry granola with pecans, 54
  -watermelon and toasted almond parfait, 49
bok choy, mushrooms, and cilantro, fish soup with, 120
breads, 25. *See also* pita crisps; pizza, pita
  mini whole wheat apple muffins with cinnamon glaze, 146
  mini whole wheat banana muffins with nutmeg glaze, 147
  mini whole wheat pumpkin muffins with orange drizzle, 145–46
  quick garlic croutons, 131–32
broccoli
  chicken, and sun-dried tomatoes, red sauce with, 217
  spicy chicken, and basil, creamy pasta with, 210
broccoli rabe
  sausage, and red pepper, red sauce with, 217
  and winter squash, spicy sausage and white bean soup with, 114–15
broth, chicken, 27
brussels sprouts, roasted, with Dijon and lemon, 269
burgers, turkey, seared, 108

cabbage, carrots, and caraway, ham and white bean soup with, 116

Canadian bacon
and cheese pizza with tomatoes and basil, 60
flatbread d'Alsace, 196
ham, cheddar, and caraway omelet, 76
ham, Gruyère, and nutmeg omelet, 74
ham, pear, hazelnut, and goat cheese salad, 98
meal-in-a-bowl salad; variations, 92–104
reuben flatbread, 203
cantaloupe-strawberry and Grape-Nut parfait, 50
capers, 27
caramel crème, 288
caraway and mustard seed pita crisps, 174
cardamom pistachio cookies, 151
carrots
cabbage, and caraway, ham and white bean soup with, 116
and cilantro, Thai chicken flatbread with, 198
cashew(s)
cinnamon cookies, 153
roasted, and pineapple-banana parfait, 50
tropical granola, 53
cauliflower puree, rich and creamy, 275
cereal. *See also* granola
overnight oven oatmeal, 57–58
overnight refrigerator oatmeal, 57
cheese, 29. *See also* cream cheese; feta; goat cheese; Parmesan; Swiss cheese
barbecue chicken flatbread, 202
blue, and red onion, seared turkey burger salad with, 100
blue, bacon, and watercress omelet, 75
blue, chicken, grape, and walnut salad, 101
and Canadian bacon pizza with tomatoes and basil, 60
chicken flatbread with salsa verde, white beans, and corn, 197
crustless quiche; variations, 78–81
ham, cheddar, and caraway omelet, 76
meal-in-a-bowl salad; variations, 92–104
Pecorino, pepper, and oregano pita crisps, 175
and scallions, microwave scrambled eggs with, 70
slaw-topped Mexican flatbread with refried beans and pepper Jack, 200
tomato, mozzarella, and basil omelet, 75
cheesecakes
chocolate orange, 296
creamy, 294–95
lemon, 295
lime, 295
tiramisu, 295
cherry(ies)
almond biscotti, 163
almond cookies, 153
and almond granola, 53
-apricot bars, miniature, with oatmeal crumble topping, 156–57
-balsamic pan sauce with toasted almonds, 233–34
black forest smoothie, 45
chocolate 'n', 282
-peach and toasted pecan parfait, 50
pear granola with hazelnuts and vanilla, 54
chicken
apricot, chickpea, and red onion salad, 97
and black beans, creamy chili-corn soup with, 136
broccoli, and sun-dried tomatoes, red sauce with, 217
broth, for soups, 27
buying, 29
and cranberry flatbread with caramelized onions and goat cheese, 201
create-your-own-creamy-pasta combo, 211
create-your-own-red-sauce combo, 218–19
cutlets, sear-and-sauce, 222–23
flatbread, barbecue, 202
flatbread, curried, with chutney and yogurt drizzle, 199
flatbread, Thai, with carrots and cilantro, 198
flatbread with salsa verde, white beans, and corn, 197
grape, walnut, and blue cheese salad, 101
and hominy (or black bean) soup, Mexican, 113
meal-in-a-bowl salad; variations, 92–104
meal-in-a-bowl soup; variations, 111–20
mix-and-match foil packets, 243–45
noodle soup, Asian, 137
and orzo soup, lemon, with spinach, 115–16
pasta with just-right red sauce; variations, 213–17
salad, Asian, 101
sausage pizza with spinach and feta, 61
soup with lima beans and corn, 112
spiced-up grilled boneless, 248–49
spicy, broccoli, and basil, creamy pasta with, 210
thighs, sear-and-sauce, 224
tomato, black bean, and corn salad, 97

chicken sausage(s)
apples, and sage, quiche with, 80
broccoli rabe, and red pepper, red sauce with, 217
and caramelized onion flatbread with kale and Parmesan, 194
roasted pepper, olive, and feta salad, 98
and shrimp gumbo, 114
chili-corn soup, creamy, with chicken and black beans, 136
chocolate
-coconut "cookies," 155
double, pudding, 289
fruit smoothies; variations, 45
hazelnut cookies, 152
'n' cherries, 282
orange cheesecake, 296
and peanut butter, banana pizza with, 63
tartlets, 292
trail mix granola, 54
cinnamon cashew cookies, 153
clams
create-your-own-creamy-pasta combo, 211
create-your-own-red-sauce combo, 218–19
Italian herbs, and parsley, creamy pasta with, 209–10
coconut
cherries and almond granola, 53
-chocolate "cookies," 155
classic granola, 52
cream tartlets, 293
lemon bars, 161
lime cookies, 152
miniature apricot-cherry bars with oatmeal crumble topping, 156–57
toasted, and grapefruit-orange parfait, 49
trail mix granola, 54
tropical granola, 53
collards and peppers, pork and Hoppin' John soup with, 117
cookies. *See also* bars; biscotti
all-purpose slice-and-bake butter, 150–51
anise, with pine nuts, 154
banana peanut, 152
cardamom pistachio, 151
cherry almond, 153
chocolate hazelnut, 152
cinnamon cashew, 153
cranberry-orange walnut, 152
gingerbread straws, 158–59
ginger sesame, 152
lemon pistachio, 151
lime coconut, 152
low-fat, buying, 27
orange pecan, 153
rosemary, with almonds and currants, 153
"cookies," chocolate-coconut, 155
corn
chicken, black bean, and tomato salad, 97
-chili soup, creamy, with chicken and black beans, 136
crab, bell peppers, and basil, quiche with, 79
crab, roasted pepper, and avocado salad, 102
and crab soup, summer, 118–19
and lima beans, chicken soup with, 112
multigrain pancakes, 68
white beans, and salsa verde, chicken flatbread with, 197
crab, 25
bell peppers, basil, and corn, quiche with, 79
cakes, light, 107
corn, roasted pepper, and avocado salad, 102
and corn soup, summer, 118–19
create-your-own-creamy-pasta combo, 211
create-your-own-red-sauce combo, 218–19
meal-in-a-bowl salad; variations, 92–104
meal-in-a-bowl soup; variations, 111–20
mushrooms, and basil, red sauce with, 215
and roasted peppers, creamy pasta with, 209
cranberry(ies)
and chicken flatbread with caramelized onions and goat cheese, 201
orange-berry granola with pecans, 54
orange (or lemon) biscotti, 163
-orange walnut cookies, 152
cream cheese
chocolate orange cheesecake, 296
creamy cheesecake, 294–95
lemon cheesecake, 295
lime cheesecake, 295
smoked salmon, and fresh dill omelet, 76
tiramisu cheesecake, 295
croutons, quick garlic, 131–32
cumin and coriander pita crisps, 175
cumin and coriander spice rub, 251
currants and almonds, rosemary cookies with, 153
curry(ied)
and cayenne, roasted pumpkin seeds with, 171
chicken flatbread with chutney and yogurt drizzle, 199
pita crisps, 174
tandoori paste, 252
custard cups, 32

dates, pistachios, and mangoes, orange granola with, 55
desserts. *See also* bars; biscotti; cookies

banana cream tartlets, 292
caramel crème, 288
chocolate 'n' cherries, 282
chocolate orange cheesecake, 296
chocolate tartlets, 292
coconut cream tartlets, 293
creamy cheesecake, 294–95
crisp mini tart shells, 291
double chocolate pudding, 289
lemon cheesecake, 295
lemon curd tartlets, 293
light orange panna cotta with fresh raspberries, 287
lime cheesecake, 295
mango fruit salad with mint and honey-lime dressing, 285
peach melba, 284
perfect berry sauce with sour cream mounds or angel food cake, 283
strawberry mousse, 286
tiramisu cheesecake, 295
vanilla pudding, 290

drinks. *See* smoothies, fruit

egg(s), 30. *See also* omelet; quiche
deviled, for two, 179
hard-boiled, perfect, 72
microwave "boiled," 71
microwave poached, 71
microwave scrambled, with scallions and cheese, 70

equipment, 32–33

extracts, 27

fennel garlic spice rub, 251

feta, 29
sausage, roasted pepper, and olive salad, 98
shrimp, bacon, and cherry tomato salad, 103
spinach, and olives, Greek flatbread with, 195
spinach, mushrooms, and tomatoes, quiche with, 81
and spinach, chicken sausage pizza with, 61

fish. *See also* salmon; tuna
baked, with asparagus, lemon, and fresh herbs, 236
baked, with green beans and capers, 238
baked, with mushrooms and thyme, 239
baked, with oven-sautéed tomatoes, basil, and garlic, 237
baked, with spinach and Asian drizzle, 240
create-your-own-creamy-pasta combo, 211
create-your-own-red-sauce combo, 218–19
grilled swordfish or tuna steaks, 254
meal-in-a-bowl salad; variations, 92–104
meal-in-a-bowl soup; variations, 111–20
pasta with just-right red sauce; variations, 213–17
soup with bok choy, mushrooms, and cilantro, 120

flatbread pizzas. *See* pizza, flatbread

flour, 27

foil packets, mix-and-match, 243–45

fruit, 30. *See also* smoothies, fruit; *specific fruits*
bars, simplest; variations, 160–61
grilled, 263
meal-in-a-bowl salad; variations, 92–104
parfait with yogurt and drizzled honey; variations, 49–50
pizza, 62
salsa, create-your-own, 256

garlic croutons, quick, 131–32

garlicky Chinese five-spice rub, 252

gas grills, 32

gingerbread multigrain pancakes, 67

gingerbread straws, 158–59

ginger-lime drizzle, 241

ginger sesame cookies, 152

goat cheese, 29
bacon, and leeks, quiche with, 78–79
and caramelized onions, chicken and cranberry flatbread with, 201
fresh, prosciutto, and tomato omelet, 76
ham, pear, and hazelnut salad, 98

grains. *See also* oats; whole wheat
brown rice, buying, 28
creamy grits with Parmesan and prosciutto, 58
great granola; variations, 52–55
multigrain pancakes; variations, 66–68
scallop and rice soup with tomato, 118

granola
cherries and almond, 53
classic, 52
crunchy, 53
great, 52
and honeydew-blackberry parfait, 50
orange, with pistachios, mangoes, and dates, 55
orange-berry, with pecans, 54
pear, with hazelnuts and vanilla, 54
trail mix, 54
tropical, 53

grapefruit-orange and toasted coconut parfait, 49

Grape-Nut and cantaloupe-strawberry parfait, 50

grape(s)
-apple and toasted walnut parfait, 50
chicken, walnut, and blue cheese salad, 101
green, salsa with scallions and mint, 257
mango fruit salad with mint and honey-lime dressing, 285
green beans
and capers, baked fish with, 238
roasted, with cherry tomatoes and oregano, 268
greens. *See also* arugula; spinach
baby, buying, 29
bacon, watercress, and blue cheese omelet, 75
meal-in-a-bowl salad; variations, 92–104
pork and Hoppin' John soup with collards and peppers, 117
red sauce with white beans, kale, and rosemary, 216–17
sausage and caramelized onion flatbread with kale and Parmesan, 194
grills, gas, 32
grits, creamy, with Parmesan and prosciutto, 58
gumbo, shrimp and sausage, 114

ham, 30. *See also* Canadian bacon; prosciutto
and black bean soup, Brazilian, 112–13
create-your-own-creamy-pasta combo, 211
and lentil soup with tomatoes and arugula, 133
meal-in-a-bowl salad; variations, 92–104
meal-in-a-bowl soup; variations, 111–20
and rosemary, mushroom-flavored creamy pasta with, 210
Swiss cheese, and asparagus, quiche with, 80
and white bean soup with cabbage, carrots, and caraway, 116
hazelnut(s)
chocolate cookies, 152
toasted, and pear-raspberry parfait, 49
and vanilla, pear granola with, 54
hominy and chicken soup, Mexican, 113
honey, 27
honeydew-blackberry and granola parfait, 50

ingredients, 25–32

jams, preserves, and jellies, 27

kale
and Parmesan, sausage and caramelized onion flatbread with, 194
white beans, and rosemary, red sauce with, 216–17

leeks, bacon, and goat cheese, quiche with, 78–79
lemon, 28
-blueberry multigrain pancakes, 67
cheesecake, 295
coconut bars, 161
cranberry biscotti, 163
curd tartlets, 293
dill foil packet flavoring, 243
pistachio biscotti, 163
pistachio cookies, 151
–poppy seed multigrain pancakes, 67
lentil and ham soup with tomatoes and arugula, 133
lentil soup, Moroccan, 134
lettuce, romaine, 29
lime
cheesecake, 295
coconut cookies, 152
flavoring with, 28
-ginger drizzle, 241

mango(es)
fruit salad with mint and honey-lime dressing, 285
peanut salsa, 258
pistachios, and dates, orange granola with, 55
smoothie, 47
tropical smoothie, 47
Marsala pan sauce with raisins or prunes, 233
mayonnaise, buying, 30
meat. *See also* pork
meal-in-a-bowl salad; variations, 92–104
meal-in-a-bowl soup; variations, 111–20
seared steak with rosemary and garlic, 255
meatball, turkey, soup, Italian, 119–20
microplane, 32
milk, evaporated, 27
milk, soy, 30
mousse, strawberry, 286
muffins, mini whole wheat
apple, with cinnamon glaze, 146
banana, with nutmeg glaze, 147
pumpkin, with orange drizzle, 145–46
muffin tins, mini, 32
multigrain pancakes. *See* pancakes, multigrain
mushroom(s)
bok choy, and cilantro, fish soup with, 120
crab, and basil, red sauce with, 215
dried, 27
-flavored creamy pasta with ham and rosemary, 210
roasted, with garlic and thyme, 270

seared tuna, artichoke heart, and shaved Parmesan salad, 104
soup, cream of, 127
spinach, tomatoes, and feta, quiche with, 81
and thyme, baked fish with, 239
-thyme cream sauce, 231

mustard
Caribbean spice paste, 252
cream sauce with tarragon, 231
Dijon, buying, 29
tarragon cream foil packet flavoring, 243

nuts. *See also* almond(s); cashew(s); hazelnut(s); peanut(s); pecan(s); pistachio(s); walnut(s)
bar, à la Union Square Cafe, 173
buying, 27
fruit parfait with yogurt and drizzled honey; variations, 49–50
my favorite biscotti; variations, 162–63
pine, anise cookies with, 154
simplest fruit bars; variations, 160–61

oats
buying, for oatmeal, 28
great granola; variations, 52–55
miniature apricot-cherry bars with oatmeal crumble topping, 156–57
multigrain pancakes; variations, 66–68
overnight oven oatmeal, 57–58
overnight refrigerator oatmeal, 57

olive oil, 28

olive oil–vinegar drizzle, 93

olives, 28
garlic, and oregano, red wine pan sauce with, 234
green, and capers, cherry tomato relish with, 258
kalamata, tuna, and onions, red sauce with, 216
spinach, and feta, Greek flatbread with, 195

omelet, open-faced, 74
bacon, watercress, and blue cheese, 75
BLT, 75
ham, cheddar, and caraway, 76
ham, Gruyère, and nutmeg, 74
prosciutto, tomato, and fresh goat cheese, 76
sausage, cilantro, and creamy salsa verde, 75
smoked salmon, cream cheese, and fresh dill, 76
tomato, mozzarella, and basil, 75

onion(s)
caramelized, and goat cheese, chicken and cranberry flatbread with, 201
caramelized, and sausage flatbread with kale and Parmesan, 194
flatbread d'Alsace, 196

orange
-berry granola with pecans, 54
-cardamom multigrain pancakes, 67
chocolate cheesecake, 296
cranberry biscotti, 163
-Dijon pan sauce, 232
dressing, sweet-and-sour, 96
flavoring with, 28
granola with pistachios, mangoes, and dates, 55
-grapefruit and toasted coconut parfait, 49
panna cotta, light, with fresh raspberries, 287
pecan cookies, 153
pistachio biscotti, 163
seared scallop, black bean, and avocado salad, 100
sliced pork tenderloin, dried cranberry, and pecan salad, 102

pancakes, multigrain, 68
almond, 67
banana-nutmeg, 67
corn, 68
gingerbread, 67
lemon-blueberry, 67
lemon–poppy seed, 67
orange-cardamom, 67

panna cotta, light orange, with fresh raspberries, 287

pan sauces. *See* sauces, pan

paprika garlic spice rub, basic, 251

parfaits
apple-grape and toasted walnut, 50
cantaloupe-strawberry and Grape-Nut, 50
fruit, with yogurt and drizzled honey, 49
grapefruit-orange and toasted coconut, 49
honeydew-blackberry and granola, 50
peach-cherry and toasted pecan, 50
pear-raspberry and toasted hazelnut, 49
pineapple-banana and roasted cashew, 50
watermelon-blueberry and toasted almond, 49

Parmesan, 29
fresh tomato flatbread with arugula and prosciutto, 193
and herb dressing, creamy low-fat, 96
and kale, sausage and caramelized onion flatbread with, 194
and prosciutto, creamy grits with, 58
shaved, seared tuna, mushroom, and artichoke heart salad, 104

pasta, 28
  Asian chicken noodle soup, 137
  creamy, combo, create-your-own, 211
  creamy, mushroom-flavored, with ham and rosemary, 210
  creamy, with clams, Italian herbs, and parsley, 209–10
  creamy, with crab and roasted peppers, 209
  creamy, with salmon, asparagus, and dill, 208
  creamy, with scallops, peas, and saffron, 209
  creamy, with shrimp, spinach, and oregano, 208
  creamy, with spicy chicken, broccoli, and basil, 210
  creamy light, 206–7
  Italian turkey meatball soup, 119–20
  with just-right red sauce, 213–14
  lemon chicken and orzo soup with spinach, 115–16
  red sauce, create-your-own combo, 218–19
  red sauce with chicken, broccoli, and sun-dried tomatoes, 217
  red sauce with crab, mushrooms, and basil, 215
  red sauce with sausage, broccoli rabe, and red pepper, 217
  red sauce with scallops, asparagus, and orange zest, 216
  red sauce with shrimp, spinach, and lemon zest, 215
  red sauce with tuna, onions, and kalamata olives, 216
  red sauce with white beans, kale, and rosemary, 216–17
  tomato-tortellini soup with spinach and Italian spices, 135
peach(es)
  -almond smoothie, 47
  -cherry and toasted pecan parfait, 50
  grilled fruit, 263
  melba, 284
  pecan bars, 161
peanut(s)
  banana cookies, 152
  butter and chocolate, banana pizza with, 63
  mango salsa, 258
  roasted, seasoned, 170
  trail mix granola, 54
pear(s)
  granola with hazelnuts and vanilla, 54
  grilled fruit, 263
  ham, hazelnut, and goat cheese salad, 98
  -raspberry and toasted hazelnut parfait, 49
peas, black-eyed
  classic Texas caviar, 178
  pork and Hoppin' John soup with collards and peppers, 117
peas, scallops, and saffron, creamy pasta with, 209
pecan(s)
  orange-berry granola with, 54
  orange cookies, 153
  peach bars, 161
  toasted, and peach-cherry parfait, 50
pepper(s)
  bell, crab, basil, and corn, quiche with, 79
  radishes, and cilantro, pineapple salsa with, 257
  roasted, and crab, creamy pasta with, 209
  roasted, sausage, olive, and feta salad, 98
piña colada smoothie, 46
pineapple
  -banana and roasted cashew parfait, 50
  grilled fruit, 263
  piña colada smoothie, 46
  salsa with radishes, peppers, and cilantro, 257
  tropical granola, 53
  tropical smoothie, 47
pine nuts, anise cookies with, 154
pistachio(s)
  apricot bars, 161
  bar nuts à la Union Square Cafe, 173
  cardamom cookies, 151
  lemon cookies, 151
  mangoes, and dates, orange granola with, 55
  orange (or lemon) biscotti, 163
pita crisps, 174
  caraway and mustard seed, 174
  cumin and coriander, 175
  curried, 174
  "everything," 175
  Pecorino, pepper, and oregano, 175
pizza, flatbread
  chicken, barbecue, 202
  chicken, curried, with chutney and yogurt drizzle, 199
  chicken, Thai, with carrots and cilantro, 198
  chicken, with salsa verde, white beans, and corn, 197
  chicken and cranberry, with caramelized onions and goat cheese, 201
  d'Alsace, 196
  dough, quick, 191
  dough, quick white whole-wheat, 191
  dough, quick whole wheat, 192
  Greek, with spinach, feta, and olives, 195

reuben, 203
sausage and caramelized onion, with kale and Parmesan, 194
slaw-topped Mexican, with refried beans and pepper Jack, 200
with smoked salmon and all the trimmings, 204
tomato, fresh, with arugula and prosciutto, 193
pizza, pita
banana, with peanut butter and chocolate, 63
Canadian bacon and cheese, with tomatoes and basil, 60
chicken sausage, with spinach and feta, 61
fruit, 62
pizza crusts, buying, 30
plum, pork tenderloin, cashew, and cilantro salad, 103
poppy seed(s)
"everything" pita crisps, 175
–lemon multigrain pancakes, 67
pork. *See also* bacon; Canadian bacon; ham; prosciutto
and Hoppin' John soup with collards and peppers, 117
loin chops, sear-and-sauce, 226
meal-in-a-bowl salad; variations, 92–104
meal-in-a-bowl soup; variations, 111–20
mix-and-match foil packets, 243–45
spiced-up grilled boneless, 248–49
spicy sausage and white bean soup with winter squash and broccoli rabe, 114–15
tenderloin, butterflying, 31
tenderloin, plum, cashew, and cilantro salad, 103
tenderloin, sear-and-sauce, 225
tenderloin, sliced, orange, dried cranberry, and pecan salad, 102
poultry. *See also* chicken; turkey
meal-in-a-bowl salad; variations, 92–104
meal-in-a-bowl soup; variations, 111–20
prosciutto, 30
and arugula, fresh tomato flatbread with, 193
and Parmesan, creamy grits with, 58
tomato, and fresh goat cheese omelet, 76
prune pan sauce with warm spices, 233
pudding, double chocolate, 289
pudding, vanilla, 290
pumpkin seeds
roasted, with chili and lime, 171
roasted, with curry and cayenne, 171
pumpkin whole wheat muffins, mini, with orange drizzle, 145–46

quiche, crustless, 78
with bacon, leeks, and goat cheese, 78–79
with crab, bell peppers, basil, and corn, 79
with ham, Swiss cheese, and asparagus, 80
with sausage, apples, and sage, 80
with spinach, mushrooms, tomatoes, and feta, 81

radishes, peppers, and cilantro, pineapple salsa with, 257
raisin(s)
biscotti, spiced, 163
classic granola, 52
Marsala pan sauce, 233
trail mix granola, 54
raspberry(ies)
-chocolate-orange smoothie, 45
fresh, light orange panna cotta with, 287
-orange smoothie, 46
peach melba, 284
-pear and toasted hazelnut parfait, 49
relish, cherry tomato, with capers and green olives, 258
reuben flatbread, 203
rice, brown, buying, 28
rice and scallop soup with tomato, 118
rosemary cookies with almonds and currants, 153
rosemary rub, spicy, 252

salad dressings
low-fat balsamic vinaigrette, 96
low-fat creamy herb and Parmesan, 96
olive oil–vinegar drizzle, 93
sweet-and-sour orange, 96
salads
chicken, apricot, chickpea, and red onion, 97
chicken, Asian, 101
chicken, grape, walnut, and blue cheese, 101
chicken, tomato, black bean, and corn, 97
crab, corn, roasted pepper, and avocado, 102
ham, pear, hazelnut, and goat cheese, 98
mango fruit, with mint and honey-lime dressing, 285
meal-in-a-bowl, preparing, 88–91
meal-in-a-bowl (recipe), 92–95
pork tenderloin, plum, cashew, and cilantro, 103
pork tenderloin, sliced, orange, dried cranberry, and pecan, 102
salmon, seared, egg, sun-dried tomato, and Melba crouton, 104
salmon, smoked, and trimmings, 99

salads *(cont.)*
sausage, roasted pepper, olive, and feta, 98
scallop, seared, black bean, orange, and avocado, 100
shrimp, bacon, cherry tomato, and feta, 103
tuna, seared, mushroom, artichoke heart, and shaved Parmesan, 104
tuna, white bean, olive, and tomato, 99
turkey burger, seared, with blue cheese and red onion, 100
salad spinners, 32
salmon, 31
asparagus, and dill, creamy pasta with, 208
create-your-own-creamy-pasta combo, 211
create-your-own-red-sauce combo, 218–19
fillets, sear-and-sauce, 229
meal-in-a-bowl salad; variations, 92–104
mix-and-match foil packets, 243–45
seared, egg, sun-dried tomato, and Melba crouton salad, 104
seared or grilled, 106
smoked, and all the trimmings flatbread, 204
smoked, and trimmings salad, 99
smoked, cream cheese, and fresh dill omelet, 76
smoked, tartare, 177
spiced-up grilled boneless, 248–49
salsas
fruit, create-your-own, 256
green grape, with scallions and mint, 257
mango peanut, 258
pineapple, with radishes, peppers, and cilantro, 257
salsa verde cream sauce with cilantro, 230
sauces. *See also* sauces, pan
berry, perfect, with sour cream mounds or angel food cake, 283
lime-ginger drizzle, 241
pasta, creamy light, 206–7
pasta, just-right red, 213–14
soy-sesame drizzle, 241
sauces, pan
apple-ginger, 234
apricot, with pistachios and cumin, 232
cherry-balsamic, with toasted almonds, 233–34
Marsala, with raisins or prunes, 233
mushroom-thyme cream, 231
mustard cream, with tarragon, 231
orange-Dijon, 232
prune, with warm spices, 233
red wine, with garlic, olives, and oregano, 234
salsa verde cream, with cilantro, 230
tomato, light, with vinegar and basil, 231–32
white wine cream, with chives, 230
sauerkraut
reuben flatbread, 203
sausage. *See also* chicken sausage(s); turkey sausage
and white bean soup, spicy, with winter squash and broccoli rabe, 114–15
scales, kitchen, 33
scallop(s), 31
asparagus, and orange zest, red sauce with, 216
meal-in-a-bowl salad; variations, 92–104
meal-in-a-bowl soup; variations, 111–20
mix-and-match foil packets, 243–45
peas, and saffron, creamy pasta with, 209
and rice soup with tomato, 118
sea, sear-and-sauce, 228
sea, seared, 105
seared, black bean, orange, and avocado salad, 100
seafood. *See* fish; shellfish
sesame seeds
"everything" pita crisps, 175
ginger sesame cookies, 152
shellfish. *See also* crab; scallop(s); shrimp
creamy pasta with clams, Italian herbs, and parsley, 209–10
create-your-own-creamy-pasta combo, 211
create-your-own-red-sauce combo, 218–19
meal-in-a-bowl salad; variations, 92–104
meal-in-a-bowl soup; variations, 111–20
pasta with just-right red sauce; variations, 213–17
shrimp, 31
bacon, cherry tomato, and feta salad, 103
create-your-own-creamy-pasta combo, 211
create-your-own-red-sauce combo, 218–19
meal-in-a-bowl salad; variations, 92–104
meal-in-a-bowl soup; variations, 111–20
mix-and-match foil packets, 243–45
and sausage gumbo, 114
sear-and-sauce, 227
spicy grilled, 250
spinach, and lemon zest, red sauce with, 215
spinach, and oregano, creamy pasta with, 208
silicone mats, 33
slaw-topped Mexican flatbread with refried beans and pepper Jack, 200
smoothies, fruit
black forest, 45
blueberry-lemon, 47

chocolate, 45
chocolate-raspberry-orange, 45
mango, 47
peach-almond, 47
piña colada, 46
raspberry-orange, 46
tropical, 47
vanilla, 46
soups
asparagus, cream of, 126
black bean, creamy, with cumin and salsa verde, 129
chicken, with lima beans and corn, 112
chicken and hominy (or black bean), Mexican, 113
chicken and orzo, lemon, with spinach, 115–16
chicken noodle, Asian, 137
chickpea, creamy, with garam masala and cilantro, 130
chili-corn, creamy, with chicken and black beans, 136
crab and corn, summer, 118–19
fish, with bok choy, mushrooms, and cilantro, 120
ham and black bean, Brazilian, 112–13
ham and lentil, with tomatoes and arugula, 133
ham and white bean, with cabbage, carrots, and caraway, 116
lentil, Moroccan, 134
meal-in-a-bowl, ingredients for, 121–23
meal-in-a-bowl, preparing, 109–10
meal-in-a-bowl (recipe), 111
mushroom, cream of, 127
pork and Hoppin' John, with collards and peppers, 117
sausage and white bean, spicy, with winter squash and broccoli rabe, 114–15
scallop and rice, with tomato, 118
shrimp and sausage gumbo, 114
tomato, cream of, quick, 125
tomato-tortellini, with spinach and Italian spices, 135
turkey meatball, Italian, 119–20
white bean, creamy, with rosemary and basil, 131–32
soy milk, 30
soy-sesame drizzle, 241
soy sesame foil packet flavoring, 243
spice rubs and pastes
basic paprika garlic spice rub, 251
Caribbean spice paste, 252
cumin and coriander spice rub, 251
fennel garlic spice rub, 251
garlicky Chinese five-spice rub, 252
spicy rosemary rub, 252
tandoori paste, 252
warm spice rub, 252
spinach
and Asian drizzle, baked fish with, 240
feta, and olives, Greek flatbread with, 195
and feta, chicken sausage pizza with, 61
and Italian spices, tomato-tortellini soup with, 135
lemon chicken and orzo soup with, 115–16
Moroccan lentil soup, 134
mushrooms, tomatoes, and feta, quiche with, 81
shrimp, and lemon zest, red sauce with, 215
shrimp, and oregano, creamy pasta with, 208
springform pans, mini, 33
squash
mini whole wheat pumpkin muffins with orange drizzle, 145–46
quick tomato-stewed zucchini with basil and garlic, 274
winter, and broccoli rabe, spicy sausage and white bean soup with, 114–15
strawberry
almond bars, 161
-cantaloupe and Grape-Nut parfait, 50
mousse, 286
sugar, brown, 25
Swiss cheese
flatbread d'Alsace, 196
ham, and asparagus, quiche with, 80
ham, Gruyère, and nutmeg omelet, 74
reuben flatbread, 203
swordfish steaks, grilled, 254

tandoori paste, 252
tarragon mustard cream foil packet flavoring, 243
tartlets
banana cream, 292
chocolate, 292
coconut cream, 293
lemon curd, 293
tart shells, crisp mini, 291
tiramisu cheesecake, 295
tomato(es), 29
and basil, Canadian bacon and cheese pizza with, 60
BLT omelet, 75
cherry, and oregano, roasted green beans with, 268
cherry, relish with capers and green olives, 258
cherry, shrimp, bacon, and feta salad, 103
fresh, flatbread with arugula and prosciutto, 193

tomato(es) *(cont.)*
Italian herbs, and capers foil packet flavoring, 243
mozzarella, and basil omelet, 75
orange, and saffron foil packet flavoring, 243–44
oven-sautéed, basil, and garlic, baked fish with, 237
pasta with just-right red sauce; variations, 213–17
prosciutto, and fresh goat cheese omelet, 76
sauce, light, with vinegar and basil, 231–32
soup, cream of, quick, 125
spinach, mushrooms, and feta, quiche with, 81
-stewed zucchini with basil and garlic, quick, 274
-tortellini soup with spinach and Italian spices, 135
tortilla chips, I can't believe they're not fried, 173
trail mix granola, 54
tuna
create-your-own-red-sauce combo, 218–19
meal-in-a-bowl salad; variations, 92–104
onions, and kalamata olives, red sauce with, 216
seared, mushroom, artichoke heart, and shaved Parmesan salad, 104
steaks, grilled, 254
white bean, olive, and tomato salad, 99
turkey
breast, buying, 30
burger, seared, salad with blue cheese and red onion, 100
burgers, seared, 108
create-your-own-red-sauce combo, 218–19
cutlets, cooking with, 31
meal-in-a-bowl salad; variations, 92–104
meal-in-a-bowl soup; variations, 111–20
meatball soup, Italian, 119–20
spiced-up grilled boneless, 248–49
turkey sausage
and caramelized onion flatbread with kale and Parmesan, 194
cilantro, and creamy salsa verde omelet, 75

vanilla fruit smoothies; variations, 46–47
vanilla pudding, 290
vegetables. *See also specific vegetables*
create-your-own-creamy-pasta combo, 211
create-your-own-red-sauce combo, 218–19
fall/winter, roasted, 265
frozen, buying, 32
grilled, 261–62
meal-in-a-bowl salad; variations, 92–104
meal-in-a-bowl soup; variations, 111–20
mix-and-match foil packets, 243–45
pasta with just-right red sauce; variations, 213–17
spring, roasted, 266
steam-sautéed, 272–73
summer, roasted, 267
vinaigrette, low-fat balsamic, 96
vinegars, 28

walnut(s)
classic granola, 52
cranberry-orange cookies, 152
toasted, and apple-grape parfait, 50
watercress, bacon and blue cheese omelet, 75
watermelon-blueberry and toasted almond parfait, 49
wheat germ
great granola; variations, 52–55
whole wheat
flatbread, quick, 192
mini muffins, apple, with cinnamon glaze, 146
mini muffins, banana, with nutmeg glaze, 147
mini muffins, pumpkin, with orange drizzle, 145–46
white, quick flatbread, 191
wine, red, pan sauce with garlic, olives, and oregano, 234
wine, white, cream sauce with chives, 230
wine biscuits with cracked black pepper, 176

yogurt, 30
and drizzled honey, fruit parfait with; variations, 49–50
tandoori paste, 252

zucchini, quick tomato-stewed, with basil and garlic, 274